Timothy Green Beckley's

CRYPTID CREATURES FROM DARK DOMAINS:

Dogmen, Devil Hounds, Phantom Canines And Real Werewolves

CRYPTID CREATURES FROM DARK DOMAINS
Dogmen, Devil Hounds, Phantom Canines And Real Werewolves

By
Timothy Green Beckley, Sean Casteel, Tim Swartz, Nick Redfern,
Brad Steiger, Clemence Housman, Andrew Gable, Claudia Cunningham,
William Kern, Butch Witkowski, Michele Lowe

Timothy Green Beckley: Editorial Director
Carol Rodriguez: Publishers Assistant
Tim Swartz: Associate Editor
Sean Casteel: Editorial Assistant
William Kern: Layout and Format

For free catalog write:
Global CommunicationsP.O. Box 753New Brunswick, NJ 08903

Free Subscription to Conspiracy Journal E-Mail
Newsletterwww.conspiracyjournal.com

CONTENTS:

Conspiracy Journal
PRODUCTIONS

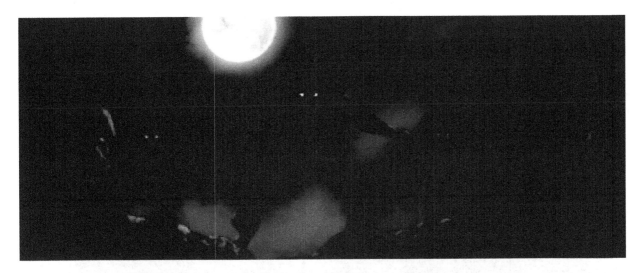

JUST WHEN YOU THOUGHT YOU'D HEARD IT ALL
By Timothy Green Beckley

Hey, I was never "Bigfoot crazy," but I have always had at least a mild interest in the topic.

Back even as early as my teens, I wrote an article for FATE Magazine on Zana, the Russian female Bigfoot who was so endearing to an entire village. She was so human – albeit smelling a bit – that she could move about on her own without any malice toward the humans who had befriended her.

I also was probably the first author to write about the Skunk-ape of the Everglades, as far back as the 1970s. The article appeared in Saga, a men's adventure magazine, and I've reprinted it a couple of times in various books because it is as timely now as when I originally researched the piece. This was the first inkling that there might be a paranormal aspect to such cryptids. This was further reinforced when I traveled to Loch Ness in Scotland and spoke with those living in the area who said they had witnessed a variety of strange flying objects over the Loch.

And, of course, I was friends with the late zoologist, Ivan T. Sanderson, who was the first national figure to champion the cause of cryptozoology in the media.

Lately, I've gotten into cryptids a bit more heavily. On the podcast I co-host with Tim Swartz (KCORradio.com, every Thursday at 10 P.M. Eastern) we've covered the topic pretty extensively. One of our favorite guests is Butch Witkowski, who first exposed our audience to the existence of the Dogmen in his home state of Pennsylvania.

The encounters with this snarling critter were so incredibly awesome that his appearance literally blew a hole in our ratings, reaching thousands of listeners beyond the audience that we normally pull in. We knew we had to do an extensive interview with Butch and put it into a book, of which you are now starting to turn the pages. The Dogmen have been seen in upwards of 20 states, I understand, and the number of witnesses that are coming forward increases every day.

So here in a very large nutshell are the latest up-to-date findings on those critters that make us warily look behind us as we hike in the woods and about which there is always a tale to tell by the campfire. We are happy that you are able to join us on our "creature quest." So grab your camera and your plaster of Paris to make casts of those unsettling footprints left in the soil and – by all means – watch your back.

HE'S A BIG, UGLY, PUG-NOSED BRUTE!
STALKING THE DOGMAN
By Sean Casteel

A new phenomenon is overtaking the land . . .

First, we had Bigfoot stomping through the underbrush and leaving tracks in the soil.

And we've had Mothman flying over our heads, poised to drop a "big one" on us at any given moment.

There are also the Thunderbirds, which fill the Native Americans with dread because the winged creatures can swoop down and grab livestock and even small babies, those sons of bitches.

Now we may have an even more deadly concern with the appearance of the Dogman, who has a well-muscled body – said to be similar in appearance to actor/politician Arnold Schwarzenegger's – and the fierceness of a grizzly.

*   *   *

Butch Witkowski has been seeking answers to the Dogman mystery since 2014. What kind of creature is it that can frighten people such that they fear for their very lives after just a glance in their direction?

A LIFE-CHANGING VISIT FROM A UFO

As often happens in Ufology and the paranormal in general, Witkowski received a sort of cosmic "tap on the shoulder" from the great beyond one day in 1989.

"While living in Arizona," he said, "I witnessed, along with seven other people, a very large object in the sky that was nothing of this Earth hovering above a mountain. It was about three football fields in length and of a burnt copper color.

3

It had a couple of very faint green lights on the side. And it just hovered silently. We all saw it for about two minutes before it raised up about 1,500 to 2,000 feet and shot off into the west."

Witkowski then forthrightly set about making inquiries with the local authorities.

"I subsequently called the Pima County Sheriff's Department," he said, "the Tucson Police Department, the Department of Public Safety, which is the state police. I also called Davis-Monthan Air Force Base and the airports. Nobody had anything."

He also contacted the local media outlets – newspapers, television and radio stations – and came up empty there as well. He was forced to conclude that "evidently, only these seven people standing in my driveway in Tucson, Arizona, in 1989, saw this object."

Despite not having any real-world support from law enforcement or the media, the sighting had made an indelible impression on Witkowski

"It piqued an interest," he recounted, "which led me to start buying books and collecting a lot of paper but which was getting me absolutely nowhere. I joined the Mutual UFO Network [MUFON] in 2007 and became a chief investigator, a state section director and a Star Team Member."

But even after rising up the ranks within MUFON, Witkowski felt he was no closer to an answer.

"I still wasn't getting the results I was looking for," he explained. "It seemed like I was becoming a data collection agency. I didn't want that. I wanted some answers and I wanted to be out in the field."

After relocating to Pennsylvania, Witkowski formed his own investigation group, called the UFO Research Center of Pennsylvania, with a gathering of like-minded researchers that he'd met over the years.

"All hardened and longtime researchers in the fields of Ufology, cryptozoology, the paranormal and Fortean research," he said. "So we took it from there in 2009, after I left MUFON, and we're now in our seventh year. We have twelve affiliates, ten in the U.S. and two over in Europe."

THE FIRST DOGMAN REPORT

Witkowski had had only a passing interest in cryptozoology, having read a little about Bigfoot and flying creatures and the Loch Ness monster. His research organization was clearly billed as UFO-oriented and that remained his primary focus.

But in November, 2014, he received his first report on a doglike creature prowling the woods of central Pennsylvania.

"A gentleman was walking his two dogs," Witkowski recounted, "in an area which he was very familiar with. He'd lived there all his life. He was a credible witness; he was a military pilot for twenty years, retired, and a commercial airline pilot for twenty years, retired. He had grown up in the area and hunted there all his life. It was state game land.

"And while he's on the fire trail," Witkowski continued, "the dogs start going bananas. They start losing their minds. They want to get to something that's on the right-hand side of the road, which he cannot see. His first inclination was that it could be a skunk, a badger, a bear or a deer. It could be anything. But the dogs were going crazier than normal. They were actually digging holes in the ground to get away from him and get to whatever it was. And then this 'creature,' we'll use that word, walks out, across the road, from one side of the tree line to the other side, and just walks into the woods."

The frenzy of the man's dogs grew even worse. But the object of their excitement didn't pay any attention to them, as though the man and his dogs didn't even exist. The witness described the creature as a tall, hairy, short-snouted "whatever the hell it was."

When Witkowski pressed for more details, the man told him he would think about it and get back to him. The man eventually returned with a picture he'd pulled off the Internet and doctored a little to make some of the details match more closely what he had seen. He told Witkowski, "I thought about it, and this is the best way I can describe it. If you would take Arnold Schwarzenegger and make him eight to ten feet tall – same body, massive chest, very thin waist, heavy-legged, muscular arms with hands."

The man didn't see any ears, but he remarked that he hadn't really looked for ears. He had taken in the whole creature, which had a short snout similar to a bulldog or pug.

After struggling to get his dogs back in his vehicle, the man retrieved a handgun out of the glovebox and walked into the woods again. He saw nothing. No broken branches or footprints. He told Witkowski he planned to return to the area with a few friends, all of whom would be heavily armed. Although Witkowski cautioned him against it, the group returned to the area, which still bore the holes made by the hunting dogs' frantic digging. The men with their high-powered rifles walked into the same section of woods that the creature had disappeared into when the man first laid eyes on it.

"They got in about 20 or 25 feet," Witkowski said, "and they all stopped at the same time, kind of looked at each other and said, 'We're out of here.' And I said to him, 'Well, what happened?' And he said, 'We all had this feeling at the same time that if we stayed there, we were going to die. Something really bad was going to happen. We saw nothing. We just had that feeling.'"

The group of men then walked back to the truck, literally walking backwards so as not to turn their back on whatever "presence" had given them that horrifying feeling.

"There is something evil in those woods," he told Witkowski, "and I'm never going back again."

The man was also adamant about refuting any notion that what he saw might have been a Bigfoot.

"I know what a Bigfoot is," he insisted, "and I know what a Bigfoot is supposed to look like. I've seen pictures and drawings of them on TV and YouTube. We're not dealing with a Bigfoot here. End of story. Nice knowing you, Mr. Witkowski. Good luck. Bye."

THE SILVER LETTER OPENER

Witkowski received his second Dogman report in July 2015. He said that two music teachers were driving home together from work in the evening on Route 22, a winding road that straightens up eventually for a long distance.

"As they round the last corner and get onto the straightaway," Witkowski said, "the driver sees what he thinks is a bear chewing on roadkill deer. So he hits his high beams, and, when he does that, the creature stands up. His description, again, was just like the first guy. 'I was looking at a werewolf,' he said. The creature had a very large wolf head, pointed ears, short hair, massive chest, a very thin waist, very heavy-legged and glowing yellow eyes."

As the music teachers drew nearer to the beast, it seemed to be taking a "defensive" posture. It stared intently at them and their vehicle as they changed lanes to avoid it. The passenger teacher continued to watch the creature, and it continued to watch them.

"It's not making a move," Witkowski continued. "And then the driver looks in the rear view mirror and sees it bound across the highway – one, two, and it's over the guardrails on the other side. Now, those roads are pretty wide. To do that in one or two bounds, that would be pretty tricky."

Empowered by their Second Amendment rights, the teachers returned home and then loaded every gun in the house, locked every door, barred every window and went downstairs.

"When this guy is describing this to me," Witkowski said, "he's quivering and shaking the whole time and damn near on the verge of tears. Now this is how scared he was: He goes down into his basement and spends 30 minutes looking for a box that his grandfather left him when he died many years prior. Because he knew in the box there was a silver letter opener. He said his thought was, 'Maybe that will be my last defense.' A silver letter opener."

Butch Witkowski, a Pennsylvania-based cryptozoologist.

SEEING THE DEVIL

While attending a conference on Bigfoot and the paranormal in Farmington, Pennsylvania, Witkowski was approached by a married couple who wanted to tell him their story and ask him some questions. The wife told Witkowski that it was she who had seen the strange creature. Her sighting lasted ten to fifteen minutes, the longest viewing time of any of the witnesses Witkowski has heard from.

She described the creature as everyone else had except that in her case the Dogman appeared to have a swishing appendage behind it which she assumed was a tail. It was a bright, moonlit night, and so pretty outside that she lingered in her doorway to take in the pleasant scenery. In the front portion of the couple's property is a pond. To the left and rear is an apple orchard. On the right side is a section of state game lands that extends for 6,700 acres.

7

Dogman is said by witnesses to stand upright, have the body of a muscular human and the face of a pug-nosed bulldog.

"She looked through the screen door," Witkowski said. "She didn't have the porch light on. It was bright out. She said you could see for miles."

The woman saw someone standing at the edge of the pond and staring into it. Whoever it was never looked at her. She saw the entity had long arms and claws and was in fact huge. The same massive chest with the head of a wolf and short pointed ears.

"Then I started to get the feeling," she told Witkowski, "that I shouldn't even be looking at this thing. So I closed the door quietly and went in to get my husband out of bed. He looks outside and doesn't see anything. It's gone."

The next morning the couple looked for footprints or crushed grass around the pond and found nothing. But their dog, a pit bull puppy, behaved strangely that day, moving through his morning wakeup routine sheepishly in marked contrast to his usual cheerful romping. The dog urinated on every tire of both cars in the driveway and then hid behind the couch, unwilling to emerge for several hours.

"And I went, 'Now that is weird,'" the wife said. "That particular morning was totally different from anything he's ever done."

The woman had grown up in a religious family and had been taught that – if she were ever to see the devil – he would appear to her in animal form. She told Witkowski, "I truly believe that I was looking at the devil."

WHAT TO NAME THE FEARSOME BEAST

Witkowski said the woman was not alone in calling the beast "demonic."

But what are we dealing with here?

"They've said it's not of this world," Witkowski explained. "Now, there are a lot of theories about what it could be. It could be a werewolf. It could be a skin-walker. It could be a Dogman."

But for Witkowski, the appellation Dogman requires some careful "hair-splitting," if you will pardon the pun. The descriptions he has been receiving the last few years differ in some ways from the Dogman sightings reported elsewhere. In every report he has received, the physical characteristics of the creature are identical to one another.

"The same size, the same short dark brown or black hair, waist, legs, long arms with hands, glowing yellow eyes, snout and wolf-like head – everyone describes the same type of creature. Also, all these sightings take place in central and southern Pennsylvania and they're all in massive state game lands. But Dogmen are described as four to five to maybe six-feet-tall; most times they're seen on all fours, running. They may stand up, or, if they're carrying anything, like roadkill or something, they're carrying it in their paws.

"We have no description of paws. We have no descriptions of these creatures ever running on all fours in any report. Dogmen are seen on railroad tracks. They're seen in parking lots. They're seen walking streets. They're seen along the edge of the road."

Meanwhile, the creature reported to Witkowski has never been seen outside of a state game land or a heavily wooded area. The Dogmen are frequently said to have glowing red eyes, but for Witkowski the reports all mention only glowing yellow eyes. The creature has always been described as much taller than the more typical Dogman reports from other regions.

"I'm going to be perfectly honest. I don't know what I'm looking for," Witkowski admitted. "So I'm going to say, yeah, they're doglike, of course. They're canine. If I had to classify it, I would classify it as a 'bipedal canine.'"

"Bipedal," of course, means the creature walks on two legs, like a human being. But Witkowski so jealously guards the differences between the creatures reported to him and the Dogmen seen in other parts of the country that he opts for a completely different phrase with which to name it. One gets the impression that "bipedal canine" is a kind of compromise term for him that helps to preserve the uniqueness of what he's dealing with.

THE LYCAN LOOP

"We've been through so much research and talked to so many people," Witkowski said, "from the Inuit down to the Cherokee. That's another thing about all the reports we have from central and southern Pennsylvania – they were all at one time Indian lands. Until 1754, there were no white men in this state.

"So when I talked to the Cherokee, they said, 'Well, you're describing a skin-walker. It could be a skin-walker protecting the graves of warriors.' We talked to the Inuit and they said it could be the shape-shifters or 'wolf-men,' they call them, that moved down from their area and went south in what they call the 'Great Migration.' There are so many stories and all you can do is collect them and try to decipher them."

Witkowski pointed out that the area his research is focused on is a sizable amount of land.

"And the bipedal canines don't venture

PENNSYLVANIA'S 'LYCAN LOOP'

outside what we call the 'Lycan Loop.' They are never seen in a populated area. It's centralized in central Pennsylvania, north central, central, and south central Pennsylvania. It is in but a handful of counties. None of these reports are outside that loop. They are never seen going to the 7/11 to get a Slurpy. I mean, Dogmen reports from western Pennsylvania and eastern Ohio have them walking down the street, have them in parks, have them in cemeteries, have them walking along railroad tracks. We're not having that. It's a different investigation."

In his research, Witkowski ran across an 1865 account of the creature published in a long-defunct newspaper in western Pennsylvania. The headline read: "Large Dog Spotted In Field By Timbermen."

"It was in Crawford County," Witkowski said, "along the Ohio border. And their description was what nailed it for me: eight to ten feet tall, very broad-chested, thin waist, massive legs and arms, standing upright and a dog- or wolf-like head. This kind of puts it in a realm I'm not comfortable with. Could I be dealing with a 'relic'? Something that's been around for a long, long time? I don't know."

THE CONSISTENCY OF THE FEAR FACTOR

So, while Witkowski juggles the various theories as to what his bipedal canines really are, he does allow as how he was not able to find any reports of people actually being attacked by them. Nevertheless, one thing that is known is that the creatures induce in witnesses an overwhelming fear.

"When you talk to these folks," he said, "they're terrified. They're petrified. They want to tell you what they saw, but they don't want to go any further than that. One thing that stands out in every report is that the people feel 'This is not a good place to be right now. I need to get out of here or I'm going to die.' They have a fear that comes over them that just sets the impulse to fear and flee right into motion instantly, the minute they see it.

"You don't have that in other Dogmen reports. Kids have thrown stones at them and they've chased them down the railroad tracks with sticks. But the bipedal canine will stand its ground. It doesn't move. It won't follow you but it's not something you're going to chase down the railroad tracks with a stick."

A FRIGHTENING ENCOUNTER IN OHIO

In Ohio, a neighboring state to Witkowski's Pennsylvania, a creature similar in appearance to the bipedal canine was spotted on two occasions in the Silver Creek area near Norton. As reported on a website called "The Sasquatch Chronicles," a witness known only as "Andrew" told of meeting the fearsome beasts while driving late at night on darkened, quiet roads.

"I don't care if you believe me or not," Andrew told the unnamed reporter.

Andrew next launched into his story of seeing two deer run out across the street. What was of interest, however, was what was chasing them. He claimed to have seen creatures seven-feet-tall running "in formation," one in front and two behind, roughly 30 to 40 yards behind the deer. The creatures were bipedal, very muscular and fast.

Though Pennsylvania's Dogman has been seen in a specific area, sightings have now been reported in twenty states.

"Lightning fast," Andrew added. "It all happened in just a few seconds. I couldn't describe any features, unfortunately. I'm assuming it was either a new moon or cloudy because it was very dark. But they were definitely a dark color, maybe a chocolate brown or a black color."

Though controversial, the camera has captured the figure of a Dogman-like beast wandering the woods.

Many of those details are identical to reports Witkowski has received, including the dark color and the extremely muscular appearance of the creatures, as well as the fact that the sighting only lasted a few seconds. Andrew quickly dismissed the idea that he had seen a Bigfoot, which he said moves in a more humanlike way than the creatures he saw.

Less than a month later, Andrew had a second sighting. As he was passing a moonlit cornfield, something ran in front of his car. This time he saw two creatures, again, seven-feet-tall, who leapt across the road, landed about ten to fifteen feet into the field on the other side and then just kept running.

The unnamed reporter went with Andrew to investigate the scenes of the sightings and observed that the creatures had passed through areas that were sparsely populated except for a few houses. But that still seemed to imply that whatever they are had no fear of people.

The reporter also made reference to a report obtained by Wisconsin cryptozoologist Linda Godfrey about a farm family that had witnessed a similar creature.

Drew, the family's son, saw a creature lurking in the tree line. When the family's rooster began to squawk, the creature let out a fierce growl, then all went silent.

"Drew heard what sounded like something jumping back over the fence," the account continues, "and the rooster squealed as if in pain."

The youth grabbed a flashlight and ran outside, searching the fence from his front porch. He saw the rooster, but it appeared to have something dark over its middle, which Drew slowly came to realize was the muzzle of a creature with

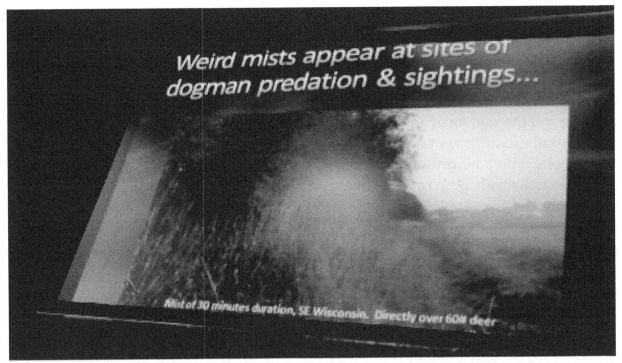

Weird mists appear at sites of dogman predation & sightings...

Mist of 30 minutes duration, SE Wisconsin. Directly over 60# deer

Pennsylvania-based researcher Butch Witkowski has now collected dozens of reports of the Dogman. He believes the beasts live quietly in the woods but have been known to confront hunters and others. The creature often appears in the middle of a fog-like mist, indicating its possible paranormal nature.

two glowing eyes.

"Whatever it was," Drew said, "it seemed to look through me. It turned my blood cold and I was paralyzed with fear. I'm a hunter. I'm used to being in the wilderness and encountering bigger animals. Those animals don't scare me like this thing did. When I encountered this thing, I got the feeling that it wanted to hurt me. After researching something I've never believed in, I'm convinced that this thing is a Dogman."

Loud howls and the sound of something walking on two legs in the gravel driveway plagued the family for many months afterward. But there is again much common ground between this story and Witkowski's accounts, primarily the deathly fear that Drew experienced. Like many witnesses, he seems to be groping for words to express just how scary the encounter was.

A DOGMAN HAUNTS THE BACKWOODS OF MICHIGAN

David Sands of "The Huffington Post" offers an account from Michigan radio personality Steve Cook, who is also a researcher of local folklore. After playing a song he had written himself, mostly for April Fools' Day laughs, about a horrifying doglike creature, he found himself flooded with reports from people claiming to have seen the real thing.

Cook told Sands he had received about 500 reports of dog man encounters.

Of those, he believes about a hundred seem plausible and credible and "just a little too weird to explain away."

One account that sticks with Cook involved a 13-year-old girl who had never heard of the Dogman. She was sneaking a smoke behind her family's home near Reed City, Michigan, in the winter of 1993, when she noticed a glint of light coming through the planks of an abandoned barn. After a few minutes, she realized a six-foot-tall creature with the head of a dog was staring at her. She ran away and later spoke with a neighbor who claimed to have seen a buffalo-sized dog in the same barn. As with Witkowski's cases, the witness's impulse to flee kicked in immediately.

An account from a Fowlerville fireman who claimed to have seen a gorilla-shaped creature with a canine head that raced over one hundred feet into a wooded area in a period of three to four seconds also reached Cook. The fact that the creature was spotted running into a wooded area is also very consistent with the reports received by Witkowski.

Sands also consulted the aforementioned Linda Godfrey, who told him that the creature is "fully canine, walks on its hind legs, and uses it forelimbs to carry chunks of roadkill or deer carcasses. They have pointed ears on top of their heads. They have big fangs. They walk – most tellingly – digit-grade, or on their toe pads, as all canines do, and that's something a human in a fur suit really can't duplicate."

Godfrey added that witnesses are usually scared to death by the creatures, but, after twenty years of receiving reports, she can't cite one serious injury from an alleged encounter. The Native Americans she consulted believe the Dogmen are spirit creatures from another place that assume a physical form while in our realm.

An elder from the Ottawa-Chippewa tribe told Cook that they believed Dogmen were members of a shape-shifting skin-walker tribe who became stuck somewhere between their human and animal forms.

"It's a unique creature," Cook told Sands. "It's not just a variation of Bigfoot. It's not a Jersey Devil. It's not some ghost. It's the Michigan Dogman, and people love to have their own homegrown folklore."

SOME CAUTIONARY WORDS FROM BUTCH WITKOWSKI

When asked if he had any final comment to make in our interview, Witkowski said, "People should keep in mind that these – whatever they are – could be dangerous. They have followed people. In one case, they charged a lady. She heard it coming at her and she was close enough to the porch to get inside when it broke the woods. But she heard it running. So I'm going to assume that these creatures could be extremely dangerous. If one is seen, I would tell people to report it to the local authorities. Don't go out with your 12-gauge shotgun and think you're going to stop something like this. You're just liable to piss it off."

Witkowski said he planned to lead an expedition of several fellow researchers into the wooded Pennsylvania areas where the bipedal canine has been seen, hoping to compensate for the creature's stealth with human technology, like surveillance cameras that can snap a photo every half second for up to sixty days as well as infrared and thermal imaging devices.

"This is a real mystery to me," Witkowski said. "You know, I thought Ufology was strange and hard to figure out, but it's kind of simple compared to this stuff."

HELTER-SKELTER REVISITED
By Michele Lowe

When I was a young adult in my late teens, early twenties, I used to hang out with my friends like most young people in Southern California. But I was a little weird. I loved all things Hollywood. I would recruit my friends all the time to go with me up to Hollywood to hang out. We would go to clubs, cruise Hollywood and Sunset Boulevards to the wee hours of the morning and get invited to wild parties that you've probably only read about! (But that's a whole other story.) We would also drive up as far as we could onto the Paramount Studios lot before we would hit the security gates and hope that we would see movie stars!

JUST SOME SHOW BIZ KIDS

I was obsessed with all things Hollywood. This included the seedier side to Hollywood also. Like the crazy Hollywood Babylon-type stories that ran rampant in Hollywood through the decades. A good example is the book written about the murder of director Desmond Taylor. It was titled "A Cast of Killers," written by Sidney D. Kirkpatrick. It is the true story about the murder of this famous director during the "Roaring Twenties." The suspects were literally all of Hollywood's elite stars of the time. People who were involved or suspects were people like Fatty Arbuckle, Charlie Chaplin and Mabel Normand, to name a few. To this day, the case has never been solved. And if you can get a copy of this book I highly recommend it.

I was also fascinated and horrified by the Manson murders. I loved Sharon Tate. She was so beautiful. I remembered her from repeats of those old crazy 1960s beach and horror movies. I couldn't believe anyone would want to kill such a beautiful woman, a pregnant woman at that. It was a horrific crime that scared all of Southern California, not only because of its brutality and pure evil, but also because of the seeming randomness of it. I remember my mother saying how she was so scared after that and how she hated being home alone with just my sister and me, both very small children, because my dad worked nights.

Flash forward to my teen years. One night my friends, including Cuz Dave (who turned out to be my cousin! Hence the name Cuz Dave), and my friend Carla and I decided to drive up to Hollywood and cruise around and hang out. While we were driving around we decided we would go over to Benedict Canyon Drive and find 10050 Cielo Drive. We knew that is where the Manson murders had taken place and so we wanted to check out the house where it happened.

We definitely were not your average teenagers hanging out and playing pool and drinking beer. No, we were a bit odd. On many nights we would go to the library and spend hours looking at books and reading about whatever tickled our fancy at the time. So we had all read about the murders at 10050 Cielo Drive, and that was why we decided to go there that night: to check the home out in person and see a little bit of history, though it was a horrific part of history.

THE MANY GHOSTS OF BENEDICT CANYON

Benedict Canyon, which is outside of Beverly Hills, is an upscale neighborhood that is and was home to some of Hollywood's most famous. During the day, it's a beautiful and tranquil place where many would love to live. But it's been said that, when the sun goes down, Benedict Canyon can become one of the spookiest places in Hollywood. Benedict Canyon Drive winds through this upscale neighborhood and at night is very dark. Without your car lights being on, it would be pitch black! This area of Hollywood is, for some reason, also notoriously haunted. Stories of the claimed hauntings on or around Benedict Canyon Drive are quite numerous.

Like on June 16th, 1959, when actor George Reeves went into his upstairs bedroom at 1579 Benedict Canyon Dr. and reportedly shot himself in the head. George Reeves was television's "Superman." He died instantly. One evening a couple who lived in the home after the tragedy saw his ghost fully materialize in front of them, wearing his Superman costume. They moved out that same night.

One of the most famous and well-documented of hauntings in Benedict Canyon was at the then-home of actress Elke Sommers and her husband, Joe Hyams. The couple witnessed paranormal activity in the dining room of their home on Benedict Canyon Drive from 1964-1968. They claimed to see the apparition of a middle-aged man, and he was seen by several guests on at least five separate occasions. Paranormal investigators from the American Society for Psychical Research and UCLA monitored the events taking place in the house. The Hymans moved out of the house, however, after being awakened one night by knocking on their bedroom door. When they opened the door, they found that the hallway was filled with smoke from a fire that started in the dining room. The house ended up being bought and sold seventeen times in the next few years!

SHARON TATE'S PRECOGNITIVE GHOSTLY VISITATION

Many people don't know this, but Sharon Tate had a glimpse of her own death three years before that horrible and tragic night at 10050 Cielo Drive with a ghostly experience and premonition. It was on the very same stretch of Benedict Canyon, about three miles away on Easton Drive, at her ex-boyfriend Jay Sebring's home. He lived in the home at 9860 Easton Drive once owned by MGM film producer Paul Bern, who was briefly married to Jean Harlow.

Paul Bern gave Jean Harlow the home as a wedding gift. She did not want the home and wanted to sell it. But Paul Bern would not allow that. It was only three months later that a butler would discover the body of Mr. Bern – nude and in Jean Harlow's entirely white bedroom – dead from an apparent gunshot wound. It was ruled a suicide initially, but controversy soon followed.

Eventually it was believed that his death was not a suicide but a murder. But, to this day, the case of Paul Bern's death has never been solved. That was not the only tragedy at that home either. Two people also drowned in the home and it was said a previous owner had committed suicide in the home as well. Jay Sebring had actually been warned that the house was "jinxed" but moved in anyway.

It was in 1966 that Sharon Tate was staying overnight at her ex-boyfriend's place. She was there alone that night and she couldn't sleep. She later told others that she was uncomfortable but could not say why. She also told a reporter that she felt "funny" and was scared by every little sound she heard in the home. While she lay there restless on the bed, she said that a "creepy little man" came into the bedroom. She said she knew the man was Paul Bern. Apparently Jay Sebring had told her of the previous occupant.

Sharon said that he was unaware that she was even in the room and that he seemed to be looking for something. Sharon was so upset by the site of Paul Bern's ghost that she quickly put on her robe and made her way to the stairs. As Sharon started to go down the stairs, she saw something horrifying that made her stop in her tracks! There, at the bottom of the staircase, was a body tied to the staircase post. She was so scared and could not tell if it was a male or a female. But she said that she could clearly see that the person's throat had been cut! She said the apparition then vanished.

Sharon was so upset by these events that she continued downstairs to the living room to make herself a drink. But she could not find where Jay kept the alcohol. She later said that she felt compelled to press on a section of the bookcase, and it opened to reveal a hidden bar. Sharon also said that she was compelled to pull away part of the wallpaper at the base of the bar. She eventually calmed down and, thinking that it was only a bad dream, went back upstairs to bed. But the next morning when she came downstairs she was shocked to see the hidden bar still open from the night before and the torn wallpaper at the base of the bar that she had been compelled to pull on the night before.

After this incident Sharon told anyone who would listen to her about this vision. Many believe that she saw a glimpse of her own horrific future that night when she, Jay Sebring and three others were brutally murdered at 10050 Cielo Drive. Sadly, her vision was exactly how her pregnant body was found. So, with all of that being said, it will help you understand what my friends and I went through on our trips up to Benedict Canyon and 10050 Cielo Dr.

RETURNING TO THE SCENE OF THE CRIME

The first time I went up there was with Cuz Dave and my friend Carla Haley. We all had that fascination with the Manson murders and decided to make the trip up to check out the infamous house. As we slowly made our way up the dark and winding Benedict Canyon Drive, we were already getting a spooky vibe. So we were all very quiet as we made our way down the dark road. Then we saw it. Cielo Drive. We turned left onto the small street that ended in a cul-de-sac. We scanned the mail boxes, looking for 10050. As we got to the end of the cul-de-sac, we saw 10040 on a mail box. But then the address on the next mail box was something like 54789 and then the one after was 10060.

So we deduced that they had changed the address because of people like us, "looky loo's" coming to check out the house. But they didn't do that great of a job, because we knew that had to be the driveway to the house. Now mind you that you could not see the houses from the street where we were. No, you had to drive up a very steep and narrow driveway to get to the area where the home was. The driveway was so narrow that only one car could drive up or down the driveway at a time. (Things were a lot more laidback when we were teenagers, and I would highly recommend that nobody go up there now. I'm sure they probably have tons of security cameras and such to protect that area and surrounding properties. Also the original home has long since been torn down.)

But we were adventurous and drove very slowly up the steep driveway that seemed to go on forever. We finally pulled up to the Iron Gate, which was near to where they found the first body. It was that of a teenage boy named Steven Parent, who did not even know anybody there in the house, but was there to visit the gatekeeper. Just beyond the gate, about 100 or so yards away, you could see the side of the house. The feeling of being so close to where such a horrific crime was committed was very sobering. The atmosphere was very heavy there, and it just didn't feel right, so we left.

A MENACING BLACK DOG CHARGES THE HORRIFIED GROUP

We navigated our way back down the long narrow driveway and back onto Cielo Drive and then made a right turn back onto Benedict Canyon Drive. As we were driving we started discussing our little adventure and decided to turn off of the dark road into one of the neighborhoods and check out some of the beautiful homes. Many of them were lit up by colored lights and it was a nice change from

the spooky home on Cielo Drive. As we were slowly driving through the neighborhood, checking out the nice homes, a giant black dog came charging at the car! Now, when I say dog, it was more like a wolf! It was huge and had this very thick black fur. The dog's back and head easily came up to the window of Cuz Dave's car, which was a Nova.

When the dog charged the car, it so startled Carla and I that we screamed, and Cuz Dave took off quickly, trying to get away from this crazed dog. Dave had gotten up to 35 mph and this dog was easily keeping up with the car. It was literally right next to the car, looking at us as if he was out to kill! It was barking violently as we tried to drive away in sheer terror. Dave finally got back to the entrance of the neighborhood and turned right back onto Benedict Canyon Drive. We drove about a mile or so before Dave finally slowed down and turned into another neighborhood so that we could calm down and regroup.

On Benedict Canyon it was so dark and there was no place to pull over so this other neighborhood seemed like the best choice at the moment. Just was we were starting to calm down and talk about what had just happened, the giant black dog literally appeared out of nowhere and came charging at the car. We again screamed and Dave took off again. We could not believe this was happening. There was no way that dog could have kept up with us when Dave took off out of that last neighborhood, much less find us again in a random neighborhood over a mile away! We quickly got out of that neighborhood and again lost the crazed dog. This time though we didn't stop. We went straight home.

A PARANORMAL MONSTER, NOT A PET

Now, you're probably thinking it was somebody's pet. But I can assure you this was not the case. The dog was enormous. I've never before or since seen a dog with the thick, pitch-black fur like we saw on this dog that night or one of its enormous size. And its speed was not that of any dog I've ever seen. It was running right next to the car and was in no way straining to keep up; it kept up with ease. Also, these neighborhoods had long streets, so Dave had time to get the car to a good speed of 30-35 mph easily.

It was clear the dog could have easily run even faster if it wanted to. And then there is the fact that we drove off as fast as we could a mile or more away to another neighborhood to try to calm down and were only there a couple minutes when, out of literally nowhere, the dog appeared again and started charging at us at full speed! How could it even find us again? We didn't even know we were going into this next neighborhood. It was just a last second decision.

Even though we didn't understand it then, we still knew that what happened was not normal. And, though we didn't know the term "paranormal," inside we knew that what happened was exactly that. Looking back at what had happened and knowing what I know now, I believe that what we encountered was a Hell Hound. I had heard of them before, but didn't know what they were. So I did some research. This is what I found:

A Hell Hound is a supernatural dog, usually very large with thick black fur. They are unnaturally strong and fast and have red eyes. Sometimes the eyes are yellow. It is said that they are assigned to guard the entrance to the home of the dead, like graveyards or burial grounds. They also have other duties to do with the afterlife, like hunting down lost souls. They can also be an omen of death.

FLEEING FROM A POOR LOST SOUL

Could these creatures be out looking for lost souls? With all of the death and haunting in this area, this could be the case. My next trip to 10050 Cielo Drive seemed to prove this.

After telling a couple of my friends of our adventure in Benedict Canyon,

they wanted to go check it out for themselves. So I got my friend Lynne Nagata to drive myself and my friend Betty Bennett up to Benedict Canyon. We found Cielo Drive once again. This time I knew exactly where I was going.

We slowly drove up the long steep narrow driveway and approached the Iron Gate. It was very dark, but Lynn's headlights illuminated the Iron Gate and part of the driveway. You could see the side of the house because of the lights on it. We had only been there a minute when out of nowhere a black silhouette of a young man appeared right before our eyes! Though the figure was black, you could tell by the slender frame that it was a teenager or young man. But with my instincts I knew that was the case also.

He was looking out from behind the gate, directly at us! And that was not the most disturbing part. It was how he didn't move at all. Just standing there looking out at us. We sat there, staring back for a moment, trying to take in what we were seeing. Then an overwhelming sence of terror struck us and I told Lynne, "Let's get out of here now!"

Now, again, there was a minimal amount of room to maneuver on that driveway where we were, even though Lynn drove a small Datsun. So it took a few times of going back and forth for her to maneuver the car and get it turned around from where we were. While she was turning the car around, Betty and I stared in horror at the shadowy silhouette. It never moved. It was motionless and still staring directly at us. Finally she got the car turned around, and, as we started to drive back down the driveway, the shadowy figure just vanished.

I believe that the figure we saw was the teenage boy who was the first to be killed that dreadful night in 1969 by Charles Manson follower Tex Watson. Steven Parent was at the wrong place at the wrong time. He had gone to the home to see the gatekeeper that evening, and, when he was leaving in his car, he was met at the gate by Tex Watson and the monsters of the Helter-Skelter crimes. Tex Watson shot him, and Parent died right there in his car in front of the Iron Gate. We were so disturbed by the incident that night that we never again returned to 10050 Cielo Drive.

Michele Lowe

Board Member\Lead Investigator Roswell Georgia Paranormal Investigations

http://roswellparanormal.com/

POSSIBLY MORE FRIGHTENING THAN THE DOGMAN
THE LOUP-GAROUS OF OLD VINCENNES, INDIANA
By Tim R. Swartz

MORE frightening than the most modern of sightings of the Dogman, the early 18th century, French fur traders making their way south from Canada, settled in what is now South-Western Indiana, and encountered their own version of this hideous beast. The area was rich with game such as beaver and buffalo, and even after the French lost their claim on the territory following the French-Indian wars, the settlers remained and founded the town of Vincennes.

Because of its early French heritage, which is robust with supernatural-based folklore, Vincennes, Indiana has become a focal point for mysterious creatures straight from the shadowy corners of the human mind. For the 18th century settler, the dark, endless forest that surrounded Vincennes was filled with all manner of unknown dangers. But it was threats of the supernatural that produced the most terror, and the most horrifying of these paranormal nightmares was the Loup-garou.

The Loup-garou, also known as the Rougarou, which haunted the dreams of early French settlers, could appear as a monstrous wolf, but it could also be someone who transformed into a cow, horse, or any other animal. Once under a spell as a Loup-garou, the unfortunate victim became an enraged animal that roamed each night through the fields and forests for a certain period of time, usually 101 days. During the day, he returned to his human form, though he was continually morose and sickly and fearful to tell of his predicament lest even a worse sentence should befall him.

According to some legends, a person could become a Loup-garou by breaking lent seven years in a row. As well, the cursed shape-shifter was especially fond of hunting down and killing Catholics who did not follow the rules of Lent. The main way the Loup-garou could be released from its spell was for someone to recognize him as a cursed creature of the night and injure him to the point of drawing blood. Only this would effectively remove the curse. However, both the victim and his rescuer could not mention the incident, even to each other. Anyone who defied this taboo could find themselves possessed and transformed into the Loup-garou.

One could also be possessed by the spirit of a Loup-garou if they were unfortunate enough to encounter a Feu Follet in the forest. A Feu Follet, also known as a will-o'-the-wisp or ghost light, was a bright ball of light that would be seen flying and hopping around trees and brush. It was thought that the Feu Follet could bewitch both man and horse to lead them off the trail and into the dark forest.

REMEMBERING THE OLD TALES

By the beginning of the 20th century, memories of the Loup-garou began to fade with each passing generation. Fortunately, many of these folk tales were recorded in the 1920''s by Anna C. O'Flynn, a teacher in the old French section of Vincennes. As well, in the 1930s a group of writers with the Federal Writers' Project of the Works Progress Administration also managed to record some of the old tales from a handful of Vincennes French descendants. These people, who at this point were in their seventies and eighties, clearly remembered the stories of the Loup-garou told to them on dark nights in front of the flickering fire of the family hearth.

One story, as recalled by Pepe Boucher, involved a man named Charlie Page who one night, as he was going home, encountered a large, black dog with gleaming red eyes. Page, a large man who feared nothing, at first tried to shoo the dog away. When the dog refused to move, Page attempted to kick it in its face. However, the dog with a stealthy, panther-like movement sprang at his throat and knocked him to the ground.

Boucher recalled: "You bet this time he tried to kick and get his knife to finish the dog whose hot breath was singeing his hair—whose great paws were tearing his shoulders and whose fangs were near his neck. With one of his powerful arms, he grab the neck of the dog until his tongue hant out. The shaggy hair on the dog's neck be lashing his face and his eyes blazing with madness. The Loup-garou be trying to bewitch Page. He know now it be Loup-garou. He know that

nothing but blood could save him. Struggling to use his knife, the beast pushed the point against Page to make him draw his own blood. Now had Page not been almost a giant he would have turned right into a Loup-garou."

Throwing his whole strength into the struggle, Page managed to push his knife through the shaggy fur, deep behind the forelegs of the savage creature. As its blood spurted from its wound, the Loup-garou vanished in a flash of light and flames, in its place stood Page's best friend, Jean Vetal.

"They look and look at each other," Boucher said. "Mais they spoke no word. Soon they part, each going to his own home. The knife had cut Jean Vetal's arm near the elbow, he doctor it and soon it be well, and then he be delivered from the Loup-garou power."

According to tradition, for 101 days Page and Vetal never spoke of the horrible animal. After the 101 days had passed the two men were free to tell their friends what had happened.

Boucher told the researchers that Jean Vetal gave Page a horse and a cow in gratitude for being freed of his curse.

THE LOUP-GAROU COW

Another tale, as recalled by Pepe Boucher, shows that the traditional Loup-garou was not always a wolf or dog. Around 1780, shortly after Gen. George R. Clark and his troops took Fort Sackville from the British, Vincennes saw an increase in American settlers coming from the east in search of homesteads. The Americans had no time for tales of ghosts, witches and Loup-garou's and openly mocked the French and their superstitions.

Soon, however, one of the new American settlers, a man who had been especially scornful of the French and their belief in the Loup-garou, started disappearing from his home every night. When questioned by his friends, he claimed that he had lost his cow and was simply out trying to find it.

This story sounded suspicious to Jean Vetal, who remembering his own misery as a cursed Loup-garou years before, was certain that supernatural forces were at work. Feeling that God had presented Vetal this opportunity to further cleanse his accursed soul, he secured a large, sharp knife and went out into the night in search for the possessed American.

After searching most of the night, Vetal heard the moan of a cow. Gathering up his courage, Vetal crept softly to the spot from where the moaning came. There, lying in a clearing was a cow, moaning like a person in great pain.

Vetal was convinced that this cow was the missing American, now a Loup-garou. The unearthly moaning made Vetal tremble in fear, as he reached out with his knife to draw blood and deliver the cursed man. Unfortunately, before Vetal could plant his knife, the cow jumped up, swung her head and knocked him onto the ground.

For over a mile the Loup-garou ran with Vetal chasing close behind. Finally he was able to get close enough to stick his knife deep enough into the cow's shoulder to draw blood.

"Oh! Oh!," Boucher said. "The blood spout out and the cow tumble down as Vetal tumble over on the grass in the common, right by the side of the American what always make fun on the French loup-garou."

As the two men walked back to town, the American begged Vetal not to tell anyone until he had died or moved away. Shortly afterwards, he moved back east and was never heard from again.

Boucher concluded his story with: "When the American be gone Vetal tell, mais some not believe, pourquei. Et quelquesunes ne pas eroire! (It is so whether you believe it or not!)

"Will 'o' the Wisp"

CURSE'S OF THE CAUCHEMARS

In old Vincennes, shape-shifters did not necessarily have to be Loup-garous. According to an article published in the January 8, 1891, issue of the *Vincennes Commercial* newspaper, there were also witches around to cast evil spells upon the early settlers of Vincennes.

It was believed that witches—called "cauchemars" (nightmares)—could turn men into horses, so that they could ride them along the Wabash River Bottoms. In the morning, when the French woke up feeling all worn out and "hag-ridden," they would say, "C'est mon cauchemar!" (It is my nightmare!)

One old man always claimed that this had happened to him. The next day he said he could see where he had stood and pawed the earth, at the place where the witch had dismounted and tied him.

And there were marks on the fence rail where he had gnawed as an impatient horse. Even the day after, he still was picking some pieces of wood out of his teeth, the bewitched man said.

It was also believed that witches could shape-shift themselves into anything that they desired, and in that shape they would torment their neighbors.

One old French farmer said that for years he had experienced nothing but bad luck because of an old hag that had been persecuting him. At length he made a silver bullet, loaded his gun, and went to a deer-lick. There he killed the witch that had taken the form of a deer. After that his luck turned around and he was never bothered again.

Nowadays the vast, wild forests that once surrounded Vincennes have been cut down to make way for shopping malls, housing developments and highways. In the harsh light of modern society, the old superstitions of the early French settlers have been all but forgotten. Nevertheless, the shape-shifters, witches and other monsters of times past still remain, quietly waiting for their chance to live once again in the nightmares of those foolish enough to travel alone into the dark, forbidding night.

The beast from the motion picture, "Driller."

THE TERRIBLE HUNGERS OF REAL-LIFE VAMPIRES, WEREWOLVES AND GHOULS
by Brad Steiger

SOMETIMES one hears it said that hell and the devil are but projections of one side of the human psyche. Without attempting to determine the truth or error of such a conjecture, it would appear that the imagination is, indeed, as Shakesphere said, capable of "seeing more devils than hell can hold."

There are, however, some things which defy even the most lurid imagination. When otherwise representative specimens of humanity develop a thirst for human blood and/or flesh, and others rob graves in order to satisfy their sexual hungers, it is enough to make even the most jaded cast about for an explanation.

Man has not always had modern psychiatry to explain such peculiar and incomprehensible behavior in terms of sadism and sexual perversion. In times past, evil spirits got the blame. This was only logical, for were not supernatural emissaries of evil responsible for such cataclysms as lightning and thunder, earthquakes, fires, sickness, and warts on the nose?

It was easy enough to lay blame for a bloodless, mutilated corpse on wild animals. But when, immediately after such a discovery, a man would be found wandering in a daze with fresh on his beard or fragments of human flesh sticking to his clothing, some other explanation was needed.

Clearly, early man reasoned, it must be the work of devils. Men simply did not do such things of their own volition. Those who did were most certainly possessed. Since those possessed behaved like wild animals, it followed that the demon-men must somehow take the form of wild animals. Belief in the transformation of men into carnivorous animals, or lycanthropy, led to the formation of the legends of the vampire, the werewolf, and the ghoul.

Vampirism is recognized today as a condition of deep psychosis in which one believes that his or her life can be sustained only by fresh blood obtained from human victims. There is also a form of sexual perversion in which the deviate is aroused by the thought of drinking or sucking human blood. In order to achieve sexual satisfaction, the deviate must somehow satisfy his terrible thirst. Those having a knowledge of sexual symbolism will readily discover a wealth of such conversions in the vampire legend.

According to legend, a vampire was the restless soul of a dead person, which needed regular draughts of human blood to sustain its existence. It was believed that the vampire did its hunting in the form of a huge bat, a form that it could assume at will. The vampire would leave its place of burial at night to suck the blood of living persons and had to return to its grave before daybreak.

It was further believed that a person who met death at the hands (or fangs, more properly) of such a creature also became a vampire. In some regions it was thought that a vampire was the soul of an excommunicate, kept by the devil for his own purposes. Vampires were reputed to favor their relatives and friends as victims, especially those who were young and healthy.

If young and healthy victims are considered choice fare for vampires, then Hungary's Countess Elizabeth Bathory must be deemed discriminating. Over six hundred girls and young women were drained of their lives in order to appease the beautiful but perverted noblewoman's strange lusts.

Except for her zest for the taste of blood, the ravishing vampire of Castle Czejthe bore little resemblance to the traditional image of her breed. The Countess' sensual body could hardly be likened to the withered cadavers that by night forsook their coffins to steal the lifeblood of others. Elizabeth's lusty blood was very much her own.

Kings and cardinals, bishops and judges were proud to call themselves Bathory, as were princes and warriors. Gyorgy Thurzo, prime minister of Hungary, was Elizabeth's cousin.

On New Year's Eve of the year 1610, Prime Minister Thurzo, the governor of the Nvitra Province, and the village priest, along with a detachment of soldiers and police, stealthily climbed the bleak hill to Castle Cezjthe. The night was cold, and the members of the company shivered as the black sky showered cold rain on them. But not all of the chill could be attributed to the weather.

As Count Thurzo stood by the castle's huge, vault-like doors, waiting for the others to join him, he thought of the day, just a little over a week earlier, when King Mattias had summoned him.

"Thurzo," the king had begun in serious tones, "isn't the Countess Nadasdy of Csejthe a kinswoman of yours?"

The prime minister had paled. So, it's come at last, he thought, then answered, "Yes, your majesty. A cousin."

"I've been hearing strange and terrible things about the countess," said the King. "The village priest says that the villagers are afraid she is a vampire, and they want something done. Do you know anything about it?"

Count Thurzo knew. He had heard many stories of the mysterious disappearances of a number of children and young women from Czejthe, and of travelers who had never been heard of after they had reached the village. He had heard, too, of the midnight sorties of Castle Csejthe's emblemed coach into the village, "which had caused the terrified peasants to lock and bolt their doors. He had remembered one trembling peasant who had come to him with a report of screams of agony and the sweet stench of burning human flesh that sometimes drifted down from the castle into the village when the wind was right.

"I've heard a few wild tales. But I'm sure there is an explana... ."

King Mattias cut him off.

"I'm not so sure the stories are wild, Thurzo. Those people are frightened, and badly. I order you to take whatever men you need and personally see what's going on in that castle!"

"Yes, your majesty."

The wind wailed through the battlements of Castle Csejthe, startling the prime minister back to the present. By this time the raiding party had assembled. Testing the castle's door and finding it ajar, Count Thurzo walked straight in, closely followed by his men. The sight that greeted them caused Thurzo's handpicked professionals to shudder.

The village priest fell to his knees and crossed himself. In the center of the great hall lay the chalk-white corpse of a young girl with a jagged cut in its throat, obviously drained of every drop of blood. A short distance away sprawled another girl, whose nude form looked as if it had been used as a cushion for giant pins. Although she, too, had been drained of a large amount of blood, this one was still alive and gasping.

Two seasoned policemen turned away in horror from the next spectacle.

Chained to a pillar at one end of the hall was the charred corpse of yet another of the vampire's victims. This one had been set afire before being bled dry. Her death had obviously been a mercy.

"Your Excellency, look here!" cried the prime minister's sergeant.

The raiders hastened down the dark stairway to the dungeon area. Horror gave way to rage when they discovered dozens of girls and young women penned up like cattle. Many were weak and thin from repeated bleedings, while others were fat and healthy. Count Thurzo's party had found a veritable human slaughterhouse. A clamor of oaths and threats rose among the band, as they went about freeing the captives.

"Silence!" ordered the prime minister in a harsh whisper. "We have not yet found everything we came for. Quickly now, upstairs!"

The raiders had not yet been discovered. Swiftly they ascended the steps leading from the dungeon, and with eyes averted, crossed the great hall once more. Count Thurzo thought for a moment, then decided to enter the banquet hall. The prime minister had chosen New Year's Eve for his expedition with the thought that the raiding party might have a better chance of gaining entrance undetected because of the probable festivities which would be taking place. But no one was prepared for the kind of celebration actually in progress.

Devils would have delighted in the vampires' orgy that the raiders interrupted.

The walls of the banquet hall fairly oozed blood. There was so much blood on the floor that the heels of the soldiers' jackboots were stained. Three nude female bodies in various stages of mutilation lay on the floor and another served as the *piece de resistance* in the center of a table, which had been spread with a gore-soaked tablecloth of the finest white linen. The Nadasdy's expensive silver lay scattered about the room. On the table stood goblets containing liquid too dense and too red to be wine.

A fifth victim hung from the ropes that bound her to a pillar near the revelers. Around the table sat Countess Elizabeth Bathory-Nadasdy; Lloona Joo, the Countess' advisor in devil worship; Barsovny and Orvos, Lesbian pplaymates and procurors to the countess; and other celebrants—completely in the nude.

The raiders, too stricken for action or words, watched as Barsovny tightened a cord around the victim's throat until the jugular vein, swollen with blood, stood out. Orvos was ready with a stiletto.

"Me!" cried out the Countess, as though in the arms of a lover. "Me!"

She sprang in front of the doomed girl. Orvos made a jab with the pointed dagger, and a stream of crimson spewed out under pressure, drenching the waiting Countess, who screamed in pleasure and rubbed her naked breasts with bloody hands.

"Hold!" choked out Count Thurzo. "In the name of God, hold!" The dagger clattered to the floor. Several of the revelers screamed.

"Hello, cousin," gurgled Elizabeth, drunk on blood or wine or both. "Welcome!"

The celebrants were placed under arrest. All were taken to a nearby jail, except Elizabeth, who was placed under heavy guard in her apartment.

When the trial convened with Theodosiue de Sluzo of the Royal Supreme Court presiding, the tale of an eleven-year reign of terror unfolded. It was revealed that the Countess Bathory had not only drunk the blood of her victims, but had bathed in it as well, in the belief that such a process would keep her skin soft and white and youthful. De Sluzo and twenty other judges heard accounts of murder, torture, human sacrifice, perverted sexual acts, orgies of blood drinking and blood baths such as seldom reach the ears of man. There could be no doubt as to the verdict.

Lloona Joo was sentenced to death by burning after having her fingers torn off one by one. The others met swift justice under the headsman's axe—all except Elizabeth.

The beautiful vampire of Csejthe was found guilty with the others, but because of her high station and noble birth, the court delayed passing sentence. She was, however, never to see the light of day again. Her castle apartment was sealed up except for narrow slits to provide ventilation and to allow her guards to pass food to her. The countess was then fifty, was said to be still beautiful and remarkably youthful for her age. Four years after the stonemasons sealed her in, the Countess Elizabeth Bathory-Nadasdy died—but not from a stake through her heart.

Perhaps in Elizabeth's case, the fury of a woman scorned was matched, even surpassed, by the wrath of one deserted while caught up in the hot whirlwind of first passion.

Would the ardent young countess have gone to such gruesome lengths if her smoldering desire had been granted satisfaction through normal sexual expression? What kind of man was Count Nadasdy, who preferred the masculine society of army camps to the bedroom of his young and beautiful bride? Was the vampire instinct already rampant in the mind of Countess Bathory?

"Vampire" conjures up for most an image quite different from that embodied by the beautiful, perverse Countess Bathory. Moviegoers of twenty years ago and late show devotees will remember Bela Lugosi's portrayal of Count Dracula, the central character of Bram Stoker's classic vampire novel of the same name. In the movie version of the book and in the subsequent films based upon it, the presentation was always the same.

The story would open with a view of the vampire's coffin hidden away in a remote burial vault or the secret chamber of a deserted mansion. And then—

"screee-e-ch!" The lid would slowly raise, revealing the cadaverous figure of Dracula, dressed somberly in black, with the Dracula family crest worn at his collar. With eyes gleaming malevolently, he would step gracefully from the casket, black cloak swirling, and transform himself into a bat.

A short time later, the bat could be seen flying through the window of a bedroom, where slept his always beautiful victim with her bare throat white in the moonlight. The sexual symbolism is obvious, and it is just as apparent today in the popular figure of television's matinee idol vampire, Barnabas Collins, of *Dark Shadows.* But real life vampires seldom operate with such dignity and poetry.

An example is the case of Italy's Vincent Verzini, whose vampiric crimes were committed during the years 1867-1871. The sexual nature of the twenty-two year old Verzini's acts is unmistakable. He achieved orgasm, it is reported, by grasping his female victim by the throat, first chocking her, and then tearing her flesh with his teeth. He then proceeded to suck the blood through the wound.

One day pretty Maria Previtali, nineteen-year-old cousin of Verzini, went out into the fields to work. Suddenly she became aware of footsteps other than her own. Frightened, she looked over her shoulder. Vincent was following.

Maria's footsteps picked up speed, as she fought back a wave of fear and panic. She thought of fourteen-year-old Johanna Motta, who had been viciously murdered the preceding December as she traveled on foot to a nearby village.

She remembered how she had lain awake that night, too frightened to sleep, and listened to Papa as he told his wife of the incident.

"Si, Mama," Papa had said, his voice filled with emotion, "her throat was black and blue, and her mouth was full of dirt. All of her clothes were ripped off and her thighs were bruised with teeth marks.

"Her belly was wide open, and her insides pulled out. And, Mama, *per Dio,* the parts that make her a woman had been torn right off!"

Maria shuddered and started to run. She remembered Mrs. Frigeni, who had gone out to work in the fields one morning, and by nightfall, had still not returned. When her husband had gone out to look for her, he found her naked and mutilated body. She had been strangled with a leather thong and flesh had been torn from her abdomen.

Maria was almost breathless now. Vincent had recently been in trouble for chocking women. Mario could run no more. Her footsteps faltered, and two powerful hands grabbed her.

She felt herself thrown to the ground. Fingers like bands of steel closed around her throat. She could not even scream. Only a miracle could save her. She started to faint, and the hasty vampire loosened his grip. Drawing in her breath, the courageous girl brought up her knee and kicked her insane cousin in the stomach.

As he staggered, Maria sprang to her feet, rubbing her burning throat.

"Vincent," she gasped, "are you crazy? You trying to kill me?"

Maria's blow had drained the erstwhile vampire of his thirst. He got to his feet, muttering obscenities and threats, then staggered off across the field. Maria ran home and told her horrified mother, who took her at once to the village prefect.

Verzini was immediately arrested, and after being questioned at length, made a full and detailed confession. He was tried, convicted, and sentenced to life imprisonment.

Although Vincent Verzini's examiners found "no evidence of psychosis," there can be little doubt that his vampirism was the expression of deep derangement and sexual perversion. That this is the case is shown lucidly by Verzini's own words:

"I had an unspeakable delight in strangling women, experiencing during the act erections and real sexual pleasure. The feeling of pleasure while strangling them was much greater than that which I experienced while masturbating. I took great delight in drinking Motta's blood. It also gave me the greatest pleasure to pull the hairpins out of the hair of my victims.

"It never occurred to me to touch or look at the genitals...*It satisfied me to seize the woman by the neck and suck their blood.*"

Not manifestly sexual were the vampirish acts of John Haigh, British killer of nine. Haigh's thirst for human blood is believed by some authorities to have been somehow linked to his religious fanaticism.

Haigh was obsessed with the Old Testament admonitions to "drink water out of thine own cistern and running waters out of thine own well." It would be fascinating to know the processes by which Haigh's twisted mind shaped this thought to cause him to start drinking his own urine and blood.

Yes, the religious vampire's first taste of human blood was that of his own. He became involved in an automobile crash in which he suffered a scalp wound which bled profusely. The blood flowed down his face and into his mouth, creating a thirst which would lead him to the gallows.

Perhaps the wound's accompanying blow deepened Haigh's psychosis. Shortly after the incident, he had a dream which he interpreted to mean that his religious fervor had sapped his strength and he could only restore his energies by the regular consumption of fresh human blood.

In keeping with the religious trend of his sickness, Haigh evolved a ritual. First he would sever the jugular vein of his victim, then he would carefully draw off the blood a glassful at a time. The actual drinking of the vital fluid was observed with great ceremony. Haigh later became convinced that his faith, too, could be sustained only by the sacrifice of others and the drinking of their blood.

35

It is accepted today that the drinking of both blood and urine are perverted sexual acts, affording gratification and pleasure to the psychotic or deeply neurotic who indulge.

It is believed that Haigh participated in homosexual acts as a youth. It is interesting to note that he claimed to have been seduced by a homosexual member of a religious sect prior to his own deviation.

Is it possible that feelings of guilt arising from these events drove the impressionable Haigh to offer such terrible propitiation? Or did he mistake the intoxication which reportedly comes from blood-drinking for religious ecstasy? As fascinating as these questions are, they will never be answered in the case of John Haigh, the vampire, who in August, 1949, was delivered to the hangman.

The vampire, the restless soul of a dead person which must drink the blood of others to sustain its "life," is highly suggestive of the pathologically immature, dependent personality, who cannot fend for himself in the business of living, but must attach himself to a more productive personality, just as the vampire attaches itself to the creatures on whose blood is feeds. Such individuals almost always subconsciously desire to return to the state of complete dependence characteristic of the prenatal state. Psychoanalysts usually disclose that, in extreme cases, the grave comes to symbolize the womb. This is often the true motive behind some individuals' incestuous desire for intercourse with their mother. The vampire's nightly return to its grave greatly resembles such a state of mind. The vampire's fangs are clearly phallic symbols, both in form and function. The vampire's predilection for its relatives resembles the incestuous cravings of the deviate, a form of infantile sexuality, as further symbolized by the vampire's relish for the young.

Blood sucking itself is significant. Psychologists say that any neurotic act involving this act is a sign of mother-fixation.

A stake through the heart to kill a vampire is strongly suggestive of fear (connected hatred) of the father figure.

It appears, therefore, that the true lair of the vampire must be sought in the hidden and forgotten areas of the human mind, rather than in secluded burial vaults and the cobweb-laced ruins of deserted mansions; and that the terrible thirst of real-life vampires must be understood in the light of the frustration and misdirection of the most basic of human needs: the need to love and reproduce one's own kind.

*****

During the Middle Ages and the period known as that of the Great Witch Mania, it was natural to explain the deviations of men in terms of demonology. Prevalent at the same time was a belief in the transformation of men into wolves (perhaps the source of the modern designation for a certain lascivious breed of male creature) and other carnivorous animals.

36

CRYPTID CREATURES FROM DARK DOMAINS

The belief that a creature half-human and half-animal was unholy reaches back into dim antiquity. Thus, the ancient Israelites are instructed through the *Book of Leviticus*: "And you should not lie with any beast and defile yourself with it, neither shall any woman give herself to a beast to lie with it... ." (18:23) Such practices were associated with worship of the pagan deity Moloch, and any offspring of such a union was classed as an evil spirit.

The most common manifestation of lycanthropy was the werewolf. A less-fastidious cousin of the vampire, this half-man half-wolf was said to go about committing murder, rape and cannibalism.

One day in the town of Dole, France, in the year 1573, a wooden stake was set up in the public square and straw and faggots piled at its base. A figure with long, matted hair and tattered remnants of clothing was dragged in chains and under heavy guard to the stake and tied securely to it.

This being accomplished, the sheriff unrolled an official looking document and read in a loud voice:

"In the name of His Majesty, by the grace of God King of France: It is proven that on a certain day, shortly after the Feast of St. Michael last, Gilles Garnier, being in the form of a wolf, seized upon in a vineyard a young girl, aged about ten or twelve years, she being in the place commonly called as Gorges, the vineyard de Chasteonoy, hard by the Bois de Serre, about a mile from Dole, and there he slew and killed her both with his hands seemingly paws, as with his teeth, and having dragged her body with his hands and teeth into the aforesaid Bois de Serre, he stripped her naked and not content with eating heartily of the flesh of her thighs and arms, he carried some of the flesh to Apolline, his wife at the hermitage of Saint-Bonnot, near Amanges, where he and his wife had their dwelling"

The official's voice cracked, and he paused to clear his throat. The crowd let out its breath as one. A priest made the sign of the cross and chanted in Latin as the sheriff began to read again.

In trite, unemotional language, a story of murder and cannibalism unfolded that caused the sale of fresh meat in Dole to fall off for a week afterwards. In revulsion the people listened as the damnation of Gilles Garnier, convicted werewolf, proceeded.

"...Unto customary place of execution, and that there by aforesaid Master Executioner he shall be burned and his body reduced to ashes."

The hooded executioner approached and with a flourish placed his torch on the dry straw. Flames shot up, and the "werewolf" screamed his way into oblivion with a cry of pain that may very well have come from either man or beast.

About a month before Christmas, 1598, Antoinette Duprey, eleven years old, paused on a Paris street to absorb the full joy of a snowflake kiss on her cheek. From the door of a tailor shop a soft voice spoke.

"Salut, Cherie."

"Bon jour, M'sieur."

"What a beautiful child you are. Do you live near?"

"No, M'sieur. It is a distance from here. It was such a nice day for a walk I lost count of the blocks."

"Tiens! You must be cold. Will you not come into my shop where it is warm? And I have some chocolate ready."

The child shook her long, blond hair. It was growing late, and Maman would be worried. But yet... .

"Merci, M'sieur. But only for a minute."

"But of course. Pretty girls should not be out after dark."

The little girl's minute turned into eternity. She never came out of the tailor shop alive. But a friend of her family had seen her enter the shop, and when he discovered that Antoinette was missing, he informed the police. At the sadistic tailor's trial it was testified that once the child entered the shop the tailor changed himself into a wolf and sprang upon her, ripping off her clothing and biting and clawing at her frail child's body.

It was further avowed that this fiend prowled the woods by night, snarling and drooling at the mouth, and tearing out the throats and entrails of helpless passersby.

Barrels of bleaching bones were found in the accused tailor's cellar, along with other things too hideous to describe.

Quickly the werewolf was condemned to the stake. His executioners, who had seen all manner of villains burned, stopped their ears, so great was this fiend's blasphemy, even as the flames burned the flesh from his bones. The magistrate ordered that the court records pertaining to the case be burned in the same fire.

If there seems to be a dearth of werewolf cases today, it is only because the beast has had his name changed by modern psychiatry. Nowadays he is called by such names as "sadist," "pervert," or "psychotic sex offender." From time to time, nevertheless, one sees the "werewolf" label attached to sex crimes by sensationalists publications. Such was the case of William Johnston.

William Johnston, alias H. Meyers, alias Harry Gordon, sadistic killer of three women, did not claw or bite his victims to death. He did his namesake justice, however, with a straight razor. Like London's infamous "Jack the Ripper," Johnston chose prostitutes for his victims.

On the night of April 6, 1935, Betty Coffin turned a corner and started to walk down San Francisco's Market Street. As she passed the streetlamp, she glanced at her wristwatch. It was 2: 30 A. M., and Betty's feet hurt. She had covered a lot of concrete during the last three hours and was about to call it a night.

Then she saw him.

It was too late to play games. She walked right up to the heavy-set, slightly drunk man, who was dressed as a seaman, and propositioned him.

"Sailor, do you know a nice place where a girl can get some rest?"

"Huh? Oh, yeah, sure," replied the man, his eyes snapping awake.

Half an hour later, Betty Coffin stood sleepily by as her "client" scribbled on a registration card in a cheap waterfront hotel. A minute "Mr. and Mrs. Harry Meyers" started up the stairs to their room. The night clerk noted later that the couple's only luggage was a bottle of whiskey and a little box that protruded from Meyers' pocket.

Two hours late Meyers came down alone.

He approached the night clerk. "Where can I get a beer and a sandwich," he yawned.

"There's a place on the corner," answered the drowsy clerk. "Just turn left after you go out the door."

"Thanks. Can I get you anything?"

"Nope."

But the big man was already on his way.

At eight o'clock a chambermaid entered the Meyers' room using a pass-key. She placed her broom against the wall and started to open the window. Then she looked at the sprawled figure on the bed. Her scream brought the manager from downstairs. The nude body of Betty Coffin lay on the blood-soaked sheets. Her face had been beaten savagely, and her mouth taped shut. The corpse was stiped with gaping wounds in regular patterns, as if she had been raked again and again by the claws of a wild beast. Bloodstained fragments of clothing were strewn about the room.

The dead girl had not been sexually assaulted—at least not in the normal way.

Said Inspector Allan McGinn of the San Francisco Police: "The man who does a job like this is the type that strikes again and again. He doesn't stop at one murder. *It just whets his appetite for more.*"

The inspector was right. The most arduous of police work failed to turn up the killer, and five years later he struck again. On June 25, 1940, the body of Mrs. Irene Chandler was found in another waterfront hotel in the same circumstance as that of Betty Coffin. Causes of death were listed as strangulation and loss of blood. Mrs. Chandler was known to the police as a "seagull," a streetwalker who catered to seafaring men. This time the "werewolf" left his claws behind: a rusty, blood-stained razor.

Time was running out for the werewolf-killer. The Sailor's Union of the Pa-

39

cific supplied to the police a picture of a man who fit the killer's description. On July 8, 1940, a San Francisco detective confronted Harry W. Gordon at a sailor's union meeting.

"We want to talk to you at headquarters," said the officer quietly.

The blond werewolf's shoulders slumped. He offered no resistance as he was taken to jail.

After intense questioning, Gordon broke down.

"I'll talk!" he cried. "I'll tell you everything. I'm glad to get it over with. I killed Betty Coffin and Irene Chandler."

The officers were not prepared for Gordon's next words: "And I killed my first wife in New York, too!"

On September 5, 1941, Harry W. Gordon took his last breath in San Quentin's lethal gas chamber. The werewolf's savage hunger was quieted at last.

*****

Stranger even than the thirst of the vampire and the hunger of the werewolf is the grisly appetite of the ghoul. A ghoul has been defined as a demon which robs graves to devour the corpse. This act is termed "necrophagia," literally "eating of the dead." But the concept of ghoulishness has been extended by custom to include a number of other practices, including sexual intercourse with and mutilation of the dead, both termed "necrophilia."

A classic case of necrophilia is that of Sergeant Bertrand, a soldier in the French army in the mid-1800s. Bertrand was only twenty-five at the time of his arrest; by then the history of his ghoulish career read like a book of the damned. His behavior eventually came to the attention of his superiors, and he was placed under the care of Dr. Marchal de Calvis.

At his first meeting with the doctor Bertrand described himself as a successful Don Juan, a claim frequently the boast of impotents and deviates.

"I have had many women," he told de Calvis, "and I have always satisfied them completely."

"But of course," cajoled the physician, "and I suppose you started at quite a young age."

Bertrand's composure was a bit ruffled.

"Very young. And even before that I was extremely active. Such was my maleness at the age of nine that I was forced to relieve myself by hand seven or eight times a day."

Dr. de Calvis made notes on a pad, then studied his pen.

"Remarkable! But at what age did you turn to women?"

"Thirteen, maybe fourteen."

"Tell me about it."

Bertrand's eyes glowed. There was no mistaking the pleasure in his voice as he spoke:

"The sight of female clothing was sufficient to arouse me. In my mind I could see a room full of women, all at my disposal. In my mind I would torture them in every possible way, according to my desire. I would imagine them as dead before me, and I would defile their corpses."

"I see," mused de Calvis. He was beginning to sense the true nature of his patient's deviation. "Was this when you first made love to a corpse?"

"No," replied the sergeant. "At first it was with the bodies of animals I found dead along the roadside. Sometimes, when I could not find one, I was forced to kill."

"Most regrettable," said the doctor, feigning sympathy. "But what about your first experience with the corpse of a human?"

"It was in 1847 at a cemetery near Bere," said Bertrand slowly. "A comrade and I happened to walk by a newly-made grave. Suddenly, I was struck with a terrific headache , and my heart began to pound. I trembled all over. As soon as I could get away, I returned to the spot and dug up the body. Then I chopped it up with a pick and spade. I kept it up until my desire was relieved. Only then did my headache leave me."

In subsequent interviews Bertrand related numerous graveside orgies similar to the foregoing. He told of the time he had swum a ditch of icy water to reach a fresh grave. So great had been his passion that night that he had not even noticed the chill.

This was Bertrand's first actual sexual contact with a corpse, that of a seventeen-year-old girl.

"I cannot describe my sensations," Bertrand told Dr. de Calvis, "but all the joy procured by possessing a living woman was as nothing with the pleasure I felt."

The sergeant went on to describe his mutilation of the body, as before, and its return to the grave. Bertrand told the doctor that he thought the motivating force behind his deeds was the urge to destroy.

"The urge to dismember the bodies was incomparably more violent in me than the urge to violate them."

Small wonder, in the light of happenings like this, that superstitious folk of earlier times whispered of drooling demons that came down from the hills to desecrate graves, assault and cannibalize even bodies in advanced stages of decay.

Another real-life ghoul by the name of Ardisoon is reported to have exhumed the bodies of females aged three to eighty, and indulged in oral sex acts with them. He was arrested after he had taken home the corpse of a three-year-old girl on whom he practiced certain abominations until the stench betrayed him.

Even more remarkable is the case of the female necrophagiac who opened the caskets in her family vault and devoured the genitals of her dead husband, her brother and her son.

In 1957, Ed Gein, a middle-aged bachelor farmer from Plainsfield, Wisconsin, confessed to stealing a dozen female bodies from fresh graves in the community cemetery. Although he replaced most of the pieces after he had dismembered the bodies, he kept a collection of sex parts and noses in a box. He also saved ten of the skulls and upholstered some of his furniture with human skin. Gein progressed from grave-robbing to murdering two women, and when the sheriff entered his farmhouse, he was horrified to find one of the victims strung up by her heels, decapitated and eviscerated. The necrophagiac's neighbors later recalled with great unpleasantness that Gein was forever bringing them portions of "venison." While under psychiatric examination, Gein told the analyst that he had never shot a deer in his life.

A mitigating case can be made for those suffering from the ghoul psychosis in that they disturb only corpses, which, of course, cannot suffer further. But this in not likely to assuage the feelings of their victims' survivors. And would ghoul suddenly turn werewolf if no cadavers were available to him? Would he turn upon the living to satisfy his strange and terrible hunger?

What is the true nature of the real-life vampires, werewolves and ghouls? Perhaps a clue is to be found in the self-evaluation of Sergeant Bertrand:

"The urge to dismember . . .was incomparably more violent in me than the urge to violate. . ."

Whatever the answer, another question remains: Can there be a vein of truth in the old beliefs, that such atrocities are the work of evil spirits who have taken possession, body and soul, of the perpetrators?

It might be argued that, as in the case of the poltergeist, a person in the appropriate frame of mind might serve as a medium through which these entities can satisfy their unholy cravings.

Older stories carry accounts of men and women changing themselves into bloodsucking bats, voracious wolves, or red-eyed, fang-toothed demons. More recent accounts report nothing of the sort. But actually, the discrepancy is of small significance. If the *mind* of the "ghoul" has undergone change to the point where he believes himself to be such a creature, it is of slight consequence if his form changes.

The Countess Bathory made a formidable vampire with the scissors from her maid's sewing kit. Harry W. Gordon's razor served most adequately as werewolf's claws and fangs. Sergeant Bertrand was not hampered in his ghoulish pleasures by the fact that he worked with a pick and shovel or sword rather than a monster's paws.

Our age of scientific reason leads us to explain the acts of these and others like them in clinical terms of psychosis and sexual perversion, and to view perversion itself as a sign of negative psychic forces at work on the mind of man. Where most logically could such forces be focused than on the instinct to propagate life? As sex produces life, so it is that perversion produces death.

"It (necrophilia) is a true perversion," writes Dr. Erich Fromm. "While being alive not life, but death is loved, not growth but destruction."

Instead of in the supernatural, then, it appears that the origin of history's recorded vampires, werewolves, and ghouls must be sought in the wastelands of man's subconscious.

Brad Steiger is the author of 200 books on the paranormal; his most relevant being *The Werewolf Book: An Encyclopedia of Shape Shifting Beings.*

Go to www.BradandSherry.com <http://www.bradandsherry.com/>
for full details of his career.

Real Life Werewolves
They're Not The Stuff Of Hollywood!

By Sean Casteel

Sean Casteel is a journalist who has interviewed numerous luminaries in the field of UFO and paranormal research. He has written several books for Inner Light/Global Communications, including "UFOs, Prophecy and the End of Time" and "The Excluded Books of the Bible." Casteel has also appeared on the popular radio programs "Coast To Coast" and "The Kevin Smith Show."

LINDA GODFREY

People come to the study of werewolves in many different ways. For Linda Godfrey, it all started when she was working as a reporter for a county newspaper called "The Week" based in Delavan, Wisconsin.

"It just came to my attention," Godfrey said, "that people around the town of Elkhorn, which is my hometown, were seeing some kind of wolf-like creature that just walked around on two legs around a stretch of county road called Bray Road, just outside of town. They were even phoning in reports to the County Animal Control Officer. When I checked with him, I found out this was true, and that in fact he had a manila file folder marked 'werewolf,' because nobody knew what else to call this thing, and he didn't either."

So Godfrey had an interesting story virtually dumped in her lap. She would eventually come to write three books dealing with these strange sightings and become a well known crypto-zoologist in her own right. But back again to the beginning.

"When I interviewed the witnesses," she said, "I became very impressed that they didn't seem like they were making it up or trying to pull a hoax or anything like that. They were a fairly diverse group. So we ran the first story and I dubbed it 'the Beast of Bray Road' because that was where the first reported sightings came up. It's certainly by far not the only place where it's been seen. But I liked the term 'beast' better than 'werewolf' because we really didn't know what it was, and I still don't know what it is. But 'beast' can refer to any kind of animal. That story ran December 1, 1991, and it's never stopped since."

EYE WITNESS ACCOUNTS

The initial stories were fascinating, to say the least.

"There was a witness," Godfrey said, "who was a young, single mother named Lori Endrizzi, and she happened to see this creature at night. She noticed it because it was kneeling by the side of the road in a way that an animal really can't normally manage. It was using its paws to hold up what looked like a chunk of road kill that it was eating from. It scared her a lot. She went to the library to look up and see what it could be, and the only thing she found that looked like it were pictures of werewolves. She was one of the ones who reported it to the Animal Control Officer."

Another young woman, named Dorothy Gipson, thought that she had hit something with her car.

"She felt a bump," Godfrey explained, "stopped and got out of the car to see if she'd hit somebody's pet dog or something like that. Then, as she described it, she said this 'thing' came running at her and she could hear its feet very heavily pounding the pavement—but only its hind feet. It was running upright at the car. At that point, she hopped back in and sped off, but it did lunge at her car and left some scratch marks, which I did see. There wasn't any way to prove, really, what they were from, but she had a set of evenly spaced scratch marks on the rear end of her car."

Equally strange is the story of a group of schoolchildren who had been out sledding on Bowers Road, which runs parallel to Bray Road, not very far away.

"They saw what they thought was a dog kneeling by a little bit of open water," Godfrey said. "They thought it was kneeling and trying to drink. When they went over to pet it, the so-called 'dog' stood up. That's when they realized it was no dog and they took off running. It actually chased them, and this is what usually happens when people are chased: it broke off the chase and they were able to continue safely home. But they were really frightened out of their wits."

One of the children who was part of the incident was a classmate of one of Godfrey's sons.

"My son told me that he really didn't think this kid was making it up," Godfrey said, "or that any of them were."

THE WEREWOLF GOES NATIONWIDE

The sightings on Bray Road continued apace for a little while after the period discussed above, and then dropped off for about the next ten years. But the sightings continued elsewhere, and Godfrey's first reports for the county newspaper soon became a national news story.

"I was on 'Inside Edition,'" she said, "and from then on, just about any time someone wanted to talk about werewolves, they would call me. Because there really aren't any other large bodies of contemporary accounts of something that sounds and looks like a werewolf."

After having a kind of crypto-zoological greatness thrust upon her, Godfrey quickly became one of the few experts on the subject of werewolves, a term she disdains, by the way.

"I like to call it a 'man-wolf' instead," she said, "because it has less Hollywood baggage. 'Werewolf' implies it's a human changing into a wolf. So much of what we think of as the werewolf legend began in Hollywood. The full moon, the silver bullets, all that sort of thing. So it's true that every indigenous people and culture around the world has its own traditions of men that can change into some other type of animal. But a lot of that is more related to shamanistic traditional tribal rites than it is to an actual physical being turning into a Lon Chaney style werewolf. There's a difference.

"The shamans are thought," she continued, "to perhaps be able to create a psychic impression or a thought form that they can throw off from themselves. I don't entirely discount that idea."

Godfrey also considers the possibility—which she calls the "Indigenous Dog-Man Theory"—that perhaps some strain of canine has managed to adapt a more upright stance because it gave them advantages in running around in swamps, for instance, which might be easier on two legs than four.

"And it's more efficient to carry prey," she said, "in your upper arms than to drag it away in your mouth. They may have adapted to this and become a little more intelligent as a result, too, and so have been able to remain very elusive. Also, it would not have changed their outward appearance very much. Many witnesses have reported seeing it running both on hind feet and four legs, and it can go back and forth between the two. We've even had track evidence of this in some other states. But if you found a dead one, you probably would just think here's a really large wolf or wolf-hybrid. So those are I think more likely explanations than the traditional Hollywood werewolf."

Godfrey said that the sightings reports pour in at the rate of one to two a week, and come to her from all over the country, including New Jersey, Georgia, Kentucky, Tennessee, Texas and Oklahoma, with more recent sightings coming from Iowa.

"They seem more confined to the Midwest and the East Coast," she said. "So I don't know if they're stopped by the Great Plains there because there's no cover for them to move around. They do seem to prefer to have some kind of cover, whether it's a forest or a cornfield or something like that. They also seem to follow water and water sources. There's almost always some source of water nearby a reported sighting."

PARANORMAL POSSIBILITIES

Again, the idea of a paranormal origin for the werewolves is a thorny one to grapple with. In medieval times, for instance, people who were accused of being a werewolf were generally believed to have achieved the transformation through magical means.

"They would apply a special salve," Godfrey said, "or they would have a belt made out of wolf hide that they could put on them. Then there were chants and rites to be performed that would transform them. But it didn't necessarily mean that their body physically transformed. Often it was understood that their spirit or their astral body would take on the form of a wolf and go out from them while their actual physical body lay sleeping. And if the wolf form was wounded somehow, say somebody shot it in the leg, then a corresponding wound would be found on the person's own leg, without the actual human body ever having changed or moved from the spot. That was the way that they would identify a werewolf. They'd say, 'Well, I shot it in the leg and then they found somebody sleeping with a bullet hole in their leg in the same spot.'

"So that's actually really very close to the idea of the shaman tradition that you have with Native Americans and other indigenous people where, through some sort of magical rite, either a thought form or a spirit double goes out from the body, or in some cases forms around the body, kind of like a supernatural costume, if you will, that the person can move around in. And underneath is his physical body, but around him is this illusion of the form of an animal. In Tibet, they call these thought forms a tulpa, but it has parallels in many other cultures as well.

"There are other people who believe that entities may be conjured up by means of other magical rites, and that these entities wouldn't be based on human beings. They would be some other type of spirit that could take on the shape of a werewolf, and hopefully go out and do things for whoever had conjured it up. Some people believe that's possible, and other people don't."

DOWNRIGHT MEAN LOOKING

Wherever the creatures come from, they consistently project an aura of evil and meanness, according to the many witnesses Godfrey has spoken to.

"Something I really get very often from people," she said, "way more often than not, is a sense of fear emanating from it. They just get really unnerved. They feel that it's glaring at them, that it's sort of sneering. That it's somehow getting across to them that it has the upper hand and that it could follow them or do bad things to them if it wanted to. But in most cases, once they're good and scared, what it does is makes its escape. Whether it's been chasing them or just watching from the roadside, there's almost always some kind of cover, and as soon as it can get to that cover, it just tries to get away."

Godfrey stopped counting after a hundred sightings and now estimates the total to be around two hundred. But in all those sightings, only one person has ever reported being injured by the werewolf. A man in Quebec told her he had had his hip grazed by the tooth of a werewolf, which left a jagged cut behind. The man sent Godfrey a photo of the wound, which of course remains inconclusive.

"In all these other cases," she said, "you would think that somebody would have been hurt by now, or reported that it ripped their arm or bit them on the leg or something like that. It just doesn't happen. It has such a consistently clear behavior that I think that that really is another indication that people aren't making this up. There's something strange that's really going on."

The werewolves, along with the aura of fear they project, also seem to make a kind of telepathic contact with some witnesses.

"People will say to me," Godfrey said, "and usually it's at the end of the report, they'll say, 'There's one other thing. I hope you don't think I'm crazy but I felt that I was getting a mental message from it.' And not in the King's English, you know. It's not like they're hearing words in their head, but they feel that they're getting a definite impression that they can understand. They usually translate it as something like, 'You shouldn't be looking at me. If you tell anyone I'll come and get you. I'm here, you're there. You can't get me,' that kind of thing. Very challenging, and it kind of shakes them up."

DON'T LAY YOUR BIGFOOT ON MY WEREWOLF

Godfrey allowed as how the Bigfoot is sometimes said to send a similar kind of telepathic message, but in the case of the Bigfoot, witnesses usually "hear" something much more benign than what is projected by the more aggressive manwolf. Meanwhile Godfrey bristles at those who say the man-wolf is just another version of the Bigfoot only with a longer snout.

"You've really got definite primate characteristics on the one hand," she said, "and really definite canine characteristics on the other hand. Not only does the werewolf have a long pointed snout—whereas even baboons can have snouts, but they're not long and pointed—they also have ears on top of their heads, sharp pointed ears that look like a German shepherd or wolf ears, from most accounts. The bodies taper towards the hips and they're much more slender than you would find on any kind of a primate. There are tails often seen, and most important, anyone who gets a clear look at it will report that the legs looked like they were bent backwards. That's because a canine walks on its toe pads and its heel is up above the ground. Where we're expecting to see a knee bending forward, we're seeing what's actually the heel, bending what looks to us like backwards but it's actually just the normal heel joint, it's just off the ground.

"So it looks very different," Godfrey continued. "We have had photos of the footprints of this thing, and they look like very large, somewhat elongated wolf or dog prints. When the track medium is the right kind, you can see claw marks, little points where the claws extend, and this would not be the case with a primate. They're not Bigfoot tracks, let's put it that way."

IS LUST IN THE PICTURE?

Godfrey was asked the inevitable question, is the werewolf or man-wolf perhaps a metaphor for human lust?

"I think that's a legitimate question," Godfrey responded. "But I believe, from everything I've read and studied, there would be more of a metaphor for human violence, the desire to shed blood that's connected with eating flesh. I think that if you're looking for the metaphor for lust, that kind of goes more with a vampire. Now, in Eastern Europe, the werewolf and the vampire are almost one and the same being. They're very close to one another, like they've morphed into the same creature.

"But I think there isn't a real big sexual connotation with these things. It's more all about power and violence and people being scared that they're going to be eaten. Whereas the vampires are seductive, they come into people's bedrooms. I can really see the lust argument much more readily with a vampire than a werewolf. I do think there is some merit to the argument that we do have these archetypes in our mind and that with all the violence that's going on in the world—it's a way of externalizing the violence that we fear.

"And there is another theory," she went on, "if you want to combine the two, that posits that perhaps they are a type of psychic vampire, feeding not on lust or blood but on fear, on the strong emotions caused by fear, and that that explains why they're interested in coming across as fearsome, making this big attack, eliciting strong emotions from people. Then they would have what they want and make their exit. This would argue for them being other-dimensional beings, if that were true."

BRAY ROAD REVISITED

After a long absence, the sightings have started up again in the Bray Road area around Elkhorn, which leads Godfrey to wonder if the man-wolf has some kind of cyclical migration route that has brought it around full-circle to the place where Godfrey first became aware of its existence. One more recent incident occurred in March, 2008.

"A man was leaving a mobile home park," Godfrey recounted, "that is maybe half a mile from one end of Bray Road, when he spotted a creature running away from that same park area. He was visiting someone there. He had heard that a lot of cats had been going missing from around the mobile home park. He saw this creature. Didn't know what it was. It was large, running on two feet. Kind of suspecting where it was going, he trailed it and caught up with it again near Bray Road, just in time to see it disappearing into some brush. But he did report that it had the same characteristics that people usually describe, which is six to seven feet tall, covered with dark gray or brown fur, and walking just as easily on two feet as four. And looking either like a very overgrown canine or a wolf."

After nearly twenty years of collecting werewolf sightings and conducting thorough research, the obvious question becomes "Just what does Godfrey herself think is really going on?

"I don't know," she said. "I still really don't know, because I haven't been able to observe it in motion. I think perhaps if I did, that might help me make up my mind. I generally go between two theories—the indigenous dog-man that I described before or some sort of inter-dimensional being that is similar to what my Native American friends think it is, a creature that can be corporeal but perhaps can pop back into another dimension when it needs to. With modern physics now saying that there probably are at least eleven dimensions if not more, you know, it opens up that possibility. I think that science is leading us to a place where we can accept that fact, that there may be worlds beyond our own five senses, beyond what we can see.

"So I kind of go back and forth between those two. I can see a good case for either one of them. And until I can lay eyes on one myself, I'm probably not going to be able to say with any conclusiveness that I feel it's one thing or the other. I just hope to keep researching."

WHAT ABOUT UFOs? DEMONS? BLACK MAGIC?

There are even more alternate theories that also tantalize. Is there any direct connection to UFOs, for instance?

"I've never run across a direct link between werewolves and UFOs," Godfrey said. "It's true that odd phenomena tend to occur within the same geographical area. I know in *Hunting the American Werewolf*, I talk about the Jefferson County Square of Weirdness. I've identified a 13-square mile area that includes all kinds of strangeness, from UFO sightings to weird large birds being seen, to Bigfoot sightings and man-wolf sightings. And all of this stuff is going on within the same confined area.

"It's very similar to what Fortean researcher John Keel referred to as a 'window area,'" she continued. "His belief was that there are certain places where dimensions perhaps intersect and that things can go back and forth, if they know where to look. It's like something crawling out the window from another dimension. So perhaps there is a relationship in that way. But I don't have any kind of report of someone saying they saw the werewolf come out of a UFO or that a UFO was hovering directly overhead when they saw it or anything like that to directly link the two."

And what about the idea that a werewolf is some kind of demon?

"Demon is another one of those very loaded words," Godfrey answered. "I think maybe a better way to describe that would be the idea of some sort of pre-existing entity or an entity that is somehow conjured up from somewhere else. Christians might call that a demon; people of other religions might call it an evil spirit. There are different terms for it. I think that's another possibility. I can't say for sure, but there are many people who believe that's what it is."

As to the idea that some kind of "conjuring" is involved, wouldn't that imply an awful lot of black magicians skulking around out there in the Wisconsin woods?

"I don't know if there are that many black magicians," Godfrey replied, "who have done this over the ages, too. Because you're talking about not only two thirds of the United States, and other countries—I mean, I get reports from France and Australia and other places—so if that were true, there would have to be a wide-spread cadre of people with this amount of esoteric knowledge and skill, adept at pulling this kind of thing off. And they would have to be doing it rather regularly and for their own reasons. I would suspect that a much smaller number of people, if this were possible, would be interested in pursuing such a thing."

Whether we're dealing here with a recent form of more highly evolved Dog-Man type creature, or thought forms created by certain shamanistic adepts and then turned loose on an unsuspecting world, or Man-Wolves crossing over from other dimensions than our own, or even wolf-like demons conjured by black magicians with a darkly malevolent intent, the mystery of the werewolf persists in haunting the imagination, but is keeping its secrets nonetheless.

[More information can be found on Linda Godfrey's website at beastofbrayroad.com You can also email Linda from the site and tell her about your own sightings of werewolf-type creatures. Her books include The Beast of Bray Road, Hunting the American Werewolf and most recently Werewolf.]

Werewolf and Monster Hunter Nick Redfern Goes Wild in the Jungle

NICK REDFERN

When he was five years old, British researcher and author Nick Redfern went on a family vacation to Scotland and visited Loch Ness. He was told the story of the alleged monster that dwelt there by his father. That initial brush with the paranormal made a lasting impression on Redfern, and he has devoted his adult life to the pursuit of strange animals, UFOs, and other "out there" entities, including collecting sightings reports of werewolves on both sides of the Atlantic.

Redfern has authored three books on crypto-zoology: Three Men Seeking Monsters, Memoirs of a Monster Hunter and Man Monkey, and he comes with admirable credentials for an interview about werewolves.

CRYPTID CREATURES FROM DARK DOMAINS

THE HEXHAM HEADS

Redfern started off with an interesting werewolf story from the early 1970s that took place in England.

"There was a very, very strange werewolf case," Redfern said, "in a town in the north of England called Hexham, and this involved something that came to be known as the Hexham Heads. Two young boys were playing in their backyard one day and dug up these two small stone heads from the garden. They were shown to various archeological experts who concluded that the heads were probably ancient Celtic in origin, so going back a very long time. Well, the heads were brought into the house and examined. One looked like an obviously male-type head; the other one looked female and almost witchlike, with a beaked nose as well, like a classic witch from folklore.

"And after the heads were brought into the house," he continued, "a lot of weird paranormal activity began to happen. Not just in that house but in the neighboring house as well. The family that found it experienced strange noises and doors slamming, things like that. But the people who lived next door actually were awakened in the middle of the night by—for want of a better term—this manifestation of a werewolf in the bedroom. Literally a manlike figure, hairy, but with a large, imposing, wolf-like head. This went on on several occasions, and again it was accompanied by poltergeist-type activity, with the creature just appearing and vanishing in the blink of an eye. So it had kind of an air of the paranormal or the occult to it rather than just a straightforward flesh and blood animal that science hasn't identified."

Redfern said that the heads were next turned over to an expert in Celtic history and archeology named Dr. Anne Ross. She began to experience the same poltergeist manifestations in her own home, as well as the appearance of the identical hairy, manlike figure with the wolf's head. The Hexham Heads went through several subsequent owners before they were lost completely to the pages of history.

But not before they piqued the boundless curiosity of the young Redfern, who heard the story when it was first reported by the BBC, implanting a deep desire to know more about werewolves. He began to collect stories on the subject whenever and wherever he could.

REPORTS FROM THE UNDERGROUND

"Over time," he said, "digging into the issue of mystery animals in general, people would say to me, 'Oh, I saw a lake monster in this particular lake, or I saw a Bigfoot-type creature.' But for every 20 or 30 cases like that, you get one where somebody said, 'Well, I was driving home late one night and I saw this weird, wolf-like creature at the side of the road. As I got close to it, it seemed to rear up on its hind legs from a four-legged position, as if it could walk on four legs and two. It backed off into the trees and it looked like the closest thing you could imagine to a werewolf.'

"And these stories were all coming in from people," he continued, "none of whom knew each other, just up and down the country. And then over time, I began to realize there was like a whole underground collection of reports, but nobody had made the connection that these things were being seen all over the place."

Having collected werewolf reports for many years, Redfern has come to prize most the stories that have paranormal overtones, as if the sheer strangeness makes them more believable.

"One that I investigated," he said, "involved a guy who said he'd seen this werewolf-type creature chasing and attacking a herd of sheep. This was in Dartmoor, a very windswept, spooky, foggy moorland. He'd seen this creature pursuing the sheep, but the weirdest thing of all—it was as if the bottom part of the creature's legs, from the knees down, was missing or transparent, as if it was almost spectral rather than like a three-dimensional animal. But he said that it was as if the creature was obviously in our realm of existence because it was chasing the sheep. But it was as if it was blinking out as well and just flickering on and off almost like a faulty light bulb or something like that."

Another similar incident took place in the same county as the previous one, Devon. The rather frightening creature seen there has come to be called the Abbottsham Werewolf and was sighted in the early 1970s.

"People reported seeing this large wolf-like creature," Redfern said, "but in some of the cases there were stories of this creature again kind of striding purposefully on four legs and then, when it needed to get out of the area quickly, you know, if somebody had seen it with their car headlights late at night, it would rear up on to its hind legs and just fly off at high speed."

Rendlesham Forest is a location famous for the UFO sightings that took place there over the holidays in 1980-81, and which continue to be controversial in the present day, with various military witnesses still at odds with debunkers over what really happened there.

"But Rendlesham Forest has been a hotbed of weirdness for years," Redfern said. "Black cat reports, ghostly black dogs, and a weird creature that's come to be known as the 'Shug Monkey.' And 'shug' is a mutation on an old English word that means 'demon' and goes back centuries. Most people describe the Shug Monkey as looking like a cross between a large ape and a huge dog, the body being like a dog but the head being like a silver-backed gorilla or something like that.

"I interviewed one guy about seven years ago," he continued, "who told me that he'd been walking through Rendlesham Forest in the mid-1970s and he'd seen this creature. The body was like a very, very shiny silky black cat, but huge, ten to twelve feet long, a massive animal, but he said the head was clearly canine. It looked very much like a German shepherd, pointed ears, elongated jaw line, etc. He was just literally petrified, rooted to the spot, and didn't know what to do.

"He realized of course that it wasn't a normal animal of the sort that probably anyone had seen before, certainly in the physical world, shall we say. He just watched it. He said it was about 20 or 30 feet in front of him and just came looming out of the bushes and kind of turned towards him and glared in his direction. He said the glare was kind of strange. It almost gave off a feeling of intelligence as if it was saying, 'Well, come on then, if you think you can take me on.' Almost like goading him and confronting him. Eventually it just went on its way, ignored him, and vanished into the trees."

The person who told the story to Redfern also said that he didn't feel he had seen the Shug Monkey because the creature he did see definitely had a canine-type head as opposed to a primate one. Like Linda Godfrey said earlier in this chapter, we are dealing with something much different than a Bigfoot or any type of apelike creature.

INVOKING THE WEREWOLF

Many of the cases reported to Redfern occur in areas where there has been a whole range of other weird activity, as with Rendlesham Forest, which is also home to a certain amount of occult activity, like witchcraft and people holding ancient black rites and rituals in the woods, including the sacrifice of animals.

"We're not entirely sure," he said, "what the nature of all these incidents are, but certainly there appears to be a high degree of invoking involved in some respects. That even applies to the Hexham Heads case, with these heads having been found buried in the backyard. Where you have invoking and you have black arts groups, doing rites and rituals in the woods, invariably, these are the same locations where these wolf-like entities appear.

"And I think it would be stupid," he added, "to ignore that fact and just try to follow the flesh and blood angle, or the mysterious animal that science hasn't identified yet. I think it's far stranger. Now, we could address all sorts of areas: are they literally demonic? Are they something from another realm of existence? It could be explained by quantum physics, for example, which is looking into the feasibility of things like parallel universes, parallel realms. Is it possible that ancient man knew something about this and was able to tap into these realms of existence?

"Another theory that I find interesting is the Tulpa theory," he said, "the idea that we're literally able to conjure these things up, creating, in simplistic terms, mind monsters. There's a long history of that. It's particularly prevalent in Tibetan cultures, the idea that deep meditation and thoughts, where you focus on one particular image, and over weeks of preparation and ritual you can externalize something you've been heavily concentrating on and give it some sort of quasi-existence in the real world."

The problem then becomes that these mind monsters cling very tenaciously to life and can actually free themselves from their creator, like giving birth to an insane child.

"So that's another theory," Redfern said, "the idea that we ourselves are creating them and then they're getting out of hand."

REDFERN MEETS A WEREWOLF

Redfern has a story of his own personal encounter with a werewolf-type creature.

"Now people have said," he began, "and maybe they're right, that because I investigate these things and write about them—I was actually ironically writing about werewolves when this experience happened—people say, well, it was on your mind and it could have been your mind playing tricks, which it could have been. I always admit that before I tell people this story."

It was late 2002, and Redfern had been doing some investigations and was deeply into writing and researching. He had even been trying to conjure a werewolf himself, what he called "controversial attempts to raise these things."

"Me and my wife had gone to bed," he recounted, "and it was about three in the morning. I had what I can only term a classic example of sleep paralysis. You're in bed, you're semi-awake, but you're literally unable to move. And more often than not, these experiences are accompanied by a feeling of dread, a feeling that there's an evil, menacing force in the room."

Redfern, in his semi-comatose state, began to see the image of a wolf-like creature walking on two legs down the corridor towards his bedroom.

"The best way I can describe it," he said, "was as if it was wearing a black cloak from the neck to the feet, buttoned up or pulled tight, with the collar turned up, with a hood, and poking out of the hood was this large, wolf-like face. The closer it got to the bedroom, the more I struggled to move, the more the feeling of dread built up and built up. I had this feeling of it getting closer to the door and coming in the room and making like a very weird and ominous—like a fast guttural growl. But if you can imagine, instead of just an animal growling, the growl would sound like language almost. I know that sounds strange, but if you imagine that a dog could talk when it growls and it actually had inflection in its voice. It was a growl but you could understand it was a fast-spoken language as well. That's when the intensity got to fever pitch point, at which point I managed to wake up and got this fleeting glimpse of this thing just vanishing backwards into the hallway."

There was a very oppressive atmosphere in the Redferns' apartment for the next two days, and the couple performed a cleansing ceremony using sage to sort of clear the air, which apparently worked for them.

"That was a very weird situation to be in," he said, "and that made me appreciate the enormity of what potentially you could do if you are able to manifest these things. If they're not necessarily good and again tenacious of life and then they start stalking you or whatever. A lot of people roll their eyes when I tell them that story, but that's honestly from the heart how it happened."

Redfern plans to continue trying to conjure these creatures himself, however.

"Particularly with werewolves," he said, "I think that because of the nature of the reports, I don't think we can say we're dealing with normal flesh and blood animals. So my next hope would be, by continuing to do these investigations, that if I can for the most part rule out the flesh and blood angle, the next step is to really try and invoke one myself. I actually do stuff like this quite a lot, and it disturbs some people when I tell them."

For instance, Redfern will go into the woods and get his mind focused, by chanting or just trying to achieve an altered state of thought, after which he envisions what he seeks to manifest in the hope that he can conjure something up.

"My hope would be that I would be able to get past the point of just doing that," he explained, "and then try to understand where they're actually coming from. Is it that the human mind has the ability to externalize something and give birth to a mind monster? Or is it that we're opening a doorway to somewhere else? Even if we don't understand how we're doing it or why we're doing it. I would hope that in time I might be able to understand what that is, where it is, and how it works. It's a long shot, but I think unless we take the time to do it, we'll never get the answers. All we'll end up with is reports, and yes, reports are great. You can fill book after book with reports, but at the end of the day, all you've got is testimony. I would like to get past that point to where we can say that now we've got an idea of where they're coming from."

THE LUST QUESTION

When asked the obligatory question about werewolves as a metaphor for human lust, Redfern responded by saying, "The human mind is a complex thing. I think that culturally, at a kind of sociological level, there are certain archetypes that everybody's brain locks onto. I don't doubt the possibility that in some cases some of the reports could fall into that category. But I would have to say honestly that the ones I've looked into, I don't think so. No one's ever said to me that there's been like a sexual aspect to it. It's just been outright menace, more than anything else. To put it bluntly, I've never come across anyone who's had like a psychic experience and said, 'I got f***ed by a werewolf.' That's not happened yet.

"Now I will tell you," he continued, "that I did interview someone who was a member of a Goth group of people who lived in Glasgow, in Scotland. They were into werewolves and would hold werewolf parties, and they'd make drinks that looked like blood out of tomato juice, that sort of thing. Basically that was an excuse to have a good old time, orgies, swinging or whatever. They kind of did it on the full moon, and they would have these parties and watch old Hollywood movies and howl and everything else.

"But that is an example of where werewolves have been used in relation to sexuality. But I think the important thing is that these were just a bunch of twenty-something Goths wanting to have a good time on a Saturday night. These weren't the werewolves themselves."

DON'T TRY THIS AT HOME, FOLKS!

Redfern unequivocally says that, of all the many strange things he has investigated, werewolves are the strangest of all.

"Purely and simply," he said, "because they seem to possess attributes of physical animals—people see them walking, getting up on two legs or getting on four legs—yet they also seem to possess paranormal aspects or attributes as well. And I think the fact that they seem to exude this air of menace is a pretty significant one, a unique one, and for that reason I tread carefully when I'm investigating these things, because, no pun intended, they come back and bite you on the ass. In the same way that you screw around with some of these weirder things and then it can start affecting you.

"And so I treat these cases and reports carefully and I would urge anyone who's had experiences with these things or is thinking about investigating them to tread equally carefully. Don't go into it thinking, 'Oh, all I need is a gun and a silver bullet and it's all going to be like some jolly Hollywood film.' It's not like that. It gets very, very weird and deep and dark the more you get into it. So I'd just say tread carefully."

[Doing a Google search for Nick Redern will turn up a plethora of information on a great many paranormal subjects, but for starters, his home page is at www.nickredfern.com/index.htm]

Werewolves in the Cinema by Tim Swartz

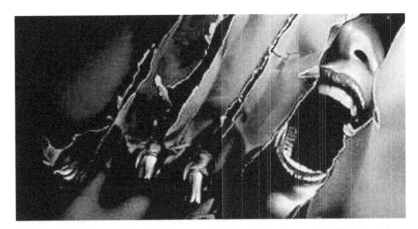

One of the most popular recurring screen monsters after the vampire is the werewolf. The werewolf in films has little to do with the "traditional" werewolf in history, which was more akin to a witch or satanic worshiper. In the movies, a werewolf is usually the unfortunate victim of fate and has little control of his transformations and subsequent actions.

The process of transmogrification from man to wolf is portrayed in films to be painful and the resulting wolf is typically cunning, merciless, and prone to killing and eating people without compunction regardless of the moral character of the person when human. The form a werewolf takes is not always an ordinary wolf, but is often more humanoid, powerful and larger than an ordinary wolf.

The first major Hollywood film to feature a werewolf was The Werewolf of London, starring Henry Hull. This film was also the first to use camera special effects, the multiple dissolve, to show the transformation from man to wolf. The werewolf, as portrayed by Hull, is less hairy and more akin to a "Dr. Jekyll and Mr. Hyde" character as he dons a cap for a night of hunting.

It wasn't until the 1941 Universal film The Wolf Man starring Lon Chaney Jr. The Wolf Man became firmly established as a horror classic. The Wolf Man was important for the mythos it added to the genre courtesy of the movie's writer, Curt Siodmak. The full moon and physical transformation was already vaguely in place, but Siodmak added the pentagram as the sign of the werewolf, the wolf's bane plant and the potential for silver to kill the werewolf. It is interesting that these points are now firmly routed in the mythology and taken almost as "fact" even though they were invented by a screenwriter.

Since that time the werewolf in film has enjoyed international popularity and rarely does a year go by without at least one film that features a lycanthrope. Each new decade brings a fresh reinterpretation on the werewolf film, the most recent influential film is 2003's Underworld that contains a rich mythology involving werewolves and their mortal enemies the vampire.

It has been fascinating watching the werewolf in film evolve. It will be even more interesting to see what new innovations will take place that will further carry the wolfman genre onto future movie screens.

The Werewolf: 1913
Bison Films (Canada)
A Navajo Witch Woman transforms her daughter into a wolf in order to attack the invading white men. An actual wolf was used in the transformation sequence.

Le Loup Garou: 1923
(France)
aka The Werewolf
Cast: Jean Marau, Madeleine Guitty
A murderer is cursed to be a werewolf by a priest.

Wolf Blood: 1925
Ryan Brothers Productions
Directors: George Chesebro, George Mitchell
Cast: George Chesebro, Marguerite Clayton
A transfusion of wolf's blood turns a man into a beast.

The Werewolf: 1932
(Germany)
Director: Friedrich Frier
Cast: Magda Sonja, Vladimir Sokolov
This is the first talkie to feature a werewolf. From the novel "Der Schwarze Mann" by Alfred Machard.

The Werewolf of London: 1935
Universal Pictures
Director: Stuart Walker
Cast: Henry Hull, Warner Oland
Wilfred Glendon (Hull) is an English botanist who journeys to Tibet in 1935 to find the elusive mariphasa plant. While there, he is attacked and bitten by a creature later revealed to be a werewolf. After he returns to London, Glendon is overcome by lycanthropy and tries to use the mariphasa flower to cure him before he kills the one he loves most.

The Wolf Man: 1941
Universal Pictures
Director: George Waggner
Cast: Lon Chaney Jr., Claude Rains, Ralph Bellamy, Maria Ouspenskaya, Bela Lugosi
Larry Talbot (Chaney) is bitten by a werewolf (Lugosi) while visiting a gypsy camp. He turns into a werewolf and is killed by his father (Rains) using a silver wolf's head cane. This movie brought silver, wolf's Bane, and the pentagram into the werewolf film genre.

The Mad Monster: 1942
Producers Releasing Corporation
Director: Sam Newfield
Cast: George Zucco, Glen Strange
An insane, but patriotic, scientist (Zucco) injects wolf's blood into a farmer (Strange) in order to create a superhuman soldier. The experiment goes awry and the farmer becomes a werewolf.

The Undying Monster: 1942
Fox Films
Director: John Brahm
Cast: James Ellison, Heather Angel, John Howard
The Hammonds are cursed with Lycanthropy, something that is found out after Howard goes on a rampage through the town, and is eventually shot by the police.

Frankenstein Meets the Wolf Man: 1943
Universal Pictures
Director: Roy Niel
Cast: Lon Chaney Jr., Bela Lugosi, Patric Knowles
Larry Talbot returns from his original role in The Wolf Man (1941), when his grave is broken into during a full moon. He locates the gypsy woman who goes with him to find Dr. Frankenstein. When they arrive Frankenstein is dead and his monster is trapped. Talbot accidentally releases him and the two monsters fight to the death.

Le Loup des Malveneur: 1943
(France)
aka The Wolf of the Malveneurs
Director: Guillaume Radot
Cast: Madeleine Sologne, Pierre Renoir, Gabrielle Dorziat
Reginald de Malveneur is a scientist attempting to discover the secret of total cellular rejuvenation. When a young governess, Monique Valory, arrives at the castle of the Malveneurs, she learns that Reginald has disappeared along with the gamekeeper. With the help of a young painter, Philippe, she begins to suspect that there is something strange at work in the household.

Cry of the Werewolf: 1944
Columbia Pictures
Director: Henry Levin
Cast: Nina Foch, Stephen Crane
Celeste La Tour (Foch) is a gypsy werewolf who tries to silence anyone that comes close to uncovering her secret.

House of Frankenstein: 1944
Universal Pictures
Director: Earle Kenton
Cast: Lon Chaney Jr., Boris Karloff
A mad doctor (Karloff) murders the proprietor of a carnival of horrors and captures Dracula, along with directions to Frankenstein's castle. There, he find the bodies of the Frankenstein Monster and Lawrence Talbot, the Wolf Man preserved in the frozen waters. After unthawing the two monsters things quickly get out of hand.

Idle Roomers: 1944
Columbia Pictures Corporation
Director: Del Lord
Cast: Moe Howard, Curly Howard, Larry Fine
The stooges are working as bellboys in a large hotel when a side show promoter shows up with "Lupe," a wild wolfman who promptly escapes. The stooges try to capture the wolfman by playing music to calm him, but music makes the wolfman go berserk and soon the stooges are the ones trying to run away. The boys end up caught in an elevator with the wolfman who shoots them into the sky.

Return of the Vampire: 1944
Columbia
Black and White
Director: Lew Landers
Cast: Bela Lugosi, Nina Foch, Matt Willis
Vampire Armand Tesla (Lugosi) is unearthed by a stray bomb. Workers, having no knowledge of vampire lore, remove the stake from his heart bringing him back to life. He becomes a part of the London elite and eventually enslaves a werewolf (Willis). The werewolf gets tired of being a slave and drags Tesla into the sun where he dissolves into a skeleton.

House of Dracula: 1945
Universal Pictures
Director: Erle Kenton
Cast: Lon Chaney, John Carradine, Lionel Atwill
Universal Pictures once again pairs a Mad Doctor (Onslow Stevens), Dracula (Carradine), the Wolfman (Chaney) and the rest of the gang for one final get together. Talbot (Chaney) is finally cured by the doctor whose attempts to also cure Dracula backfire, turning himself into a vampire as well. Much like both Frankenstein Meets the Wolfman (1943) and House of Frankenstein (1944), Frankenstein's monster is revived and there's a lot of action at the end. Talbot finally walks away cured, that is until he makes a reappearance in Abbot and Costello Meet Frankenstein.

She Wolf of London: 1946
Universal Pictures
Director: Jean Yarbrough
Cast: June Lockhart, Don Porter, Sara Haden
The Allenbys are haunted by the curse of lycanthropy, which Lockhart suspects she has inherited after several murders. However, in a plot twist, the killings were actually committed by a demented murderer.

Abbott and Costello Meet Frankenstein: 1948
Universal Pictures
Director: Charles Barton
Cast: Bud Abbot, Lou Costello, Lon Chaney Jr.
A parody of the Universal monster movies featuring Abbot and Costello as delivery men who stumble into the weird world of Count Dracula, Frankenstein's monster and Larry Talbot (Chaney) once again as the Wolfman.

The Werewolf: 1956
Clover Films
Director: Fred Sears
Cast: George Lynn, Steven Rich
Steven Rich plays a man with radiation poisoning who, when looking for an experimental treatment, instead is turned into a werewolf.

The Daughter of Dr. Jekyll: 1957
Scope
Director: Edgar Ulmer
Cast: John Anger, Gloria Talbott
Gloria Talbott goes to England in order to claim an inheritance from her deceased father who it turns out is the infamous Dr. Jekyll. A series of murders occur after she is arrived, thus leaving her the suspect. However the criminal is her father's former aid who is a werewolf. He's found, and strangely, is killed by a stake driven through his heart by villagers.

I Was a Teenage Werewolf: 1957
Sunset Productions
Director: Gene Fowler Jr.
Cast: Michael Landon, Whit Bissell, Tony Marshall
Michael Landon is a teenager who is sent to a psychiatrist in order to control his outbreaks. Instead, the psychiatrist uses hypnosis and a special serum to turn into a werewolf. His transformations occur whenever he is aroused and hears a loud noise, such as a doorbell or a telephone.

CRYPTID CREATURES FROM DARK DOMAINS

El Castillo de los Monstruos: 1957
Producciones Sotomayor
aka Castle of the Monsters
Director: Julian Soler
Cast: Antonio Espino, Evangelina Elizondo
The Mexican equivalent to the string of Universal Films in the mid-forties such as House of Dracula (1945) in which for some reason or another every imaginable movie monster converges on one castle to cause terror. In this case, the reason is to disrupt the honeymoon of a couple (Espino and Elizondo). Featured in the castle are: The Creature from the Black Lagoon, Frankenstein's Monster, the Mummy, and the Wolfman.

How to Make a Monster: 1958
AIP
Director: Herbert Strock
Cast: Robert Harris, Paul Brinegar, Gary Conway
In one of the more interesting monster movie plots, a studio costumer is dejected after production is changed from horror to movie musicals. In order to fight the men at the top he uses special makeup and hypnosis in order to turn two of his actors into Frankenstein's Monster and the Wolfman.

El Hombre y El Monstruo: 1958
Cinematographa Absa
aka The Man and the Monster
Director: Rafeal Baledon
Cast: Enrique Rabal, Abel Salazar
A concert pianist turns into a werewolf whenever he plays and only his mother's touch can change him back to human form.

La Casa del Terror: 1959
Diana Films
aka Face of the Screaming Werewolf
Director: Gilberto Martines Solares
Cast: Lon Chaney Jr., German Valdes
Lon Chaney Jr. plays not only a werewolf, but a mummified werewolf, who is resurrected by a thunderstorm and then terrifies the town.

The Curse of the Werewolf: 1960
Hammer Films
Director: Terence Fisher
Cast: Oliver Reed, Yvonne Romain
This is one of the few werewolf movies that use actual folklore and mythology in its plot. An adaptation of Guy Ender's novel The Werewolf of Paris, Leon (Reed) is born on Christmas Eve by a mute servant girl who was raped by a beggar. He is born with a patch of hair on his arm, which along with the Christmas Eve birth signifies lycanthropy. When he reaches adulthood the curse takes affect.

La Loba: 1964
Producciones Sotomayor
aka The She Wolf
Director: Rafael Baledon
Cast: Kitty de Hoyos, Joaquin Cordero
A young doctor (Cordero) who specializes in lycanthropy cases, but is a lycanthrope himself, meets the family of doctor Fernandes, who's daughter de Hoyas is also a werewolf. The werewolves fall in love, but the specially trained werewolf hunting dog and the doctor's assistant (Canedo) kill both werewolves, who die in each others arms.

Frankenstein's Bloody Terror: 1967
Maxper Producciones Cinematogrficas
Director: Enrique Eguiliz
Cast: Paul Naschy, Diane Konopka, Julian Ugarte, Rossana Yanni, Michael Manz
This movie marks the introduction of Count Waldemar Daninsky (Naschy), who happens to be a werewolf. In this, the first of many many to come, he meets a strange Hungarian couple (Ugarte and Yanni) who turn out to be vampires. Another couple (Konopka and Manz) befriend the werewolf who then kills the vampires and is then killed by Konopka.

Las Noches del Hombre Lobo: 1968
Kin Films (Spain/France)
aka Nights of the Werewolf
Director: Rene Govar
Cast: Paul Naschy, Monique Brainvill
In this film, Daninsky (Naschy) is a werewolf who is used by a mad scientist to kill his colleagues, but instead everyone ends up dying, including Daninsky.

Blood of Dracula's Castle: 1969
Paragon International Pictures
Directors: Al Adamson, Jean Hewitt
Cast: John Carradine, Paula Raymond, Alex D'Arcy
Count and Countess Dracula (D'Arcy and Raymond) live in a castle in the Mojave Desert. Their butler George (Carradine) keeps the basement stocked full of fresh victims. Things get interesting when a werewolf shows up along with a couple who claim to have inherited the estate.

El Hombre que Vino de Ummo: 1969
Producciones Jaime Prades/Eichberg Film/International Jaguar Cinematografica
Director: Tulio Demichelli
Cast: Michael Rennie, Paul Naschy, Karen Dor
An alien lands from the planet Ummo, and revives monsters in order to conquer the world. This includes Paul Naschy reprising his role as wolfman Count Waldemar Daninsky.

The Maltese Bippy: 1969
Metro-Goldwyn-Mayer
Director: Norman Panama
Cast: Dick Martin, Dan Rowan
A Rowan and Martin parody of monster movies where Dick Martin becomes convinced he is a werewolf.

The Werewolf vs. the Vampire Woman: 1970
Plata Films S.A.
Director: Leon Klimovsky
Cast: Paul Naschy, Paty Shepard, Gaby Fuchs
Paul Naschy returns after being resurrected when doctors remove a silver bullet from his corpse. He travels with two women to his castle in search of the vampire woman, who is revived by a drop of blood falling on her face. One girl is killed, the other is held until Walpurgis Night for a ritual. She is saved by Daninsky who dies in her place.

Dr. Jekyll and the Werewolf: 1971
Arturo Gonz:lez Producciones Cinematogrficas S.A
Director: Leon Klimovsky
Cast: Paul Naschy, Shirley Corrigan, Jack Taylor
Count Waldemar Daninsky (Paul Naschy) seeks the help of Dr. Jekyll to cure his lycanthropy.

The Fury of the Wolfman: 1971
Maxper Producciones Cinematogrficas
Director: Jose Maria Zabalza
Cast: Paul Naschy, Perla Cristal, Veronica Lujan
Following right on the heels of Dr. Jekyll y el Hombre Lobo (1971) Count Waldemar Daninsky (Naschy) returns from Tibet as a werewolf. He seeks the help of a female doctor (Cristal) but ends up turning her into a werewolf as well.

Werewolves on Wheels: 1971
Southstreet Productions
Director: Michel Levesque
Cast: Stephen Oliver, Severen Darden, Duece Berry
In this biker movie the leather-clad motorcyclists turn into werewolves thanks to a spell cast by a Satanist high priest (Severn Darden). Adam (Stephen Oliver) is the leader of a gang called The Devil's Advocates. His girl (D.J. Anderson) receives a request from a cult to offer herself to the Devil. She dances naked with a snake and before long is chomping on lover-boy Adam, which turns him into a werewolf too. The only one who can put an end to the mayhem is Tarot (Duece Barry), a biker with a background in the supernatural.

Frankenstein's Bloody Terror: 1972
Fenix/Comptoir Francais Du Film
Director: Jesus Franco
Cast: Dennis Price, Howard Vernon, Alberto Dalbes
Dracula is initially killed by Jonathan (Dalbes) only to be later brought back to life by a Baron, thus giving the Baron control of a horde of vampires. In order to once again stop the vampires Jonathan sets out with a werewolf to kill the Baron. He fails, however the Baron ends up killing the vampire horde and Count Dracula anyway. Jonathan rewards him by burning down his castle and killing him with the help from some gypsies.

Moon of the Wolf: 1972
Filmways Pictures
Director: Daniel Petrie
Cast: David Janssen, Barbara Rush, Bradford Dillman
A sheriff (Janssen) suspects that a werewolf is brutally killing off locals in his Louisiana town.

The Rats are Coming, The Werewolves are Here: 1972
Constitution Films Inc.
Director: Andy Milligan
Cast: Hope Stansbury, Jacqueline Skarvellis, Berwick Kaler
The Mooneys are struggling with genetic lycanthropy. One daughter, Diana, is sent to a Scottish medical school in order to help save the family, and returns with a new husband. The full moon causes the entire family to turn into werewolves, attacking Diana and her husband. The two manage to survive, but Diana later tells her husband that his only purpose had been to get her pregnant, she then changes into a werewolf and kills him.

The Return of Walpurgis: 1973
Lotus Films/Atlas International
Director: Carlos Aured
Cast: Paul Naschy, Faye Falcon, Vinc Molina, May Oliver
Paul Naschy as Daninsky is bitten by a beautiful woman (Oliver) and becomes a werewolf. His lover (Falcon) kills him with a knife fashioned from a melted silver cross, thus ending the curse.
The Boy Who Cried Werewolf: 1973
RKF/Universal
Director: Nathan Juran
Cast: Kerwin Mathews, Elain Devry, Scott Sealy
A boy witnesses his father being attacked by a werewolf, and then tries to convince both his mother and his therapist that his father is now a werewolf.

The Werewolf of Washington: 1973
Millco
Director: Milton Ginsberg
Cast: Dean Stockwell, Biff McGuire, Clifton James
A presidential aide turns into a werewolf after a trip to Hungary, and the U.S government then tries to cover it up.

Blood: 1974
Damiano Film Productions Inc./Bryanston Films Ltd
Director: Andy Milligan
Cast: Allen Berendt, Paula Adams, Eve Crosby
Dr. Orlovski (Allan Berendt), who is afflicted with lycanthropy, lives with the daughter of Dracula. There are also hordes of rabid bats flying around, turning the locals into blood-drooling cannibals.

The Beast Must Die: 1974
Amicus Productions
Director: Paul Annett
Cast: Calvin Lockhart, Peter Cushing, Charles Gray
An eccentric millionaire with a taste for the extravagant invites a group of people, who are all connected to a strange death, to his mansion. One of the invitees is supposedly a werewolf and the prey for the host's hunting party.

Legend of the Werewolf: 1974
Tyburn Film Productions Limited
Director: Freddie Francis
Cast: Peter Cushing, Ron Moody, Hugh Griffith
A traveling circus in 19th century France adopts and showcases a feral "wolf boy." He runs off to Paris, where he develops a jealous, overprotective crush on a prostitute, leading him to attack her client, incurring a pursuit by a determined police surgeon.

Scream of the Wolf: 1974
Metromedia Productions
Director: Dan Curtis
Cast: Philip Carey, Peter Graves, Don McGowan
An author is being stalked by a terrifying, mysterious beast. The creature is also being tracked by a big game hunter, who has come out of retirement to make one final big kill.

The Werewolf and the Yeti: 1975
Profilmes/Profilms
Director: Miguel Iglesias Bonns
Cast: Paul Naschy, Grace Mills, Castillo Escalona
Naschy reprises his role as Count Waldemar Daninsky who is bitten by a woman and turned into a werewolf. This time, however, he is eventually cured, but not before he gets into a fight with the Yeti.

Nazareno Cruz y el lobo (1975)
Choila Producciones Cinematogrˈficas
aka The Nazarene Cross and the Wolf
Director: Leonardo Favio
Cast: Juan JosÈ Camero, Marina Magali, Alfredo AlcÛn, Lautaro Murˈa
Nazareno Cruz is the seventh son of a couple living in a high mountain village. According to a myth, a seventh son will become a wolf on nights of the full moon. Everyone in the village is relieved when this doesn't happen. The boy grows up and falls in love with a beautiful girl, Griselda. When he's 20 years old, he is visited by the Devil, who offers him the wealth of the world if he will turn his back on his love for Griselda, and if he fails to do this, he will become a wolf.

Werewolf of Woodstock: 1975
American Broadcasting Company
Cast: Tige Andrews, Belinda Balaski, Ann Doran, Meredith McRae, Andrew Stevens
After Woodstock has ended, a hippie-hating farmer (Tige Andrews) gets turned into a werewolf when he gets a massive jolt of electricity from a leftover piece of equipment one of the bands left behind. The farmer keeps transforming during electrical storms and killing everyone who gets in his way. After being chased to the top of a power station, he is shot with a silver bullet and falls to his death.

Wolfman: 1979
EO Productions
Director: Worth Keeter
Cast: Earl Owensby, Kristina Reynolds, Ed Grady
Colin Glasgow (Owensby) inherits the "Devil's curse," when his father dies. He soon discovers that his father was a werewolf and that he is to follow in his footsteps.

The Return of the Wolfman: 1980
Dalmata Films
Director: Jacinto Molina (Paul Naschy)
Cast: Paul Naschy, Silvia Aguilar, Azucena Hernandez
In this film, Paul Naschy makes his directorial debut. Once again Count Waldemar Daninsky is resurrected as a werewolf and uses his limited time to kill Countess Bathory.

The Howling: 1980
AVCO Embassy Pictures
Director: Joe Dante
Cast: Dee Wallace, Patrick Macnee, Dennis Dugan
Possibly one of the most influential werewolf movies ever made. News anchor Karen (Wallace) is used as a decoy to catch a psychopath. It is later found that the psychopath is a werewolf. Karen follows up on the story which leads her to the Colony, a remote spa that's sole population is a coven of werewolves. She escapes after burning the werewolves in a barn. As she reports her story, she transforms into a wolf on air, only to be shot to death by her lover.

An American Werewolf in London: 1981
Lycanthrope Films
Director: John Landis
Cast: David Naughton, Jenny Agutter, Griffin Dunne
A movie that really broke new ground using special effects to transform a man into a wolf. Two American students (Naughton and Dunne) come across the Slaughtered Lamb Pub while traveling through England. They are warned to stay on the roads and off the moors but stray from the road. They are attacked by a werewolf who kills Dunne and mauls Naughton. He wakes up in a hospital and has reoccurring nightmares through which he learns that he has become a werewolf. Naughton has a relationship with his nurse and eventually dies when he is in wolf form.

Wolfen: 1981
Orion Pictures
Director: Michael Wadleigh
Cast: Albert Finney, Diane Verona, Gregory Hines
Wilson (Finney) is a police detective who investigates a series murders in the Bronx. Along with his partner (Verona) and Hines, they soon discover that the killers are 'wolfen,' descendants of Indians who prey on the white man.

Full Moon High: 1982
Filmways Pictures/ Larco Productions
Director: Larry Cohen
Cast: Adam Arkin, Alan Arkin, Ed McMahon
Tony, a high school quarterback is taken on a trip to Romania where, as a direct quote from the video box states: "Tony (Arkin) is bitten by a werewolf - and that's when things really start to get hairy!"

The Beast and the Magic Sword: 1983
Aconito Films
Director: Jacinto Molina (Paul Naschy)
Cast: Shigeru Amachi, Beatriz Escudero, Junko Asahina
Naschy returns as director and once again plays wolfman Count Waldemar Daninsky. This time he is in sixteenth century Japan seeking a cure for his curse.

Children of the Full Moon: 1984
ITC Entertainment
Director: Tom Clegg
Cast: Christopher Cazenove, Diana Dors
A couple discovers a remote mansion whose occupants are a kindly old woman and very mysterious children, all who turn out to be werewolves.

Leviatan: 1984
Continental Motion Pictures
Director: Claudio Fragasso
Cast: Alice Cooper, Victoria Vera
Rock superstar Vincent Raven (Alice Cooper) returns to his boyhood home for a video shoot. The sheriff warns him that there have been several grisly murders lately. The authorities think it is wild dogs, but Raven (the werewolf) knows the truth.

The Company of Wolves: 1984
Palace Pictures
Director: Neil Jordan
Cast: Angela Lansbury, Sarah Patterson, David Warner
This movie is dreamlike and full of symbolic folklore about werewolves. Grandmother (Lansbury) tells her granddaughter (Patterson) strange tales about maidens falling in love with handsome strangers with a smoldering look in their eyes. All the stories are somehow reducible to loss of innocence, and fear of/hunger for a newly acquired sense of sexuality.

Silver Bullet: 1985
Paramount
Director: Daniel Attias
Cast: Gary Busey, Everett McGill, Corey Haim, Megan Follows
Based on Stephen King's book "Cycle of the Werewolf." A new Minister (McGill) moves into town and at the same time a series of grizzly murders occur. A paraplegic boy (Haim) believes that a werewolf is responsible for the murders, and tries to convince his family likewise. Only his sister (Follows) believes him, and together they seek out the identity of the werewolf.

The Howling II - Your Sister is a Werewolf: 1985
Hemdale
Director: Philippe Mora
Cast: Christopher Lee, Annie McEnroe, Reb Brown
Plot: Christopher Lee and Reb Brown are werewolf hunters who travel to Transylvania and run across an entire village of werewolves. This coven is led by Striba (Danning) the queen witch of Transylvania. A really bad sequel to a great movie.

Teen Wolf: 1985
Atlantic
Director: Rod Daniel
Cast: Michael J. Fox, James Hampton, Susan Ursitti
Michael J Fox plays a high school student who finds out that because of a family curse, he is a werewolf. However, instead of seeing it as a curse he uses it to become the most popular kid in school.

She Wolf: 1987
K-Beech Video Inc.
Cast: Anne Borel, Frank Stafford
Daniella (Borel) has inherited the werewolf curse from an ancestor. When the moon turns full, the she-wolf stalks the night.

Howling III the Marsupials: 1987
Bacannia
Director: Phillipe Mora
Cast: William Yang, Deby Wrightman, Christopher Pate
In one of the weirdest werewolf movies ever conceived, a mutant strain of werewolves survives as an Australian species. Full of strange concepts that include marsupial werewolves with pouches to carry their young!

Werewolf: 1987
Fox TV
Director: David Hemmings
Cast: John York, Lance LeGault, Chuck Connors
One of the first series carried by the newly formed Fox TV. A graduate student is bitten by his best friend who is a werewolf. Consequently, he turns into a werewolf himself, and to break the curse he must find and kill the original werewolf.

Teen Wolf 2: 1987
Atlantic
Director: Christopher Leitch
Cast: Jason Bateman, Kim Darby, John Astin, Paul Sand
Todd (Bateman) is accepted to a university on a boxing scholarship, although his boxing abilities are questionable. What he doesn't know is that he was accepted in hopes that he would have the same curse (lycanthropy) as his cousin Scott.

The Howling 4 - The Original Nightmare: 1988
Allied Entertainment
Director: John Hough
Cast: Romy Windsor, Michael Weiss, Anthony Hamilton
Marie (Windsor) is an author plagued by dreams of werewolves. Thinking the dreams are caused by stress, she and her husband (Weiss) take a holiday to the town of Drago. She soon discovers that her dreams were premonitions of the future, as everyone in Drago is a werewolf.

Lone Wolf: 1988
Prisim Entertainment (Uk)
Director: John Callas
Cast: Shelly Beatie, Dyan Brown, Ann Douglas, Kevin Hart
A computer genius puts his talents to work to expose the werewolf that's been preying on local high-school students.

My Mom's a Werewolf: 1989
Crown International
Director: Michael Fischa
Cast: Diana Barrows, Ruth Buzzi, Tina Caspary
When a lonely housewife decides to lunch with a pet shop owner, she is unaware that he is a werewolf. Things go too far and she soon becomes one as well.

The Howling V- The Rebirth: 1989
Allied Vision/Lane Pringle
Director: Neal Sundstrom
Cast: Ben Cole, William Shockley, Mark Sivertsen, Clive Turner, Phillip Davis
In the Middle ages, residents of a castle in Budapest committed suicide to severe the bloodline of a werewolf. However, a baby survives. In 1989 the Count summons a variety of people to the castle to discover the werewolf's descendant. Shortly after they arrive, the suspects are eliminated one by one by the real werewolf.

Mom: 1990
Trans World Entertainment
Director: Patrick Rand
Cast: Jeanne Bates, Art Evans, Stella Stevens
During a time when the city of Los Angeles is terrorized by animal attack style murders, a kindly elderly lady provides a nomad with room and board. It turns out that he is a werewolf and is responsible for the recent killings. He bites the elderly woman, turning her into a hungry werewolf. Now her son must try to prevent the both of them from doing any more harm.

The Howling 6 - The Freaks: 1991
Allied Vision/Lane Pringle
Director: Hope Perello
Cast: Bruce Martin Payne, Brendaan Hughes
A drifter Ian (Hughes) ventures into the town of Canton Bluff seeking work. He soon finds work restoring the town's church. He seems distant to the townsfolk and when a traveling freak show ventures into town, the reason becomes clear, Ian is a werewolf. He is kidnapped by the show's proprietor Harker (Payne who is a vampire himself) and put on display. After the carnival is stormed by the townspeople Ian kills Harker and once again takes to the road.

Huntress - Spirit of the Night: 1991
Torchlight Entertainment / New City Releasing
Director: Mark Manos
Cast: Jenna Bodnar, Charles Copper, Ion Siminie
Tara returns to her ancestral estate only to have her clothes explode off her body and a white light enter her chest. Afterwards she's tormented by strange desires and dreams of running through the woods. Her cave-dwelling boyfriend is no help to her. Meanwhile, false friends plot to steal her inheritance and a determined hunter seeks to slay the new werewolf in town.

Full Eclipse: 1993
HBO/Tapestry Films/Citadel Entertainment
Director: Anthony Hickox
Cast: Mario Van Peebles, Patsy Kensit, Bruce Payne
Peebles is recruited to be a part of an elite Los Angeles police team comprised of werewolves.

Wolf: 1994
Columbia
Director: Mike Nichols
Cast: Shirin Devrim, Jack Nicholson, Allison Janney
Will Randal (Nicholson) is bitten by a wolf that he encounters while driving late at night. From that point on, his life begins to change. Using his newly acquired wolf instincts, he gains an advantage over colleagues and foes alike.

The Howling - New Moon Rising: 1995
Allied Vision
Director: Clive Turner
Cast: Clive Turner, John Huff, John Ramsden, Cheryl Allen
Ted (Turner) arrives in Pioneer Town and discovers that there has been a mysterious murder. A priest (Huff) explains to the detective (Ramsden) the history of the werewolf curse, and that Ted was once present at the slaughter at a Budapest castle. More deaths occur, and Ted is arrested. A young woman (Allen) helps Ted escape, and then reveals to him that she is in-fact the werewolf.

Project Metalbeast: 1995
Blue Ridge Entertainment/Prison Pictures
Director: Alessandro de Gaetano
Cast: Barry Bostwick, Kim Delaney, John Marzilli
In Hungary, CIA agent Donald Butler (Marzilli) heads an operation in search of werewolf blood, in hopes of using it to create a superior soldier. After killing the werewolf, and injecting himself with the blood, Butler is turned into a werewolf and is killed by his partner (Bostwick). Twenty years later, scientist Anna De Carlo experiments with a new metallic flesh called BioFerron. Butler's corpse is grafted with the BioFerron, and the Metal Beast is created.

Bad Moon: 1996
Badwolf Productions/Morgan Creek
Director: Eric Red
Cast: Michael Pare, Mariel Hemmingway, Mason Gamble
An adventurous photojournalist, Ted (Pare), encounters a horrific, half-human beast that savagely murders his girlfriend. In a violent battle, Ted manages to kill the creature - but not before he receives a vicious bite that leaves him scarred forever. Ted returns to the home of his sister, Janet (Hemmingway), his beloved 10-year-old nephew, Brett (Gamble) and their dog Thor. Things soon begin to go bad, especially when the family dog, a big German Shepherd named Thor, just can't accept the werewolf among them.

American Werewolf in Paris: 1997
Hollywood Pictures
Director: Anthony Walker
Cast: Tom Everett Scott, Julie Delpy
Three friends are on a thrill seeking tour across Europe where they meet the daughter conceived in "An American Werewolf In London" (1981) and save her from jumping off the Eifel Tower. They get involved in a plot for an underground group of werewolves who want to use a serum to transform whenever they want.

Werewolf Reborn: 1998
Full Moon/Tempe Video
Director: Jeff Burr
Cast: Bogdan Cambera , Len Lesser, Robin Downes
Fourteen-year-old Eleanor Crane goes to visit her older cousin Peter in a remote Eastern European village, and receives an unexpectedly cold welcome from the villagers, who are plagued by a deadly curse - and from her cousin, who hides a deadly secret of his own.

Eyes of the Werewolf: 1999
Sterling Entertainment/SNJ Productions
Director: Jeff Leroy
Cast: Stephanie Beaton, Mark Sawyer, Deborah Hurber
An industrial accident leaves Rich (Sawyer) blind and at the mercy of an unscrupulous surgeon who performs an experimental eye transplant. Unknown to everyone, including the doctor's band of organ snatching murderers, the eyes were pulled from the sockets of a werewolf. All hell breaks loose, for Rich and everyone he comes in contact with, during the next full moon.

Rage of the Werewolf: 1999
Brimestone Productions
Director: Kevin Lindenmuth
Cast: Tom Nondorf, Joe Zaso, Santo Marotta
New York, sometime in the future; an asteroid collides into the moon which causes it to orbit closer to the Earth - causing a proliferation of werewolves.

Ginger Snaps: 2001
TVA International
Director: John Fawcett
Cast: Katharine Isabelle, Emily Perkins, Mimi Rogers
On the night of Ginger's first period, she is savagely attacked by a wild creature. Ginger's wounds miraculously heal but something is not quite right. Now Brigitte must save her sister and save herself.

Dog Soldiers: 2002
Kismet Entertainment Group
Director: Neil Marshall
Cast: Sean Pertwee, Kevin McKidd, Emma Cleasby, Liam Cunningham, Thomas Lockyer
A squad of British soldiers on training in the lonesome Scottish wilderness discovers a wounded Special Forces captain and the savaged remains of his team. As they encounter ranger Megan it turns out that werewolves are active in the region. They have to prepare for some action as the there will be a full moon tonight.

Wolves of Wall Street: 2002
A.C.H. GmbH
Director: David DeCoteau
Cast: Eric Roberts, Elisa Donovan, Michael Bergin, William Gregory Lee, Jason-Shane Scott
On the advice of a bartender familiar with the Wall Street crowd, Jeff applies to the Wolfe Brothers brokerage firm for his dream job as a stock broker. He is forced to abandon his love and values for cunning and instinct. After a change of heart, he finds that leaving the brotherhood is harder than joining.

Dark Wolf: 2003
20th Century Fox
Director: Richard Friedman
Cast: Samaire Armstrong, Ryan Alosio, Andrea Bogart, Kane Hodder
Josie, a waitress who discovers that the blood in her veins is of noble werewolf descent and that a werewolf is after her because it needs to mate.

Underworld: 2003
Lakeshore Entertainment
Director: Len Wiseman
Cast: Kate Beckinsale, Scott Speedman, Michael Sheen
A war has been going on for centuries between vampires and werewolves, never seen by human eyes, until one of the werewolves by the name of Lucian (Michael Sheen) finds out about one human that can bond with vampire blood and Lycans blood, Michael (Scott Speedman). Selene (Kate Beckinsale) is the vampire Death dealer that finds out why the Lycans are following Micheal and falls in love with him. Kraven (Shane Brolly) is the leader of the vampire house after Viktor (Bill Nighy) dies and wants Selene by his side.

Ginger Snaps 2: Unleashed: 2004
49th Parallel Productions
Director: Brett Sullivan
Cast: Emily Perkins, Katharine Isabelle, Tatiana Maslany
The second part of the "Ginger Snaps" trilogy picks up after the first one. Ginger has turned into a werewolf and her sister Bridgitte has infected herself with Ginger's blood. In order to keep herself from becoming like her sister, she must inject herself daily with monkshood. After barely escaping a werewolf that has found her, she awakes in a clinic that treats drug addiction. With her monkshood taken away, Bridgitte can't escape what she is becoming.

Ginger Snaps Back: The Beginning: 2004
Combustion Inc.
Director: Grant Harvey
Cast: Katharine Isabelle, Emily Perkins, Nathaniel Arcand, JR Bourne, Hugh Dillon
Set in 19th Century Canada, Brigette and her sister Ginger take refuge in a Traders' Fort which later becomes under siege by some savage werewolves. And an enigmatic Indian hunter decides to help the girls, but one of the girls has been bitten by a werewolf. Brigitte and Ginger may have no one to turn to but themselves.

Romasanta: 2004
Lions Gate Films Home Entertainment
Director: Paco Plaza
Cast: Julian Sands, Elsa Pataky, John Sharian
In 1850 wolves plague the forests and people are disappearing. The mutilated cadavers present precise surgical cuts along with savage gashes. It's a contradiction that terrorizes the local villagers, who are too frightened to enter the forests. Rumors about the legend of the "Werewolf of Allariz" spread. Barbara and her sister Josephine live in an isolated house in the forest. They only feel safe when a traveling vendor by the name of Manuel Romasanta comes to visit. But why is Manuel not afraid to enter the forest and what secrets are hidden under the roof of his wagon?

Van Helsing
Universal Pictures: 2004
Director: Stephen Sommers
Cast: Hugh Jackman, Kate Beckinsale, David Wenham, Will Kemp
Based on a version of the character of Abraham Van Helsing from Bram Stoker's novel Dracula, the film also incorporates characters from other works such as the film The Wolfman into the narrative, and draws particularly on literary classics of the gothic horror canon such as Mary Shelley's novel Frankenstein.

The Beast of Bray Road: 2005
The Asylum
Director: Leigh Slawner
Cast: Jeff Denton, Thomas Downey, Sarah Lieving, Joel Hebner
Based on actual accounts of werewolf sightings in Walworth County, Wisconsin, the film follows a local sheriff who is finally forced to accept that a string of horrifying deaths is linked to a predator which possesses DNA of both man and wolf.

Cursed: 2005
Dimension Films
Director: Wes Craven
Cast: Christina Ricci, Jessie Eisenberg, Joshua Jackson, Shannon Elizabeth
Ellie has been taking care of her younger brother Jimmy since their parent's death. One night after picking him up from a party they are involved in a car accident on Mullholland Drive. While trying to rescue a woman from the other car a creature attacks and kills her, also injuring both Ellie and Jimmy. After some research Jimmy realizes the creature could only have been a werewolf.

Wolfsbayne: 2005
Bloody Moon Films
Director: Ben Dixon
Cast: Jim O'Rear, Gunnar Hansen, Linnea Quigley
In 1590, the Diet of Augsburg ruled that gypsies were the spawn of Satan and, therefore, had no rights whatsoever. The ruling allowed Christians to kill gypsies without penalty, which sparked the church to organize a small group of religious assassins to carry out the dirty work. Unfortunately, the band of killer priests were not informed that the gypsies had made a pact of protection with a powerful werewolf clan, so all hell broke loose. Four hundred years later, the bloody war between the church, gypsies and werewolves rages on and it's up to a small-town police chief to end it or die trying.

Underworld: Evolution: 2006
Lakeshore Entertainment
Director: Len Wiseman
Cast: Kate Beckinsale, Scott Speedman, Bill Nighy, Shane Brolly
The movie continues the saga of war between the Death Dealers (vampires) and the Lycans (werewolves). The film traces the beginnings of the ancient feud between the two tribes as Selene (Kate Beckinsale) and Michael (Scott Speedman), the lycan hybrid, try to discover the secrets of their bloodlines. All of this takes them into the battle to end all wars as the immortals must finally face their retribution.

Skinwalkers: 2007
Lions Gate Films
Color 110 min
Director: James Issac
Cast: Jason Behr, Elias Koteas, Rhona Mitra, Kim Coates, Natassia Malthe
Creatures, bound by the blood of the wolf, that can kill with curses and move at lightening speed, watching the night sky for the rise of the blood-rd crescent moon. They are Skinwalkers. They feed on our flesh and thirst for the taste of human blood. The red moon signals each pack, divided by principles, hell bent to survive an ancient prophecy.

Werewolf: The Devil's Hound: 2007)
Lionsgate Films
Director: Gregory C. Parker & Christian Pindar
Cast: Kirsten Babich, Christy O. Cianci, Michael Dionne, Phil Gauvin
Kevin has a late night encounter with the blood thirsty Christine that prompts him to slowly turn against his family and co-workers. Now, with the help of the quirky werewolf hunter Kwan, two families will unite for one common cause.

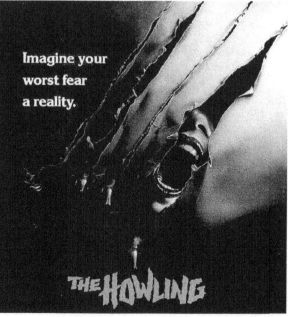

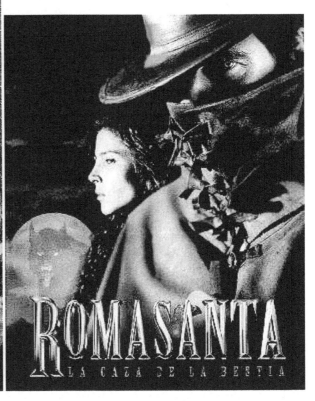

Skinwalkers

THE
MONSTER

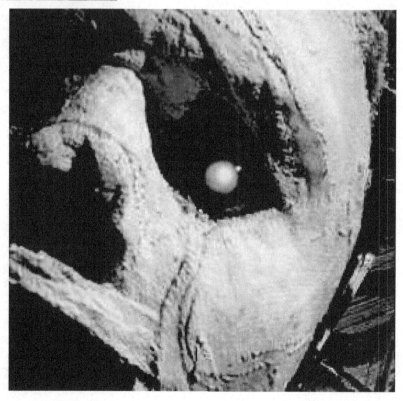

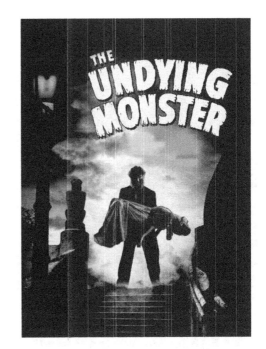

THE WOLFMAN

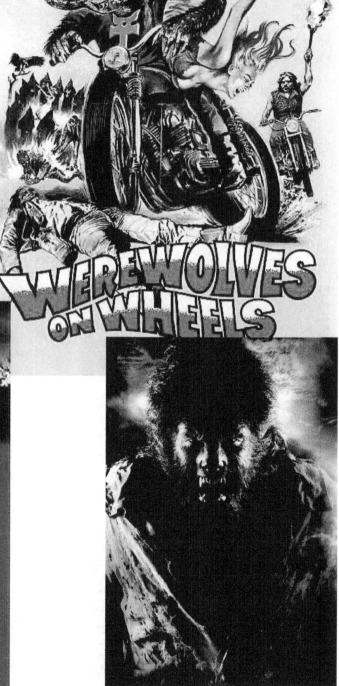

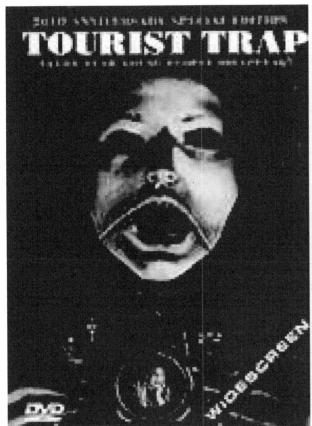

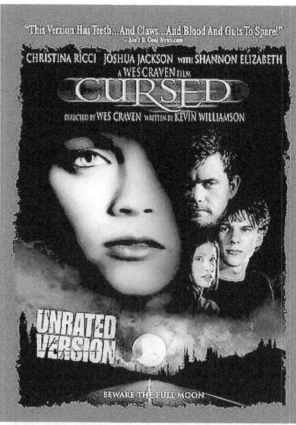

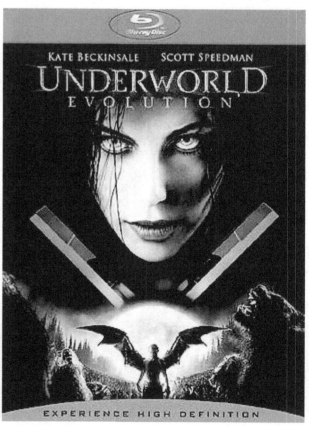

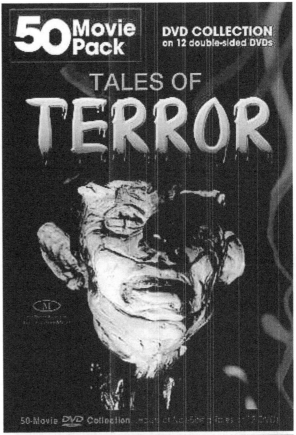

Werewolf of Ansbach Execution

Werewolfs (300 Women) in Julich (Germany)
woodcut, Augsburg 1591

18th Century Engraving

Fredrick Madden
Cambridge, 1832

Beast of LeGermudan

Beast of LeGevaudan

Hartmann Schedel
Liber Cronicarum
Numberg Germany, 1493

Marco Polo: Lykanthrope, Island auf Andaman;
Painting in manuscript, France, 15th Century

Werewolf in Battle
woodcut colored, 15th Century

Hans Weiditz
Straburg, 1516

Maurice Sand
Les Lupins
from Légendes Rustiques

Werewolf (magician) and Cat (witch)
woodcut Mailand, Italy
from E-M. Guazzo: Compendium_1628

"He soon emerged in the form of a wolf"
THE WERE-WOLVES.

Scene from a Russian Tale

Ch. Le Brun
France, 17th Century

Beast of LeGezaudan

The Werewolf
A Short Story
Clemence Housman

The great farm hall was ablaze with the fire-light, and noisy with laughter and talk and many-sounding work. None could be idle but the very young and the very old: little Rol, who was hugging a puppy, and old Trella, whose palsied hand fumbled over her knitting. The early evening had closed in, and the farm- servants, come from their outdoor work, had assembled in the ample hall, which gave space for a score or more of workers. Several of the men were engaged in carving, and to these were yielded the best place and light; others made or repaired fishing-tackle and harness, and a great seine net occupied three pairs of hands. Of the women most were sorting and mixing eider feather and chopping straw to add to it. Looms were there, though not in present use, but three wheels whirred emulously, and the finest and swiftest thread of the three ran between the fingers of the house-mistress. Near her were some children, busy too, plaiting wicks for candles and lamps. Each group of workers had a lamp in its centre, and those farthest from the fire had live heat from two braziers filled with glowing wood embers, replenished now and again from the generous hearth. But the flicker of the great fire was manifest to remotest corners, and prevailed beyond the limits of the weaker lights.

Little Rol grew tired of his puppy, dropped it incontinently, and made an onslaught on Tyr, the old wolf- hound, who basked dozing, whimpering and twitching in his hunting dreams. Prone went Rol beside Tyr, his young arms round the shaggy neck, his curls against the black jowl. Tyr gave a perfunctory lick, and stretched with a sleepy sigh. Rol growled and rolled and shoved invitingly, but could only gain from the old dog placid toleration and a half-observant blink. 'Take that then!' said Rol, indignant at this ignoring of his advances, and sent the puppy sprawling against the dignity that disdained him as playmate. The dog took no notice, and the child wandered off to find amusement elsewhere.

The baskets of white eider feathers caught his eye far off in a distant corner. He slipped under the table, and crept along on all-fours, the ordinary commonplace custom of walking down a room upright not being to his fancy. When close to the women he lay still for a moment watching, with his elbows on the floor and his chin in his palms. One of the women seeing him nodded and smiled, and presently he crept out behind her skirts and passed, hardly noticed, from one to another, till he found opportunity to possess himself of a large handful of feathers. With these he traversed the length of the room, under the table again, and emerged near the spinners. At the feet of the youngest he curled himself round, sheltered by her knees from the observation of the others, and disarmed her of interference by secretly displaying his handful with a confiding smile. A dubious nod satisfied him, and presently he started on the play he had devised. He took a tuft of the white down, and gently shook it free of his fingers close to the whirl of the wheel. The wind of the swift motion took it, spun it round and round in widening circles, till it floated above like a slow white moth. Little Rol's eyes danced, and the row of his small teeth shone in a silent laugh of delight. Another and another of the white tufts was sent whirling round like a winged thing in a spider's web, and floating clear at last. Presently the handful failed.

Rol sprawled forward to survey the room, and contemplate another journey under the table. His shoulder, thrusting forward, checked the wheel for an instant; he shifted hastily. The wheel flew on with a jerk, and the thread snapped. 'Naughty Rol!' said the girl. The swiftest wheel stopped also, and the house-mistress, Rol's aunt, leaned forward, and sighting the low curly head, gave a warning against mischief, and sent him off to old Trella's corner.

Rol obeyed, and after a discreet period of obedience, sidled out again down the length of the room farthest from his aunt's eye. As he slipped in among the men, they looked up to see that their tools might be, as far as possible, out of reach of Rol's hands, and close to their own. Nevertheless, before long he managed to secure a fine chisel and take off its point on the leg of the table. The carver's strong objections to this disconcerted Rol, who for five minutes thereafter effaced himself under the table.

During this seclusion he contemplated the many pairs of legs that surrounded him, and almost shut out the light of the fire. How very odd some of the legs were: some were curved where they should be straight, some were straight where they should be curved, and, as Rol said to himself. 'they all seemed screwed on differently.' Some were tucked away modestly under the benches, others were thrust far out under the table, encroaching on Rol's own particular domain. He stretched out his own short legs and regarded them critically, and, after comparison, favourably. Why were not all legs made like his, or like *his*?

These legs approved by Rol were a little apart from the rest. He crawled opposite and again made comparison. His face grew quite solemn as he thought of the innumerably days to come before his legs could be as long and strong. He hoped they would be just like those, his models, as straight as to bone, as curved as to muscle.

A few moments later Sweyn of the long legs felt a small hand caressing his foot, and looking down, met the upturned eyes of his little cousin Rol. Lying on his back, still softly patting and stroking the young man's foot, the child was quiet and happy for a good while. He watched the movement of the strong deft hands, and the shifting of the bright tools. Now and then, minute chips of wood, puffed off by Sweyn, fell down upon his face. At last he raised himself, very gently, lest a jog should wake impatience in the carver, and crossing his own legs round Sweyn's ankle, clasping with his arms too, laid his head against the knee. Such act is evidence of a child's most wonderful hero-worship. Quite content when Sweyn paused a minute to joke, and pat his head and pull his curls. Quiet he remained, as long as quiescence is possible to limbs young as his. Sweyn forgot he was near, hardly noticed when his leg was gently released, and never saw the stealthy abstraction of one of his tools.

Ten minutes thereafter was a lamentable wail from low on the floor, rising to the full pitch of Rol's healthy lungs; for his hand was gashed across, and the copious bleeding terrified him. Then was there soothing and comforting, washing and binding, and a modicum of scolding, till the loud outcry sank into occasional sobs, and the child, tear-stained and subdued, was returned to the chimney-corner settle, where Trella nodded.

In the reaction after pain and fright, Rol found that the quiet of that fire-lit corner was to his mind. Tyr, too, disdained him no longer, but, roused by his sobs, showed all the concern and sympathy that a dog can by licking and wistful watching. A little shame weighed also upon his spirits. He wished he had not cried quite so much. He remembered how once Sweyn had come home with his arm torn down from the shoulder, and a dead bear; and how he had never winced nor said a word, though his lips turned white with pain. Poor little Rol gave another sighing sob over his own faint-hearted shortcomings.

The light and motion of the great fire began to tell strange stories to the child, and the wind in the chimney roared a corroborative note now and then. The great black mouth of the chimney, impending high over the hearth, received as into a mysterious gulf murky coils of smoke and brightness of aspiring sparks; and beyond, in the high darkness, were muttering and wailing and strange doings, so that sometimes the smoke rushed back in panic, and curled out and up to the roof, and condensed itself to invisibility among the rafters. And then the wind would rage after its lost prey, and rush round the house, rattling and shrieking at window and door.

In a lull, after one such loud gust, Rol lifted his head in surprise and listened. A lull had also come on the babel of talk, and thus could be heard with strange distinctness a sound outside the door—the sound of a child's voice, a child's hands. 'Open, open; let me in!' piped the little voice from low down, lower than the handle, and the latch rattled as though a tiptoe child reached up to it, and soft small knocks were struck. One near the door sprang up and opened it. 'No one is here,' he said. Tyr lifted his head and gave utterance to a howl, loud, prolonged, most dismal.

Sweyn, not able to believe that his ears had deceived him, got up and went to the door. It was a dark night; the clouds were heavy with snow, that had fallen fitfully when the wind lulled. Untrodden snow lay up to the porch; there was no sight nor sound of any human being. Sweyn strained his eyes far and near, only to see dark sky, pure snow, and a line of black fir trees on a hill brow, bowing down before the wind. 'It must have been the wind,' he said, and closed the door.

Many faces looked scared. The sound of a child's voice had been so distinct—and the words 'Open, open; let me in!' The wind might creak the wood, or rattle the latch, but could not speak with a child's voice, nor knock with the soft plain blows that a plump fist gives. And the strange unusual howl of the wolf-hound was an omen to be feared, be the rest what it might. Strange things were said by one and another, till the rebuke of the house-mistress quelled them into far-off whispers. For a time after there was uneasiness, constraint, and silence; then the chill fear thawed by degrees, and the babble of talk flowed on again.

Yet half-an-hour later a very slight noise outside the door sufficed to arrest every hand, every tongue. Every head was raised, every eye fixed in one direction. 'It is Christian; he is late,' said Sweyn.

No, no; this is a feeble shuffle, not a young man's tread. With the sound of uncertain feet came the hard tap-tap of a stick against the door, and the high-pitched voice of eld, 'Open, open; let me in!' Again Tyr flung up his head in a long doleful howl.

Before the echo of the tapping stick and the high voice had fairly died away, Sweyn had sprung across to the door and flung it wide. 'No one again,' he said in a steady voice, though his eyes looked startled as he stared out. He saw the lonely expanse of snow, the clouds swagging low, and between the two the line of dark fir-trees bowing in the wind. He closed the door without a word of comment, and re- crossed the room.

A score of blanched faces were turned to him as though he must be solver of the enigma. He could not be unconscious of this mute eye-questioning, and it disturbed his resolute air of composure. He hesitated, glanced towards his mother, the house-mistress, then back at the frightened folk, and gravely, before them all, made the sign of the cross. There was a flutter of hands as the sign was repeated by all, and the dead silence was stirred as by a huge sigh, for the held breath of many was freed as though the sign gave magic relief.

Even the house-mistress was perturbed. She left her wheel and crossed the room to her son, and spoke with him for a moment in a low tone that none could overhear. But a moment later her voice was high- pitched and loud, so that all might benefit by her rebuke of the 'heathen chatter' of one of the girls. Perhaps she essayed to silence thus her own misgivings and forebodings.

No other voice dared speak now with its natural fulness. Low tones made intermittent murmurs, and now and then silence drifted over the whole room. The handling of tools was as noiseless as might be, and suspended on the instant if the door rattled in a gust of wind. After a time Sweyn left his work, joined the group nearest the door, and loitered there on the pretence of giving advice and help to the unskilful.

A man's tread was heard outside in the porch. 'Christian!' said Sweyn and his mother simultaneously, he confidently, she authoritatively, to set the checked wheels going again. But Tyr flung up his head with an appalling howl.

'Open, open; let me in!'

It was a man's voice, and the door shook and rattled as a man's strength beat against it. Sweyn could feel the planks quivering, as on the instant his hand was upon the door, flinging it open, to face the blank porch, and beyond only snow and sky, and firs aslant in the wind.

He stood for a long minute with the open door in his hand. The bitter wind swept in with its icy chill, but a deadlier chill of fear came swifter, and seemed to freeze the beating of hearts. Sweyn stepped back to snatch up a great bearskin cloak.

'Sweyn, where are you going?'

'No farther than the porch, mother,' and he stepped out and closed the door.

He wrapped himself in the heavy fur, and leaning against the most sheltered wall of the porch, steeled his nerves to face the devil and all his works. No sound of voices came from within; the most distinct sound was the crackle and roar of the fire.

It was bitterly cold. His feet grew numb, but he forbore stamping them into warmth lest the sound should strike panic within; nor would he leave the porch, nor print a foot-mark on the untrodden white that declared so absolutely how no human voices and hands could have approached the door since snow fell two hours or more ago. 'When the wind drops there will be more snow,' thought Sweyn.

For the best part of an hour he kept his watch, and saw no living thing—heard no unwonted sound. 'I will freeze here no longer,' he muttered, and re-entered.

One woman gave a half-suppressed scream as his hand was laid on the latch, and then a gasp of relief as he came in. No one questioned him, only his mother said, in a tone of forced unconcern, 'Could you not see Christain coming?' as though she were made anxious only by the absence of her younger son. Hardly had Sweyn stamped near to the fire than clear knocking was heard at the door. Tyr leapt from the hearth, his eyes red as the fire, his fangs showing white in the black jowl, his neck ridged and bristling; and overleaping Rol, ramped at the door, barking furiously.

Outside the door a clear mellow voice was calling. Tyr's bark made the words undistinguishable.

No one offered to stir towards the door before Sweyn.

He stalked down the room resolutely, lifted the latch, and swung back the door.

A white-robed woman glided in.

No wraith! Living—beautiful—young.

Tyr leapt upon her.

Lithely she baulked the sharp fangs with folds of her long fur robe, and snatching from her girdle a small two-edged axe, whirled it up for a blow of defence.

Sweyn caught the dog by the collar, and dragged him off yelling and struggling.

The stranger stood in the doorway motionless, one foot set forward, one arm flung up, till the house- mistress hurried down the room; and Sweyn, relinquishing to others the furious Tyr, turned again to close the door, and offer excuse for so fierce a greeting. Then she lowered her arm, slung the axe in its place at her waist, loosened the furs about her face, and shook over her shoulders the long white robe—all as it were with the sway of one movement.

She was a maiden, tall and fair. The fashion of her dress was strange, half masculine, yet not unwomanly. A fine fur tunic, reaching but little below the knee, was all the skirt she wore; below were the cross-bound shoes and leggings that a hunter wears. A white fur cap was set low upon the brows, and from its edge strips of fur fell lappet-wise about her shoulders; two of these at her entrance had been drawn forward and crossed about her throat, but now, loosened and thrust back, left unhidden long plaits of fair hair that lay forward on shoulder and breast, down to the ivory-studded girdle where the axe gleamed.

Sweyn and his mother led the stranger to the hearth without question or sign of curiosity, till she voluntarily told her tale of a long journey to distant kindred, a promised guide unmet, and signals and landmarks mistaken.

'Alone!' exclaimed Sweyn in astonishment. 'Have you journeyed thus far, a hundred leagues, alone?'

She answered 'Yes' with a little smile. 'Over the hills and the wastes! Why, the folk there are savage and wild as beasts.'

She dropped her hand upon her axe with a laugh of some scorn.

'I fear neither man nor beast; some few fear me.' And then she told strange tales of fierce attack and defence, and of the bold free huntress life she had led.

Her words came a little slowly and deliberately, as though she spoke in a scarce familiar tongue; now and then she hesitated, and stopped in a phrase, as though for lack of some word.

She became the centre of a group of listeners. The interest she excited dissipated, in some degrees, the dread inspired by the mysterious voices. There was nothing ominous about this young, bright, fair reality, though her aspect was strange.

Little Rol crept near, staring at the stranger with all his might. Unnoticed, he softly stroked and patted a corner of her soft white robe that reached to the floor in ample folds. He laid his cheek against it caressingly, and then edged up close to her knees.

'What is your name?' he asked.

The stranger's smile and ready answer, as she looked down, saved Rol from the rebuke merited by his unmannerly question.

'My real name,' she said, 'would be uncouth to your ears and tongue. The folk of this country have given me another name, and from this' (she laid her hand on the fur robe) 'they call me "White Fell."'

Little Rol repeated it to himself, stroking and patting as before. 'White Fell, White Fell.'

The Fair face, and soft, beautiful dress pleased Rol. He knelt up, with his eyes on her face and an air of uncertain determination, like a robin's on a doorstep, and plumped his elbows into her lap with a little gasp at his own audacity.

'Rol!' exclaimed his aunt; but, 'Oh, let him!' said White Fell, smiling and stroking his head; and Rol stayed.

He advanced farther, and panting at his own adventurousness in the face of his aunt's authority, climbed up on to her knees. Her welcoming arms hindered any protest. He nestled happily, fingering the axe head, the ivory studs in her girdle, the ivory clasp at her throat, the plaits of fair hair; rubbing his head against the softness of her fur-clad shoulder, with a child's full confidence in the kindness of beauty.

White Fell had not uncovered her head, only knotted the pendant fur loosely behind her neck. Rol reached up his hand towards it, whispering her name to himself, 'White Fell, White Fell,' then slid his arms round her neck, and kissed her—once—twice. She laughed delightedly, and kissed him again.

'The child plagues you?' said Sweyn.

'No, indeed,' she answered, with an earnestness so intense as to seem disproportionate to the occasion.

Rol settled himself again on her lap, and began to unwind the bandage bound round his hand. He paused a little when he saw where the blood had soaked through; then went on till his hand was bare and the cut displayed, gaping and long, though only skin deep. He held it up towards White Fell, desirous of her pity and sympathy.

At sight of it, and the blood-stained linen, she drew in her breath suddenly, clasped Rol to her—hard, hard—till he began to struggle. Her face was hidden behind the boy, so that none could see its expression. It had lighted up with a most awful glee.

Afar, beyond the fir-grove, beyond the low hill behind, the absent Christian was hastening his return. From daybreak he had been afoot, carrying notice of a bear hunt to all the best hunters of the farms and hamlets that lay within a radius of twelve miles. Nevertheless, having been detained till a late hour, he now broke into a run, going with a long smooth stride of apparent ease that fast made the miles diminish.

He entered the midnight blackness of the fir-grove with scarcely slackened pace, though the path was invisible; and passing through into the open again, sighted the farm lying a furlong off down the slope. Then he sprang out freely, and almost on the instant gave one great sideways leap, and stood still. There in the snow was the track of a great wolf.

His hand went to his knife, his only weapon. He stooped, knelt down, to bring his eyes to the level of a beast, and peered about; his teeth set, his heart beat a little harder than the pace of his running insisted on. A solitary wolf, nearly always savage and of large size, is a formidable beast that will not hesitate to attack a single man. This wolf-track was the largest Christian had ever seen, and, so far as he could judge, recently made. It led from under the fir-trees down the slope. Well for him, he thought, was the delay that had so vexed him before: well for him that he had not passed through the dark fir-grove when that danger of jaws lurked there. Going warily, he followed the track.

It led down the slope, across a broad ice-bound stream, along the level beyond, making towards the farm. A less precise knowledge had doubted, and guessed that here might have come straying big Tyr or his like; but Christian was sure, knowing better than to mistake between footmark of dog and wolf.

Straight on—straight on towards the farm.

Surprised and anxious grew Christian, that a prowling wolf should dare so near. He drew his knife and pressed on, more hastily, more keen-eyed. Oh that Tyr were with him!

Straight on, straight on, even to the very door, where the snow failed. His heart seemed to give a great leap and then stop. There the track ended.

Nothing lurked in the porch, and there was no sign of return. The firs stood straight against the sky, the clouds lay low; for the wind had fallen and a few snowfiakes came drifting down. In a horror of surprise, Christian stood dazed a moment: then he lifted the latch and went in. His glance took in all the old familiar forms and faces, and with them that of the stranger, fur-clad and beautiful. The awful truth flashed upon him: he knew what she was.

Only a few were startled by the rattle of the latch as he entered. The room was filled with bustle and movement, for it was the supper hour, when all tools were laid aside, and trestles and tables shifted. Christian had no knowledge of what he said and did; he moved and spoke mechanically, half thinking that soon he must wake from this horrible dream. Sweyn and his mother supposed him to be cold and dead-tired, and spared all unnecessary questions. And he found himself seated beside the hearth, opposite that dreadful Thing that looked like a beautiful girl; watching her every movement, curdling with horror to see her fondle the child Rol.

Sweyn stood near them both, intent upon White Fell also; but how differently! She seemed unconscious of the gaze of both—neither aware of the chill dread in the eyes of Christian, nor of Sweyn's warm admiration.

These two brothers, who were twins, contrasted greatly, despite their striking likeness. They were alike in regular profile, fair brown hair, and deep blue eyes; but Sweyn's features were perfect as a young god's, while Christian's showed faulty details. Thus, the line of his mouth was set too straight, the eyes shelved too deeply back, and the contour of the face flowed in less generous curves than Sweyn's. Their height was the same, but Christian was too slender for perfect proportion, while Sweyn's well-knit frame, broad shoulders, and muscular arms, made him pre-eminent for manly beauty as well as for strength. As a hunter Sweyn was without rival; as a fisher without rival. All the countryside acknowledged him to be the best wrestler, rider, dancer, singer. Only in speed could he be surpassed, and in that only by his younger brother. All others Sweyn could distance fairly; but Christian could outrun him easily. Ay, he could keep pace with Sweyn's most breathless burst, and laugh and talk the while. Christian took little pride in his fleetness of foot, counting a man's legs to be the least worthy of his members. He had no envy of his brother's athletic superiority, though to several feats he had made a moderate second. He loved as only a twin can love—proud of all that Sweyn did, content with all that Sweyn was; humbly content also that his own great love should not be so exceedingly returned, since he knew himself to be so far less love-worthy.

Christian dared not, in the midst of women and children, launch the horror that he knew into words. He waited to consult his brother; but Sweyn did not, or would not, notice the signal he made, and kept his face always turned towards White Fell. Christian drew away from the hearth, unable to remain passive with that dread upon him.

'Where is Tyr?' he said suddenly. Then, catching sight of the dog in a distant corner, 'Why is he chained there?'

'He flew at the stranger,' one answered.

Christian's eyes glowed. 'Yes?' he said, interrogatively.

'He was within an ace of having his brain knocked out.'

'Tyr?'

'Yes; she was nimbly up with that little axe she has at her waist. It was well for old Tyr that his master throttled him off.'

Christian went without a word to the corner where Tyr was chained. The dog rose up to meet him, as piteous and indignant as a dumb beast can be. He stroked the black head. 'Good Tyr! brave dog!'

They knew, they only; and the man and the dumb dog had comfort of each other.

Christian's eyes turned again towards White Fell: Tyr's also, and he strained against the length of the chain. Christian's hand lay on the dog's neck, and he felt it ridge and bristle with the quivering of impotent fury. Then he began to quiver in like manner with a fury born of reason, not instinct; as impotent morally as was Tyr physically. Oh! the woman's form that he dare not touch! Anything but that, and he with Tyr would be free to kill or be killed.

Then he returned to ask fresh questions.

'How long has the stranger been here?'

'She came about half-an-hour before you.'

'Who opened the door to her?'

'Sweyn: no one else dared.'

The tone of the answer was mysterious.

'Why?' queried Christian. 'Has anything strange happened? Tell me.'

For answer he was told in a low undertone of the summons at the door thrice repeated without human agency; and of Tyr's ominous howls; and of Sweyn's fruitless watch outside.

Christian turned towards his brother in a torment of impatience for a word apart. The board was spread, and Sweyn was leading White Fell to the guest's place. This was more awful: she would break bread with them under the roof-tree!

He started forward, and touching Sweyn's arm, whispered an urgent entreaty. Sweyn stared, and shook his head in angry impatience.

Thereupon Christian would take no morsel of food.

His opportunity came at last. White Fell questioned of the landmarks of the country, and of one Cairn Hill, which was an appointed meeting-place at which she was due that night. The house-mistress and Sweyn both exclaimed.

'It is three long miles away,' said Sweyn; 'with no place for shelter but a wretched hut. Stay with us this night, and I will show you the way tomorrow.'

White Fell seemed to hesitate. 'Three miles,' she said; 'then I should be able to see or hear a signal.'

'I will look out,' said Sweyn; 'then, if there be no signal, you must not leave us.'

He went to the door. Christian rose silently, and followed him out.

'Sweyn, do you know what she is?'

Sweyn, surprised at the vehement grasp, and low hoarse voice, made answer:

'She? Who? White Fell?'

'Yes.'

'She is the most beautiful girl I have ever seen.'

'She is a werewolf.'

Sweyn burst out laughing. 'Are you mad?' he asked.

'No; here, see for yourself.'

Christian drew him out of the porch, pointing to the snow where the footmarks had been. Had been, for now they were not. Snow was falling fast, and every dint was blotted out.

'Well?' asked Sweyn.

'Had you come when I signed to you, you would have seen for yourself.'

'Seen what?'

'The footprints of a wolf leading up to the door; none leading away.'

It was impossible not to be startled by the tone alone, though it was hardly above a whisper. Sweyn eyed his brother anxiously, but in the darkness could make nothing of his face. Then he laid his hands kindly and re-assuringly on Christian's shoulders and felt how he was quivering with excitement and horror.

'One sees strange things,' he said, 'when the cold has got into the brain behind the eyes; you came in cold and worn out.'

'No,' interrupted Christian. 'I saw the track first on the brow of the slope, and followed it down right here to the door. This is no delusion.'

Sweyn in his heart felt positive that it was. Christian was given to day-dreams and strange fancies, though never had he been possessed with so mad a notion before.

'Don't you believe me?' said Christian desperately. 'You must. I swear it is sane truth. Are you blind? Why, even Tyr knows.'

'You will be clearer headed tomorrow after a night's rest. Then come too, if you will, with White Fell, to the Hill Cairn; and if you have doubts still, watch and follow, and see what footprints she leaves.'

Galled by Sweyn's evident contempt Christian turned abruptly to the door. Sweyn caught him back.

'What now, Christian? What are you going to do?'

'You do not believe me; my mother shall.'

Sweyn's grasp tightened. 'You shall not tell her,' he said authoritatively.

Customarily Christian was so docile to his brother's mastery that it was now a surprising thing when he wrenched himself free vigorously, and said as determinedly as Sweyn, 'She shall know!' but Sweyn was nearer the door and would not let him pass.

'There has been scare enough for one night already. If this notion of yours will keep, broach it tomorrow.' Christian would not yield.

'Women are so easily scared,' pursued Sweyn, 'and are ready to believe any folly without shadow of proof. Be a man, Christian, and fight this notion of a werewolf by yourself.'

'If you would believe me' began Christian.

'I believe you to be a fool,' said Sweyn, losing patience. 'Another, who was not your brother, might believe you to be a knave, and guess that you had transformed White Fell into a werewolf because she smiled more readily on me than on you.'

The jest was not without foundation, for the grace of White Fell's bright looks had been bestowed on him, on Christian never a whit. Sweyn's coxcombery was always frank, and most forgiveable, and not without fair colour.

'If you want an ally,' continued Sweyn, 'confide in old Trella. Out of her stores of wisdom, if her memory holds good, she can instruct you in the orthodox manner of tackling a werewolf. If I remember aright, you should watch the suspected person till midnight, when the beast's form must be resumed, and retained ever after if a human eye sees the change; or, better still, sprinkle hands and feet with holy water, which is certain death. Oh! never fear, but old Trella will be equal to the occasion.'

Sweyn's contempt was no longer good-humoured; some touch of irritation or resentment rose at this monstrous doubt of White Fell. But Christian was too deeply distressed to take offence.

'You speak of them as old wives' tales; but if you had seen the proof I have seen, you would be ready at least to wish them true, if not also to put them to the test.'

'Well,' said Sweyn, with a laugh that had a little sneer in it, 'put them to the test! I will not object to that, if you will only keep your notions to yourself. Now, Christian, give me your word for silence, and we will freeze here no longer.'

Christian remained silent.

Sweyn put his hands on his shoulders again and vainly tried to see his face in the darkness.

'We have never quarrelled yet, Christian?'

'I have never quarrelled,' returned the other, aware for the first time that his dictatorial brother had sometimes offered occasion for quarrel, had he been ready to take it.

'Well,' said Sweyn emphatically, 'if you speak against White Fell to any other, as tonight you have spoken to me—we shall.'

He delivered the words like an ultimatum, turned sharp round, and re-entered the house. Christian, more fearful and wretched than before, followed.

'Snow is falling fast: not a single light is to be seen.'

White Fell's eyes passed over Christian without apparent notice, and turned bright and shining upon Sweyn.

'Nor any signal to be heard?' she queried. 'Did you not hear the sound of a sea-horn?'

'I saw nothing, and heard nothing; and signal or no signal, the heavy snow would keep you here perforce.'

She smiled her thanks beautifully. And Christian's heart sank like lead with a deadly foreboding, as he noted what a light was kindled in Sweyn's eyes by her smile.

That night, when all others slept, Christian, the weariest of all, watched outside the guest-chamber till midnight was past. No sound, not the faintest, could be heard. Could the old tale be true of the midnight change? What was on the other side of the door, a woman or a beast? he would have given his right hand to know. Instinctively he laid his hand on the latch, and drew it softly, though believing that bolts fastened the inner side. The door yielded to his hand; he stood on the threshold; a keen gust of air cut athim; the window stood open; the room was empty.

So Christian could sleep with a somewhat lightened heart.

In the morning there was surprise and conjecture when White Fell's absence was discovered. Christian held his peace. Not even to his brother did he say how he knew that she had fled before midnight; and Sweyn, though evidently greatly chagrined, seemed to disdain reference to the subject of Christian's fears.

The elder brother alone joined the bear hunt; Christian found pretext to stay behind. Sweyn, being out of humour, manifested his contempt by uttering not a single expostulation.

All that day, and for many a day after, Christian would never go out of sight of his home. Sweyn alone noticed how he manoeuvred for this, and was clearly annoyed by it. White Fell's name was never mentioned between them, though not seldom was it heard in general talk. Hardly a day passed but little Rol asked when White Fell would come again: pretty White Fell, who kissed like a snowflake. And if Sweyn answered, Christian would be quite sure that the light in his eyes, kindled by White Fell's smile, had not yet died out.

Little Rol! Naughty, merry, fair-haired little Rol. A day came when his feet raced over the threshold never to return; when his chatter and laugh were heard no more; when tears of anguish were wept by eyes that never would see his bright head again: never again, living or dead.

He was seen at dusk for the last time, escaping from the house with his puppy, in freakish rebellion against old Trella. Later, when his absence had begun to cause anxiety, his puppy crept back to the farm, cowed, whimpering and yelping, a pitiful, dumb lump of terror, without intelligence or courage to guide the frightened search.

Rol was never found, nor any trace of him. Where he had perished was never known; how he had perished was known only by an awful guess—a wild beast had devoured him.

Christian heard the conjecture 'a wolf'; and a horrible certainty flashed upon him that he knew what wolf it was. He tried to declare what he knew, but Sweyn saw him start at the words with white face and struggling lips; and, guessing his purpose, pulled him back, and kept him silent, hardly, by his imperious grip and wrathful eyes, and one low whisper.

That Christian should retain his most irrational suspicion against beautiful White Fell was, to Sweyn, evidence of a weak obstinacy of mind that would but thrive upon expostulation and argument. But this evident intention to direct the passions of grief and anguish to a hatred and fear of the fair stranger, such as his own, was intolerable, and Sweyn set his will against it. Again Christian yielded to his brother's stronger words and will, and against his own judgement consented to silence.

Repentance came before the new moon, the first of the year, was old. White Fell came again, smiling as she entered, as though assured of a glad and kindly welcome; and, in truth, there was only one who saw again her fair face and strange white garb without pleasure. Sweyn's face glowed with delight, while Christian's grew pale and rigid as death. He had given his word to keep silence; but he had not thought that she would dare to come again. Silence was impossible, face to face with that Thing, impossible. Irrepressibly he cried out:

'Where is Rol?'

Not a quiver disturbed White Fell's face. She heard, yet remained bright and tranquil. Sweyn's eyes flashed round at his brother dangerously. Among the women some tears fell at the poor child's name; but none caught alarm from its sudden utterance, for the thought of Rol rose naturally. Where was little Rol, who had nestled in the stranger's arms, kissing her; and watched for her since; and prattled of her daily?

Christian went out silently. One only thing there was that he could do, and he must not delay. His horror overmastered any curiosity to hear White Fell's smooth excuses and smiling apologies for her strange and uncourteous departure; or her easy tale of the circumstances of her return; or to watch her bearing as she heard the sad tale of little Rol.

The swiftest runner in the country-side had started on his hardest race: little less than three leagues and back, which he reckoned to accomplish in two hours, though the night was moonless and the way rugged. He rushed against the still cold air till it felt like a wind upon his face. The dim homestead sank below the ridges at his back, and fresh ridges of snowlands rose out of the obscure horizon-level to drive past him as the stirless air drove, and sink away behind into obscure level again. He took no conscious heed of landmarks, not even when all sign of a path was gone under depths of snow. His will was set to reach his goal with unexampled speed; and thither by instinct his physical forces bore him, without one definite thought to guide.

And the idle brain lay passive, inert, receiving into its vacancy restless siftings of past sights and sounds; Rol, weeping, laughing, playing, coiled in the arms of that dreadful Thing: Tyr—O Tyr!—white fangs in the black jowl: the women who wept on the foolish puppy, precious for the child's last touch: footprints from pine wood to door: the smiling face among furs, of such womanly beauty—smiling—smiling: and Sweyn's face.

'Sweyn, Sweyn, O Sweyn, my brother!'

Sweyn's angry laugh possessed his ear within the sound of the wind of his speed; Sweyn's scorn assailed more quick and keen than the biting cold at his throat. And yet he was unimpressed by any thought of how Sweyn's anger and scorn would rise, if this errand were known.

Sweyn was sceptic. His utter disbelief in Christian's testimony regarding the footprints were based upon positive scepticism. His reason refused to bend in accepting the possibility of the supernatural materialised. That a living beast could ever be other than palpably bestial—pawed, toothed, shagged, and eared as such, was to him incredible; far more that a human presence could be transformed from its god-like aspect, upright, freehanded, with brows, and speech, and laughter. The wild and fearful legends that he had known from childhood and then believed, he regarded now as built upon facts distorted, overlaid by imagination, and quickened by superstition. Even the strange summons at the threshold, that he himself had vainly answered, was, after the first shock of surprise, rationally explained by him as malicious foolery on the part of some clever trickster, who witheld the key to the enigma.

To the younger brother all life was a spiritual mystery, veiled from his clear knowledge by the density of flesh. Since he knew his own body to be linked to the complex and antagonistic forces that constitute one soul, it seemed to him not impossibly strange that one spiritual force should possess divers forms for widely various manifestation. Nor, to him, was it great effort to believe that as pure water washes away all natural foulness, so water, holy by consecration, must needs cleanse God's world from that supernatural evil Thing. Therefore, faster than ever man's foot had covered those leagues, he sped under the dark, still night, over the waste, trackless snow-ridges to the far-away church, where salvation lay in the holy-water stoup at the door. His faith was as firm as any that wrought miracles in days past, simple as a child's wish, strong as a man's will.

He was hardly missed during these hours, every second of which was by him fulfilled to its utmost extent by extremest effort that sinews and nerves could attain. Within the homestead the while, the easy moments went bright with words and looks of unwonted animation, for the kindly, hospitable instincts of the inmates were roused into cordial expression of welcome and interest by the grace and beauty of the returned stranger.

But Sweyn was eager and earnest, with more than a host's courteous warmth. The impression that at her first coming had charmed him, that had lived since through memory, deepened now in her actual presence. Sweyn, the matchless among men, acknowledged in this fair White Fell a spirit high and bold as his own, and a frame so firm and capable that only bulk was lacking for equal strength. Yet the white skin was moulded most smoothly, without such muscular swelling as made his might evident. Such love as his frank self-love could concede was called forth by an ardent admiration for this supreme stranger. More admiration than love was in his passion, and therefore he was free from a lover's hesitancy and delicate reserve and doubts. Frankly and boldly he courted her favour by looks and tones, and an address that came of natural ease, needless of skill by practice.

Nor was she a woman to be wooed otherwise. Tender whispers and sighs would never gain her ear; but her eyes would brighten and shine if she heard of a brave feat, and her prompt hand in sympathy fall swiftly on the axe-haft and clasp it hard. That movement ever fired Sweyn's admiration anew; he watched for it, strove to elicit it, and glowed when it came. Wonderful and beautiful was that wrist, slender and steel-strong; also the smooth shapely hand, that curved so fast and firm, ready to deal instant death.

Desiring to feel the pressure of these hands, this bold lover schemed with palpable directness, proposing that she should hear how their hunting songs were sung, with a chorus that signalled hands to be clasped. So his splendid voice gave the verses, and, as the chorus was taken up, he claimed her hands, and, even through the easy grip, felt, as he desired, the strength that was latent, and the vigour that quickened the very fingertips, as the song fired her, and her voice was caught out of her by the rhythmic swell, and rang clear on the top of the closing surge.

Afterwards she sang alone. For contrast, or in the pride of swaying moods by her voice, she chose a mournful song that drifted along in a minor chant, sad as a wind that dirges:

'Oh, let me go!
Around spin wreaths of snow;
The dark earth sleeps below.
Far up the plain
Moans on a voice of pain:
"Where shall my babe be lain?"
In my white breast
Lay the sweet life to rest!
Lay, where it can lie best!
"Hush! hush its cries!
Dense night is on the skies:
Two stars are in thine eyes."
Come, babe, away!
But lie thou till dawn be grey,
Who must be dead by day.
This cannot last;
But, ere the sickening blast,
All sorrow shall be past;
And kings shall be
Low bending at thy knee,
Worshipping life from thee.
For men long sore
To hope of what's before,—

To leave the things of yore.

Mine, and not thine,

How deep their jewels shine!

Peace laps thy head, not mine.'

Old Trella came tottering from her corner, shaken to additional palsy by an aroused memory. She strained her dim eyes towards the singer, and then bent her head, that the one ear yet sensible to sound might avail of every note. At the close, groping forward, she murmured with the high-pitched quaver of old age:

'So she sang, my Thora; my last and brightest. What is she like, she whose voice is like my dead Thora's? Are her eyes blue?'

'Blue as the sky.'

'So were my Thora's! Is her hair fair, and in plaits to the waist?'

'Even so,' answered White Fell herself, and met the advancing hands with her own, and guided them to corroborate her words by touch.

'Like my dead Thora's,' repeated the old woman; and then her trembling hands rested on the fur-clad shoulders, and she bent forward and kissed the smooth fair face that White Fell upturned, nothing loth, to receive and return the caress.

So Christian saw them as he entered.

He stood a moment. After the starless darkness and the icy night air, and the fierce silent two hours' race, his senses reeled on sudden entrance into warmth, and light, and the cheery hum of voices. A sudden unforeseen anguish assailed him, as now first he entertained the possibility of being overmatched by her wiles and her daring, if at the approach of pure death she should start up at bay transformed to a terrible beast, and achieve a savage glut at the last. He looked with horror and pity on the harmless, helpless folk, so unwitting of outrage to their comfort and security. The dreadful Thing in their midst, that was veiled from their knowledge by womanly beauty, was a centre of pleasant interest. There, before him, signally impressive, was poor old Trella, weakest and feeblest of all, in fond nearness. And a moment might bring about the revelation of a monstrous horror—a ghastly, deadly danger, set loose and at bay, in a circle of girls and women and careless defenceless men; so hideous and terrible a thing as might crack the brain, or curdle the heart stone dead.

And he alone of the throng prepared!

For one breathing space he faltered, no longer than that, while over him swept the agony of compunction that yet could not make him surrender his purpose.

He alone? Nay, but Tyr also; and he crossed to the dumb sole sharer of his knowledge.

So timeless is thought that a few seconds only lay between his lifting of the latch and his loosening of Tyr's collar; but in those few seconds succeeding his first glance, as lightning-swift had been the impulses of others, their motion as quick and sure. Sweyn's vigilant eye had darted upon him, and instantly his every fibre was alert with hostile instinct; and, half divining, half incredulous, of Christian's object in stooping to Tyr, he came hastily, wary, wrathful, resolute to oppose the malice of his wild-eyed brother.

But beyond Sweyn rose White Fell, blanching white as her furs, and with eyes grown fierce and wild. She leapt down the room to the door, whirling her long robe closely to her. 'Hark!' she panted. 'The signal horn! Hark, I must go!' as she snatched at the latch to be out and away.

For one precious moment Christian had hesitated on the half-loosened collar; for, except the womanly form were exchanged for the bestial, Tyr's jaws would gnash to rags his honour of manhood. Then he heard her voice, and turned—too late.

As she tugged at the door, he sprange across grasping his flask, but Sweyn dashed between, and caught him back irresistibly, so that a most frantic effort only availed to wrench one arm free. With that, on the impulse of sheer despair, he cast at her with all his force. The door swung behind her, and the flask flew into fragments against it. Then, as Sweyn's grasp slackened, and he met the questioning astonishment of surrounding faces, with a hoarse inarticulate cry: 'God help us all!' he said. 'She is a werewolf.'

Sweyn turned upon him, 'Liar, coward!' and his hands gripped his brother's throat with deadly force, as though the spoken word could be killed so; and as Christian struggled, lifted him clear off his feet and flung him crashing backward. So furious was he, that, as his brother lay motionless, he stirred him roughly with his foot, till their mother came between, crying shame; and yet then he stood by, his teeth set, his brows knit, his hands clenched, ready to enforce silence again violently, as Christian rose staggeringand bewildered.

But utter silence and submission were more than he expected, and turned his anger into contempt for one so easily cowed and held in subjection by mere force. 'He is mad!' he said, turning on his heel as he spoke, so that he lost his mother's look of pained reproach at this sudden free utterance of what was a lurking dread within her.

Christian was too spent for the effort of speech. His hard-drawn breath laboured in great sobs; his limbs were powerless and untrusting in utter relax after hard service. Failure in his endeavour induced a stupor of misery and despair. In addition was the wretched humiliation of open violence and strife with his brother, and the distress of hearing misjudging contempt expressed without reserve; for he was aware that Sweyn had turned to allay the scared excitement half by imperious mastery, half by explanation and argument, that showed painful dis-

121

regard of brotherly consideration. All this unkindness of his twin he charged upon the fell Thing who had wrought this their first dissension, and, ah! most terrible thought, interposed between them so effectually, that Sweyn was wilfully blind and deaf on her account, resentful of interference, arbitrary beyond reason.

Dread and perplexity unfathomable darkened upon him; unshared, the burden was overwhelming: a foreboding of unspeakable calamity, based upon his ghastly discovery, bore down upon him, crushing out hope of power to withstand impending fate.

Sweyn the while was observant of his brother, despite the continual check of finding, turn and glance when he would, Christian's eyes always upon him, with a strange look of helpless distress, discomposing enough to the angry aggressor. 'Like a beaten dog!' he said to himself, rallying contempt to withstand compunction. Observation set him wondering on Christian's exhausted condition. The heavy labouring breath and the slack inert fall of the limbs told surely of unusual and prolonged exertion. And then why had close upon two hours' absence been followed by open hostility against White Fell?

Suddenly, the fragments of the flask giving a clue, he guessed all, and faced about to stare at his brother in amaze. He forgot that the motive scheme was against White Fell, demanding derision and resentment from him; that was swept out of remembrance by astonishment and admiration for the feat of speed and endurance. In eagerness to question he inclined to attempt a generous part and frankly offer to heal the breach; but Christian's depression and sad following gaze provoked him to self-justification by recalling the offence of that outrageous utterance against White Fell; and the impulse passed. Then other considerations counselled silence; and afterwards a humour possessed him to wait and see how Christian would find opportunity to proclaim his performance and establish the fact, without exciting ridicule on account of the absurdity of the errand.

This expectation remained unfulfilled. Christian never attempted the proud avowal that would have placed his feat on record to be told to the next generation.

That night Sweyn and his mother talked long and late together, shaping into certainty the suspicion that Christian's mind had lost its balance, and discussing the evident cause. For Sweyn, declaring his own love for White Fell, suggested that his unfortunate brother, with a like passion, they being twins in loves as in birth, had through jealousy and despair turned from love to hate, until reason failed at the strain, and a craze developed, which the malice and treachery of madness made a serious and dangerous force.

So Sweyn theorised, convincing himself as he spoke; convincing afterwards others who advanced doubts against White Fell; fettering his judgement by his advocacy, and by his staunch defence of her hurried flight silencing his own inner consciousness of the unaccountability of her action.

122

But a little time and Sweyn lost his vantage in the shock of a fresh horror at the homestead. Trella was no more, and her end a mystery. The poor old woman crawled out in a bright gleam to visit a bed-ridden gossip living beyond the fir-grove. Under the trees she was last seen, halting for her companion, sent back for a forgotten present. Quick alarm sprang, calling every man to the search. Her stick was found among the brushwood only a few paces from the path, but no track or stain, for a gusty wind was sifting the snow from the branches, and hid all sign of how she came by her death.

So panic-stricken were the farm folk that none dared go singly on the search. Known danger could be braced, but not this stealthy Death that walked by day invisible, that cut off alike the child in his play and the aged woman so near to her quiet grave.

'Rol she kissed; Trella she kissed!' So rang Christian's frantic cry again and again, till Sweyn dragged him away and strove to keep him apart, albeit in his agony of grief and remorse he accused himself wildly as answerable for the tragedy, and gave clear proof that the charge of madness was well founded, if strange looks and desperate, incoherent words were evidence enough.

But thenceforward all Sweyn's reasoning and mastery could not uphold White Fell above suspicion. He was not called upon to defend her from accusation when Christian had been brought to silence again; but he well knew the significance of this fact, that her name, formerly uttered freely and often, he never heard now: it was huddled away into whispers that he could not catch.

The passing of time did not sweep away the superstitious fears that Sweyn despised. He was angry and anxious; eager that White Fell should return, and, merely by her bright gracious presence, reinstate herself in favour; but doubtful if all his authority and example could keep from her notice an altered aspect of welcome; and he foresaw clearly that Christian would prove unmanageable, and might be capable of some dangerous outbreak.

For a time the twins' variance was marked, on Sweyn's part by an air of rigid indifference, on Christian's by heavy downcast silence, and a nervous apprehensive observation of his brother. Superadded to his remorse and foreboding, Sweyn's displeasure weighed upon him intolerably, and the remembrance of their violent rupture was a ceaseless misery. The elder brother, self-sufficient and insensitive, could little know how deeply his unkindness stabbed. A depth and force of affection such as Christian's was unknown to him. The loyal subservience that he could not appreciate had encouraged him to domineer; this strenuous opposition to his reason and will was accounted as furious malice, if not sheer insanity.

Christian's surveillance galled him incessantly, and embarrassment and danger he foresaw as the outcome. Therefore, that suspicion might be lulled, he judged it wise to make overtures for peace. Most easily done. A little kindliness, a few evidences of consideration, a slight return of the old brotherly imperiousness, and Christian replied by a gratefulness and relief that might have touched him had he understood all, but instead, increased his secret contempt.

So successful was this finesse, that when, late on a day, a message summoning Christian to a distance was transmitted by Sweyn, no doubt of its genuineness occurred. When, his errand proved useless, he set out to return, mistake or misapprehension was all that he surmised. Not till he sighted the homestead, lying low between the night-grey snow-ridges, did vivid recollection of the time when he had tracked that horror to the door rouse an intense dread, and with it a hardly-defined suspicion.

His grasp tightened on the bear-spear that he carried as a staff; every sense was alert, every muscle strung; excitement urged him on, caution checked him, and the two governed his long stride, swiftly, noiselessly, to the climax he felt was at hand.

As he drew near to the outer gates, a light shadow stirred and went, as though the grey of the snow had taken detached motion. A darker shadow stayed and faced Christian, striking his life-blood chill with utmost despair.

Sweyn stood before him, and surely, the shadow that went was White Fell.

They had been together—close. Had she not been in his arms, near enough for lips to meet?

There was no moon, but the stars gave light enough to show that Sweyn's face was flushed and elate. The flush remained, though the expression changed quickly at sight of his brother. How, if Christian had seen all, should one of his frenzied outbursts be met and managed: by resolution? by indifference? He halted between the two, and as a result, he swaggered.

'White Fell?' questioned Christian, hoarse and breathless.

'Yes?'

Sweyn's answer was a query, with an intonation that implied he was clearing the ground for action.

From Christian came: 'Have you kissed her?' like a bolt direct, staggering Sweyn by its sheer prompt temerity.

He flushed yet darker, and yet half-smiled over this earnest of success he had won. Had there been really between himself and Christian the rivalry that he imagined, his face had enough of the insolence of triumph to exasperate jealous rage.

'You dare ask this!'

'Sweyn, O Sweyn, I must know! You have!'

The ring of despair and anguish in his tone angered Sweyn, misconstruing

124

it. Jealousy urging to such presumption was intolerable.

'Mad fool!' he said, constraining himself no longer. 'Win for yourself a woman to kiss. Leave mine without question. Such an one as I should desire to kiss is such an one as shall never allow a kiss to you.'

Then Christian fully understood his supposition.

'I—I!' he cried. 'White Fell—that deadly Thing! Sweyn, are you blind, mad? I would save you from her: a werewolf!'

Sweyn maddened again at the accusation—a dastardly way of revenge, as he conceived; and instantly, for the second time, the brothers were at strife violently.

But Christian was now too desperate to be scrupulous; for a dim glimpse had shot a possibility into his mind, and to be free to follow it the striking of his brother was a necessity. Thank God! he was armed, and so Sweyn's equal.

Facing his assailant with the bear-spear, he struck up his arms, and with the butt end hit hard so that he fell. The matchless runner leapt away on the instant, to follow a forlorn hope.

Sweyn, on regaining his feet, was as amazed as angry at this unaccountable flight. He knew in his heart that his brother was no coward, and that it was unlike him to shrink from an encounter because defeat was certain, and cruel humiliation from a vindictive victor probable. Of the uselessness of pursuit he was well aware: he must abide his chagrin, content to know that his time for advantage would come. Since White Fell had parted to the right, Christian to the left, the event of a sequent encounter did not occur to him.

And now Christian, acting on the dim glimpse he had had, just as Sweyn turned upon him, of something that moved against the sky along the ridge behind the homestead, was staking his only hope on a chance, and his own superlative speed. If what he saw was really White Fell, he guessed she was bending her steps towards the open wastes; and there was just a possibility that, by a straight dash, and a desperate perilous leap over a sheer bluff, he might yet meet her or head her. And then: he had no further thought.

It was past, the quick, fierce race, and the chance of death at the leap; and he halted in a hollow to fetch his breath and to look: did she come? had she gone?

She came.

She came with a smooth, gliding, noiseless speed, that was neither walking nor running; her arms were folded in her furs that were drawn tight about her body; the white lappets from her head were wrapped and knotted closely beneath her face; her eyes were set on a far distance. So she went till the even sway of her going was startled to a pause by Christian.

'Fell!'

She drew a quick, sharp breath at the sound of her name thus mutilated, and faced Sweyn's brother. Her eyes glittered; her upper lip was lifted, and shewed the teeth. The half of her name, impressed with an ominous sense as uttered by him, warned her of the aspect of a deadly foe. Yet she cast loose her robes till they trailed ample, and spoke as a mild woman.

'What would you?'

Then Christian answered with his solemn dreadful accusation:

'You kissed Rol—and Rol is dead! You kissed Trella: she is dead! You have kissed Sweyn, my brother; but he shall not die!'

He added: 'You may live till midnight.'

The edge of the teeth and the glitter of the eyes stayed a moment, and her right hand also slid down to the axe haft. Then, without a word, she swerved from him, and sprang out and away swiftly over the snow.

And Christian sprang out and away, and followed her swiftly over the snow, keeping behind, but half-a- stride's length from her side.

So they went running together, silent, towards the vast wastes of snow, where no living thing but they two moved under the stars of night.

Never before had Christian so rejoiced in his powers. The gift of speed, and the training of use and endurance were priceless to him now. Though midnight was hours away, he was confident that, go where that Fell Thing would, hasten as she would, she could not outstrip him nor escape from him. Then, when came the time for transformation, when the woman's form made no longer a shield against a man's hand, he could slay or be slain to save Sweyn. He had struck his dear brother in dire extremity, but he could not, though reason urged, strike a woman.

For one mile, for two miles they ran: White Fell ever foremost, Christian ever at equal distance from her side, so near that, now and again, her out-flying furs touched him. She spoke no word; nor he. She never turned her head to look at him, nor swerved to evade him; but, with set face looking forward, sped straight on, over rough, over smooth, aware of his nearness by the regular beat of his feet, and the sound of his breath behind.

In a while she quicked her pace. From the first, Christian had judged of her speed as admirable, yet with exulting security in his own excelling and enduring whatever her efforts. But, when the pace increased, he found himself put to the test as never had he been before in any race. Her feet, indeed, flew faster than his; it was only by his length of stride that he kept his place at her side. But his heart was high and resolute, and he did not fear failure yet.

So the desperate race flew on. Their feet struck up the powdery snow, their breath smoked into the sharp clear air, and they were gone before the air was cleared of snow and vapour. Now and then Christian glanced up to judge, by the

126

rising of the stars, of the coming of midnight. So long—so long!

White Fell held on without slack. She, it was evident, with confidence in her speed proving matchless, as resolute to outrun her pursuer as he to endure till midnight and fulfil his purpose. And Christian held on, still self-assured. He could not fail; he would not fail. To avenge Rol and Trella was motive enough for him to do what man could do; but for Sweyn more. She had kissed Sweyn, but he should not die too: with Sweyn to save he could not fail.

Never before was such a race as this; no, not when in old Greece man and maid raced together with two fates at stake; for the hard running was sustained unabated, while star after star rose and went wheeling up towards midnight, for one hour, for two hours.

Then Christian saw and heard what shot him through with fear. Where a fringe of trees hung round a slope he saw something dark moving, and heard a yelp, followed by a full horrid cry, and the dark spread out upon the snow, a pack of wolves in pursuit.

Of the beasts alone he had little cause for fear; at the pace he held he could distance them, four-footed though they were. But of White Fell's wiles he had infinite apprehension, for how might she not avail herself of the savage jaws of these wolves, akin as they were to half her nature. She vouchsafed to them nor look nor sign; but Christian, on an impulse to assure himself that she should not escape him, caught and held the back-flung edge of her furs, running still.

She turned like a flash with a beastly snarl, teeth and eyes gleaming again. Her axe shone, on the upstroke, on the downstroke, as she hacked at his hand. She had lopped it off at the wrist, but that he parried with the bear-spear. Even then, she shore through the shaft and shattered the bones of the hand at the same blow, so that he loosed perforce.

Then again they raced on as before, Christian not losing a pace, though his left hand swung useless, bleeding and broken.

The snarl, indubitable, though modified from a woman's organs, the vicious fury revealed in teeth and eyes, the sharp arrogant pain of her maiming blow, caught away Christian's heed of the beasts behind, by striking into him close vivid realisation of the infinitely greater danger that ran before him in that deadly Thing.

When he bethought him to look behind, lo! the pack had but reached their tracks, and instantly slunk aside, cowed; the yell of pursuit changing to yelps and whines. So abhorrent was that fell creature to beast as to man.

She had drawn her furs more closely to her, disposing them so that, instead of flying loose to her heels, no drapery hung lower than her knees, and this without a check to her wonderful speed, nor embarrassment by the cumbering of the folds. She held her head as before; her lips were firmly set, only the tense nostrils gave her breath; not a sign of distress witnessed to the long sustaining of that terrible speed.

But on Christian by now the strain was telling palpably. His head weighed heavy, and his breath came labouring in great sobs; the bear spear would have been a burden now. His heart was beating like a hammer, but such a dulness oppressed his brain, that it was only by degrees he could realise his helpless state; wounded and weaponless, chasing that terrible Thing, that was a fierce, desperate, axe-armed woman, except she should assume the beast with fangs yet more formidable.

And still the far slow stars went lingering nearly an hour from midnight.

So far was his brain astray that an impression took him that she was fleeing from the midnight stars, whose gain was by such slow degrees that a time equalling days and days had gone in the race round the northern circle of the world, and days and days as long might last before the end—except she slackened, or except he failed.

But he would not fail yet.

How long had he been praying so? He had started with a self-confidence and reliance that had felt no need for that aid; and now it seemed the only means by which to restrain his heart from swelling beyond the compass of his body, by which to cherish his brain from dwindling and shrivelling quite away. Some sharp-toothed creature kept tearing and dragging on his maimed left hand; he never could see it, he could not shake it off; but he prayed it off at times.

The clear stars before him took to shuddering, and he knew why: they shuddered at sight of what was behind him. He had never divined before that strange things hid themselves from men under pretence of being snow-clad mounds or swaying trees; but now they came slipping out from their harmless covers to follow him, and mock at his impotence to make a kindred Thing resolve to truer form. He knew the air behind him was thronged; he heard the hum of innumerable murmurings together; but his eyes could never catch them, they were too swift and nimble. Yet he knew they were there, because, on a backward glance, he saw the snow mounds surge as they grovelled flatlings out of sight; he saw the trees reel as they screwed themselves rigid past recognition among the boughs.

And after such glance the stars for awhile returned to steadfastness, and an infinite stretch of silence froze upon the chill grey world, only deranged by the swift even beat of the flying feet, and his own—slower from the longer stride, and the sound of his breath. And for some clear moments he knew that his only concern was, to sustain his speed regardless of pain and distress, to deny with every nerve he had her power to outstrip him or to widen the space between them, till the stars crept up to midnight.

Then out again would come that crowd invisible, humming and hustling behind, dense and dark enough, he knew, to blot out the stars at his back, yet ever skipping and jerking from his sight.

A hideous check came to the race. White Fell swirled about and leapt to the right, and Christian, unprepared for so prompt a lurch, found close at his feet a deep pit yawning, and his own impetus past control. But he snatched at her as he bore past, clasping her right arm with his one whole hand, and the two swung together upon the brink.

And her straining away in self preservation was vigorous enough to counterbalance his headlong impulse, and brought them reeling together to safety.

Then, before he was verily sure that they were not to perish so, crashing down, he saw her gnashing in wild pale fury as she wrenched to be free; and since her right hand was in his grasp, used her axe left-handed, striking back at him.

The blow was effectual enough even so; his right arm dropped powerless, gashed, and with the lesser bone broken, that jarred with horrid pain when he let it swing as he leaped out again, and ran to recover the few feet she had gained from his pause at the shock.

The near escape and this new quick pain made again every faculty alive and intense. He knew that what he followed was most surely Death animate: wounded and helpless, he was utterly at her mercy if so she should realise and take action. Hopeless to avenge, hopeless to save, his very despair for Sweyn swept him on to follow, and follow, and precede the kiss-doomed to death. Could he yet fail to hunt that Thing past midnight, out of the womanly form alluring and treacherous, into lasting restraint of the bestial, which was the last shred of hope left from the confident purpose of the outset?

'Sweyn, Sweyn, O Sweyn!' He thought he was praying, though his heart wrung out nothing but this: 'Sweyn, Sweyn, O Sweyn!'

The last hour from midnight had lost half its quarters, and the stars went lifting up the great minutes; and again his greatening heart, and his shrinking brain, and the sickening agony that swung at either side, conspired to appal the will that had only seeming empire over his feet.

Now White Fell's body was so closely enveloped that not a lap nor an edge flew free. She stretched forward strangely aslant, leaning from the upright poise of a runner. She cleared the ground at times by long bounds, gaining an increase of speed that Christian agonised to equal.

Because the stars pointed that the end was nearing, the black brood came behind again, and followed, noising. Ah! if they could but be kept quiet and still, nor slip their usual harmless masks to encourage with their interest the last speed of their most deadly congener. What shape had they? Should he ever know? If it were not that he was bound to compel the fell Thing that ran before him into her truer form, he might face about and follow them. No—no—not so; if he might do anything but what he did—race, race, and racing bear this agony, he would just stand still and die, to be quit of the pain of breathing.

He grew bewildered, uncertain of his own identity, doubting of his own true form. He could not be really a man, no more than that running Thing was really a woman; his real form was only hidden under embodiment of a man, but what it was he did not know. And Sweyn's real form he did not know. Sweyn lay fallen at his feet, where he had struck him down—his own brother—he: he stumbled over him, and had to overleap him and race harder because she who had kissed Sweyn leapt so fast. 'Sweyn, Sweyn, O Sweyn!'

Why did the stars stop to shudder? Midnight else had surely come!

The leaning, leaping Thing looked back at him with a wild, fierce look, and laughed in savage scorn and triumph. He saw in a flash why, for within a time measurable by seconds she would have escaped him utterly. As the land lay, a slope of ice sunk on the one hand; on the other hand a steep rose, shouldering forwards; between the two was space for a foot to be planted, but none for a body to stand; yet a juniper bough, thrusting out, gave a handhold secure enough for one with a resolute grasp to swing past the perilous place, and pass on safe.

Though the first seconds of the last moment were going, she dared to flash back a wicked look, and laugh at the pursuer who was impotent to grasp.

The crisis struck convulsive life into his last supreme effort; his will surged up indomitable, his speed proved matchless yet. He leapt with a rush, passed her before her laugh had time to go out, and turned short, barring the way, and braced to withstand her.

She came hurling desperate, with a feint to the right hand, and then launched herself upon him with a spring like a wild beast when it leaps to kill. And he, with one strong arm and a hand that could not hold, with one strong hand and an arm that could not guide and sustain, he caught and held her even so. And they fell together. And because he felt his whole arm slipping, and his whole hand loosing, to slack the dreadful agony of the wrenched bone above, he caught and held with his teeth the tunic at her knee, as she struggled up and wrung off his hands to overleap him victorious.

Like lightning she snatched her axe, and struck him on the neck, deep—once, twice—his life-blood gushed out, staining her feet.

The stars touched midnight.

The death scream he heard was not his, for his teeth had hardly yet relaxed when it rang out; and the dreadful cry began with a woman's shriek, and changed and ended as the yell of a beast. And before the final blank overtook his dying eyes, he saw that She gave place to It; he saw more, that Life gave place to Death—causelessly, incomprehensibly.

For he did not presume that no holy water could be more holy, more potent to destroy an evil thing than the life-blood of a pure heart poured out for another in free willing devotion.

His own true hidden reality that he had desired to know grew palpable, recognisable. It seemed to him just this: a great glad abounding hope that he had saved his brother; too expansive to be contained by the limited form of a sole man, it yearned for a new embodiment infinite as the stars.

What did it matter to that true reality that the man's brain shrank, shrank, till it was nothing; that the man's body could not retain the huge pain of his heart, and heaved it out through the red exit riven at the neck; that the black noise came again hurtling from behind, reinforced by that dissolved shape, and blotted out for ever the man's sight, hearing, sense.

In the early grey of day Sweyn chanced upon the footprints of a man—of a runner, as he saw by the shifted snow; and the direction they had taken aroused curiosity, since a little farther their line must be crossed by the edge of a sheer height. He turned to trace them. And so doing, the length of the stride struck his attention—a stride long as his own if he ran. He knew he was following Christian.

In his anger he had hardened himself to be indifferent to the night-long absence of his brother; but now, seeing where the footsteps went, he was seized with compunction and dread. He had failed to give thought and care to his poor frantic twin, who might—was it possible?—have rushed to a frantic death.

His heart stood still when he came to the place where the leap had been taken. A piled edge of snow had fallen too, and nothing but snow lay below when he peered. Along the upper edge he ran for a furlong, till he came to a dip where he could slip and climb down, and then back again on the lower level to the pile of fallen snow. There he saw that the vigorous running had started afresh.

He stood pondering; vexed that any man should have taken that leap where he had not ventured to follow; vexed that he had been beguiled to such painful emotions; guessing vainly at Christian's object in this mad freak. He began sauntering along, half unconsciously following his brother's track; and so in a while he came to the place where the footprints were doubled.

Small prints were these others, small as a woman's, though the pace from one to another was longer than that which the skirts of women allow.

Did not White Fell tread so?

A dreadful guess appalled him, so dreadful that he recoiled from belief. Yet his face grew ashy white, and he gasped to fetch back motion to his checked heart. Unbelievable? Closer attention showed how the smaller footfall had altered for greater speed, striking into the snow with a deeper onset and a lighter pressure on the heels. Unbelievable? Could any woman but White Fell run so? Could any man but Christian run so? The guess became a certainty. He was following where alone in the dark night White Fell had fled from Christian pursuing.

131

Such villainy set heart and brain on fire with rage and indignation: such villainy in his own brother, till lately love-worthy, praiseworthy, though a fool for meekness. He would kill Christian; had he lives many as the footprints he had trodden, vengeance should demand them all. In a tempest of murderous hate he followed on in haste, for the track was plain enough, starting with such a burst of speed as could not be maintained, but brought him back soon to a plod for the spent, sobbing breath to be regulated. He cursed Christian aloud and called White Fell's name on high in a frenzied expense of passion. His grief itself was a rage, being such an intolerable anguish of pity and shame at the thought of his love, White Fell, who had parted from his kiss free and radiant, to be hounded straightway by his brother mad with jealousy, fleeing for more than life while her lover was housed at his ease. If he had but known, he raved, in impotent rebellion at the cruelty of events, if he had but known that his strength and love might have availed in her defence; now the only service to her that he could render was to kill Christian.

As a woman he knew she was matchless in speed, matchless in strength; but Christian was matchless in speed among men, nor easily to be matched in strength. Brave and swift and strong though she were, what chance had she against a man of his strength and inches, frantic, too, and intent on horrid revenge against his brother, his successful rival?

Mile after mile he followed with a bursting heart; more piteous, more tragic, seemed the case at this evidence of White Fell's splendid supremacy, holding her own so long against Christian's famous speed. So long, so long that his love and admiration grew more and more boundless, and his grief and indignation therewith also. Whenever the track lay clear he ran, with such reckless prodigality of strength, that it soon was spent, and he dragged on heavily, till, sometimes on the ice of a mere, sometimes on a wind-swept place, all signs were lost; but, so undeviating had been their line that a course straight on, and then short questing to either hand, recovered them again.

Hour after hour had gone by through more than half that winter day, before ever he came to the place where the trampled snow showed that a scurry of feet had come—and gone! Wolves' feet—and gone most amazingly! Only a little beyond he came to the lopped point of Christian's bear-spear; farther on he would see where the remnant of the useless shaft had been dropped. The snow here was dashed with blood, and the footsteps of the two had fallen closer together. Some hoarse sound of exultation came from him that might have been a laugh had breath sufficed. 'O White Fell, my poor, brave love! Well struck!' he groaned, torn by his pity and great admiration, as he guessed surely how she had turned and dealt a blow.

The sight of the blood inflamed him as it might a beast that ravens. He grew mad with a desire to have Christian by the throat once again, not to loose this time till he had crushed out his life, or beat out his life, or stabbed out his life; or all these, and torn him piecemeal likewise: and ah! then, not till then, bleed his heart with weeping, like a child, like a girl, over the piteous fate of his poor lost love.

On—on—on—through the aching time, toiling and straining in the track of those two superb runners, aware of the marvel of their endurance, but unaware of the marvel of their speed, that, in the three hours before midnight had overpassed all that vast distance that he could only traverse from twilight to twilight. For clear daylight was passing when he came to the edge of an old marlpit, and saw how the two who had gone before had stamped and trampled together in desperate peril on the verge. And here fresh blood stains spoke to him of a valiant defence against his infamous brother; and he followed where the blood had dripped till the cold had staunched its flow, taking a savage gratification from this evidence that Christian had been gashed deeply, maddening afresh with desire to do like-wise more excellently, and so slake his murderous hate. And he began to know that through all his despair he had entertained a germ of hope, that grew apace, rained upon by his brother's blood.

He strove on as best he might, wrung now by an access of hope, now of despair, in agony to reach the end, however terrible, sick with the aching of the toiled miles that deferred it.

And the light went lingering out of the sky, giving place to uncertain stars.

He came to the finish.

Two bodies lay in a narrow place. Christian's was one, but the other be-yond not White Fell's. There where the footsteps ended lay a great white wolf.

At the sight Sweyn's strength was blasted; body and soul he was struck down grovelling.

The stars had grown sure and intense before he stirred from where he had dropped prone. Very feebly he crawled to his dead brother, and laid his hands upon him, and crouched so, afraid to look or stir farther.

Cold, stiff, hours dead. Yet the dead body was his only shelter and stay in that most dreadful hour. His soul, stripped bare of all sceptic comfort, cowered, shivering, naked, abject; and the living clung to the dead out of piteous need for grace from the soul that had passed away.

He rose to his knees, lifting the body. Christian had fallen face forward in the snow, with his arms flung up and wide, and so had the frost made him rigid: strange, ghastly, unyielding to Sweyn's lifting, so that he laid him down again and crouched above, with his arms fast round him, and a low heart-wrung groan.

When at last he found force to raise his brother's body and gather it in his arms, tight clasped to his breast, he tried to face the Thing that lay beyond. The sight set his limbs in a palsy with horror and dread. His senses had failed and fainted in utter cowardice, but for the strength that came from holding dead Christian in his arms, enabling him to compel his eyes to endure the sight, and take into the brain the complete aspect of the Thing. No wound, only blood stains on the feet. The great grim jaws had a savage grin, though dead-stiff. And his kiss: he could bear it no longer, and turned away, nor ever looked again.

And the dead man in his arms, knowing the full horror, had followed and faced it for his sake; had suffered agony and death for his sake; in the neck was the deep death gash, one arm and both hands were dark with frozen blood, for his sake! Dead he knew him, as in life he had not known him, to give the right meed of love and worship. Because the outward man lacked perfection and strength equal to his, he had taken the love and worship of that great pure heart as his due; he, so unworthy in the inner reality, so mean, so despicable, callous, and contemptuous towards the brother who had laid down his life to save him. He longed for utter annihilation, that so he might lose the agony of knowing himself so unworthy such perfect love. The frozen calm of death on the face appalled him. He dared not touch it with lips that had cursed so lately, with lips fouled by kiss of the horror that had been death.

He struggled to his feet, still clasping Christian. The dead man stood upright within his arm, frozen rigid. The eyes were not quite closed; the head had stiffened, bowed slightly to one side; the arms stayed straight and wide. It was the figure of one crucified, the blood-stained hands also conforming.

So living and dead went back along the track that one had passed in the deepest passion of love, and one in the deepest passion of hate. All that night Sweyn toiled through the snow, bearing the weight of dead Christian, treading back along the steps he before had trodden, when he was wronging with vilest thought, and cursing with murderous hatred, the brother who all the while lay dead for his sake.

Cold, silence, darkness encompassed the strong man bowed with the dolorous burden; and yet he knew surely that that night he entered hell, and trod hell-fire along the homeward road, and endured through it only because Christian was with him. And he knew surely that to him Christian had been as Christ, and had suffered and died to save him from his sins.

How these papers have been placed in sequence will be made manifest in the reading of them. All needless matters have been eliminated, so that a history almost at variance with the possibilities of later-day belief may stand forth as simple fact. There is throughout no statement of past things wherein memory may err, for all the records chosen are exactly contemporary, given from the standpoints and within the range of knowledge of those who made them.

Thus Ends The Tale

ENTER THE HOUNDS –
DON'T BE AFRAID, THEY WON'T HARM YOU,
OR WILL THEY?
By Timothy Green Beckley

Oh my, _The Hound of the Baskervilles_. How the mere mention of this title brings back fond memories.

As far as I am concerned, it was the most brilliant book in the Sherlock Holmes series, written by that brilliant man whom I admire so much, Sir Arthur Conan Doyle. In fact, I wish he were alive today so that I could shake his hand and thank him for all the wonderful hours I spent reading the seemingly unsolvable mysteries he brought to the world, not only as the creator of the greatest detective of all time, but as one of the world's leading investigators of the paranormal.

For those who know the history of psychic phenomena, few others have been so influential in promoting a belief in life after death, spiritualism, levitation, spirit photography and for the overall conviction that anything is possible in the kingdom of the supernatural. At one point he wanted to give up his highly successful profession as a writer and delve into the realm of the mystical fulltime. He went on extensive lecture tours to promote numerous mediums who were being attacked by the likes of the great magician/escape artist Harry Houdini, who said that spiritualism was nothing more than a scam, a matter of "hocus pocus." Doyle went so far as to state his belief in a sensational series of photographs taken by two young girls of purported fairies beside a stream in the woods behind their home. He spent a good portion of his life trying to verify the case for the existence of the paranormal and scripted several works heavily laden with quotes from members of the scientific community who actively supported his belief in the Summerland, a sort of heavenly paradise where we go when we die if we have lead a relatively civil life and shown compassion to others not as fortunate as perhaps you and I.

Frankly, I cannot acquire an adequate amount of Sir Arthur Conan Doyle's paranormal writings. For some reason, I seem to have an overwhelming aspiration to return to print those creations of his on the subject which for the most part have been impossible to obtain during the course of the last several decades. These include:

"*The Charismatic, Martyred Life of Joan Of Arc,*" a sort of channeled essay received by psychic means through the mediumship of Leon Denis.

"*Revealing The Bizarre Powers of Harry Houdini – As Exposed By*

Sir Arthur Conan Doyle," which suggests that Houdini's fanatical debunking of psychics and mediums was a subterfuge to conceal his own remarkable paranormal powers.

"*The Paranormal World of Sherlock Holmes: Sir Arthur Conan Doyle First Ghost Buster and Psychic Sleuth,*" includes a cool selection of photographs from the period in which Doyle studied the enigmas of the unknown.

As for *The Hound of the Baskervilles*, I read the literary version when I was but a tender youth, and I must have seen the original 1939 version of the film adaptation starring Basil Rathbone a half dozen times. It would come on from time to time late on a Friday or Saturday night on one of the independent stations broadcasting out of Manhattan or Philadelphia, and I happened to live just about halfway between the two mega cities. In the rafters while I was growing up was a talented performer named John Zacherle, who was hired to host some of the worst movies imaginable in the hope that the programs he made a spectacle of himself on would somehow attract an audience. Zacherle created a name for himself in no time by donning some cheap stylistic horror makeup while sleeping in a coffin and befriending a giant amoeba that he slung around the dungeon he lived in as if he were fighting the blob. On Saturday, August 2, 1958, Zacherle aired the *The Hound of the Baskervilles* for the first time and hooked me and an entire generation on what many consider to be Sir Arthur Conan Doyle's best work. If it weren't for this broadcast "way back when," there is a good chance this very book would never have been published.

Though there is no way of knowing, it is estimated that between 40 and 50 movie and TV adaptations of *The Hound of the Baskervilles* have been made, going back as early as 1915 with a silent German version Der Hund von Baskerville. The most recent one was released only a few months ago (circa 2012) in the United Kingdom under the slightly altered title, *The Hounds of Baskerville*.

But this book is mainly about the real hounds, the bona fide devil dogs, the crazed phantom canines of the night that influenced Doyle to pen his most well-received Sherlock Holmes thriller.

In order to strengthen the case for the reality of the hounds, we have called upon several top cryptolzoologists to document the beasts' uncomfortable existence. Nick Redfern was born in England and has done a thorough job of creating an accurate timeline of the hounds' appearances throughout the British Isles, while blogger Andrew Gable hunkers down in the U.S. as he concentrates on sightings of the hounds in several eastern states.

And finally, we call upon our friend and fellow Fortean enthusiast Claudia Cunningham, who has personally heard many strange stories of the hounds in upstate New York, especially those which center about the very cemetery where Charles Fort is buried. DoDoDoDo – your next stop, the Twilight Zone!

Timothy Green Beckley, Publisher
New York City
August, 2012

mrufo8@hotmail.com

AIN'T NOTHING BUT A HOUND DOG — OR IS IT?

There is no way of knowing for sure how many editions of Sir Arthur Conan Doyle's book The Hound Of the Baskervilles have been published around the world. It is estimated, however, that somewhere near 50 motion pictures and TV adaptations have been produced, starting with the earliest 1914 silent version.

Here is but a small collection of film art, posters, TV stills and DVD box covers — in various languages — to show the immense popularity of Sherlock Holmes and his demonic canine adversary from hell.

With signature pipe in hand, Peter Cushing plays Holmes
in the Hammer version of this classic.

Even the comics cannot escape the dastardly deeds of the Hound.

A rare set of theatrical one sheets illustrating quite nicely the horror of it all.

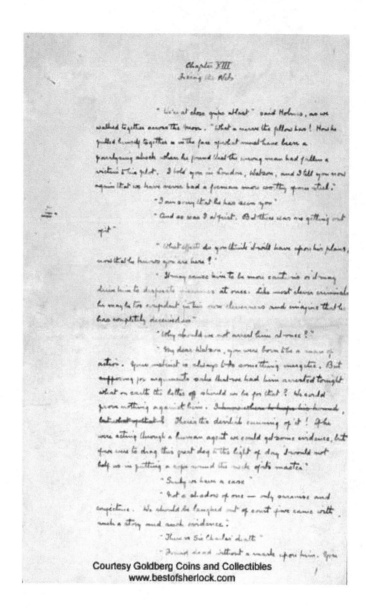

A copy of one page of the original hand-written text, valued at over one-hundred thousand dollars, from Doyle's "Hound Of The Baskervilles."

Holmes examines the victim in this rare still from the first
"Hound" film, circa 1914.

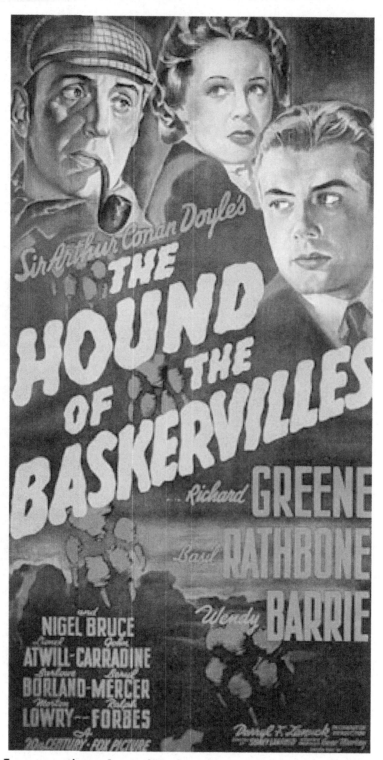

A promotion sheet for the most well known of the "Hounds" films, featuring Basil Rathbone as the famous sleuth, and Nigel Bruce as his faithful sidekick. The first English language adaptation of the Hound of the Baskervilles was an instant success.

There is only one original Sherlock Holmes as far as the author is concerned, and that is Basil Rathbone, who appeared as the detective in numerous films throughout his career.

On the Trail of Britain's Terrifying Phantom Black Dogs: Folklore, Reality, Sherlock Holmes and The Hound of the Baskervilles
By
Nick Redfern

Beware of the black dog
© Sidney Paget

BEWARE OF THE DOG!

Imagine the scene: it's late one cold, dark, winter's eve in a little old hamlet in central England. You're walking home, along a winding, tree-shrouded old road with only the light of an eerie full moon to illuminate your path. But, as you continue on your trek to your centuries-old cottage, you begin to feel uneasy.

For reasons that you are unable to fathom, as the icy wind sends a deep chill through your body, you develop the distinct feeling that you are not alone. Rather, you sense that you are being watched and followed by something terrible, something malignant, something nightmarish, and something as ancient as it is mysterious.

146

Then something truly ominous occurs: you begin to hear the vague sound of panting – animalistic panting, no less – and the unmistakable sound of heavy, beastly paws hitting the road behind you. A terrible realization suddenly hits you hard: you are being followed, *or stalked*, by some sort of large, predatory animal. It's an animal that – even though you have yet to see it up close and personal – you know deep in your heart has you firmly in its sights.

You quicken your pace, but it's no good. The panting gets louder and closer, as do those paws hitting the road. A low, guttural growl issues forth and, by now crazed with fear, you turn around to face your foe. As you do so, you are instantly frozen to the spot by the immense creature before you.

Without doubt, it is a dog. But, it's unlike any dog you have ever seen before. This hound is huge, close to the size of a small donkey. Its coat is utterly black in color. Its limbs are thick and muscular. And its giant jaws are of a definitive bone-crushing nature. But it's the eyes that are most terrifying of all: they blaze like a pair of hot coals. Fiery, red and fiendish, they bore into your soul as easily as a hot knife would cut through butter.

Summoning up all your strength, and against all the odds, you manage to make a run for it. The local inn is only a quarter of a mile away and you know you can make it. You *have* to make it. After all, you're running for your life with a definitive hellhound on your tail.

You feel the beast's hot breath on your neck as it closes in and you prepare for the absolute worst. But it doesn't come. As you reach the door of the village tavern, the animal suddenly vanishes in a flash of light. Gone, melted away, or dematerialized; however you wish to word it.

Shaking with fear, you stagger into the pub and practically collapse into an old oak chair situated near a flaming fireplace. Your friends all look on in fear: the sheer terror on your pale face has immediately caught their attention.

After a couple of pints of hearty ale to calm your nerves, you finally splutter out the incredible and awful facts of what has just occurred. And an ominous silence grips the entire clientele, barmaids and inn-keeper as you do so.

While the specific nature of the experience is shrouded in mystery, one and all know exactly what has taken place: you have had a close encounter with one of Britain's most notorious, nightmarish and devilish beasts; a creature that, for centuries, has been a staple part of the nation's folklore, mythology, culture and history: the hellhound.

The story I have related above is not fiction. Nor did it occur, as you might imagine, in the distant, fog-shrouded past of ye olde Britain. Not at all: the event in question occurred in a small, centuries-old village in central England called Ranton, which is situated in the county of Staffordshire. And, it took place in 1997, no less.

But what are these infernal creatures? Are they legend, reality, or both? And how, and under what circumstances, did they inspire the most famous, cherished and much-loved Sherlock Holmes adventure-story of all time: Sir Arthur Conan Doyle's *The Hound of the Baskervilles*? Read on: the answers to those questions – and many more – will become terrifyingly clear as we go on a wild and fear-filled hunt for hounds supernatural, horrific and, sometimes, even deadly.

A NOVEL APPROACH

Published in 1902, Conan Doyle's *The Hound of the Baskervilles* tells the memorable and atmosphere-filled saga of the noted and wealthy Baskerville family that has called Dartmoor, Devonshire, England its home for centuries. Truly, a wild, expansive, foggy and boggy locale, Dartmoor is filled with supernatural tales of terror, horror and intrigue – but leading them all is the legend of the terrible hound that haunts the Baskervilles.

After the mysterious death of Sir Charles Baskerville, the only surviving heir to the family fortune – Sir Henry Baskerville – travels to Dartmoor from Canada to take his rightful place as master of Baskerville Hall and as local, revered dignitary. And that's when darkness, murder most foul, mayhem and horror all surface from the murky depths of those old, mystery-saturated moors.

As a result, we see Sherlock Holmes and ever-faithful Dr. Watson hot on the trail of the seemingly supernatural canine that has cursed the family for generations. But, all is not as it seems in a fantastically entertaining saga that pits Holmes and Watson against a brilliant foe who has exploited the folklore of the terrible hound for equally terrible gain.

If you have not yet read *The Hound of the Baskervilles*, then you are in for a big treat. It is, without doubt, a classic unrivaled. But, there's an important question that needs answering: from where did Sir Arthur Conan Doyle find his inspiration for the story? Was it all merely his own, personal invention and imagination?

No, it most certainly was not. Conan Doyle took the lead from all-too-real supernatural occurrences of the paranormal hound variety on Dartmoor. Sometimes, the old saying that truth is stranger than fiction really is true.

It surprises many to learn that Conan Doyle took the lead from a family who owned a huge, old hall near Hay-on-Wye, a small, centuries-old town in Powys, Wales. And, being a friend of the family, Conan Doyle was a regular visitor. Thus the atmospheric abode quickly became – in Conan Doyle's mind – the ideal place for his novel to be set. So, with a few changes here and there to name and location, Baskerville Hall was duly born.

Coupled with that, the legendary creator of Sherlock Holmes had been exposed to the stories surrounding one Richard Cabell, an evil squire whose remains can be found in the Devonshire town of Buckfastleigh. So, as Devonshire folklore tells it, Cabell was a monstrously evil character – possibly one who had even entered into a pact with the Devil himself, and sold his soul for personal gain in the process.

And, when, on July 5, 1677, Cabell finally shuffled off this mortal coil and into the terrible embrace of his fork-tailed, horned master, a pack of supernatural hounds materialized on the old moors and raced for Cabell's tomb, where they howled ominously all night long, and struck cold fear into one and all that called the land their home.

Thus, the story began to develop in Conan Doyle's mind and imagination. He moved the location of the old hall that he so often frequented to Dartmoor, and changed Richard Cabell to the evil Hugo Baskerville. In the process, literary history was made and *The Hound of the Baskervilles* was born.

Beware of the Wild Hunt
© Frederick Wilhelm Hein

But there is one important factor to remember: Conan Doyle did not invent Britain's phantom, fiery-eyed hounds. He merely brought them to the attention of the public in spectacularly entertaining, fictional style.

In reality, however, the creature had been prowling around the British countryside for centuries; and particularly so Dartmoor – the fictional home of the world's most famous hound of horror, as we shall now see, in all its awful glory.

DARTMOOR'S REAL DEVIL DOGS

Bowerman's Nose is a large stack of weathered granite on Dartmoor. It can be found on the northern slopes of Hayne Down, about a mile from the intriguingly named Hound Tor and close to the village of Manaton.

According to local legend, a huntsman named Bowerman lived on the moor around one thousand years ago; and while out one day chasing a hare, he and his pack of dogs unwittingly ran into a coven of witches, overturned their cauldron and catastrophically disrupted their dark ceremony. The witches decided that punishment was due.

The next time he was out hunting, one of the witches shape-shifted into a hare, and cunningly led both Bowerman and his hounds into a deadly mire of quicksand-like proportions. And if that was not enough, as a final punishment, the old crone turned Bowerman and his dogs to stone. So the legend goes, today the dogs can be seen as a jagged chain of rocks on top of Hound Tor, while the huntsman himself became the rock formation now known as Bowerman's Nose. Notably, with a little imagination, it is indeed possible to see a human face in the rocky outline.

And the intrigue did not end there.

The same area is also rife with ancient tales and legends of a group of diabolical and unholy creatures known as the Wisht Hounds – fearsome devil-dogs with glowing eyes and large fangs. They are said to have a taste for both human flesh and human souls, and ride with the Devil himself, as he crosses the windswept wilds of Dartmoor late at night - and atop a headless, black horse, no less.

According to legend, the Wisht Hounds inhabit the nearby Wistman's Woods – a sacred grove where, in centuries past, ancient druids held pagan rituals in honor of a veritable multitude of old Earth gods and goddesses.

As I know from personal experience, even today Wistman's Woods is a strange and atmospheric locale: situated in a valley on the eastern slopes of Dartmoor's West Dart River, it is comprised of densely-packed, gnarled and dwarfish oak-trees that invoke graphic imagery of a distinctly Lovecraftian nature.

But, such creatures are not limited to Dartmoor. Rather, their exploits have been recorded across pretty much the entirety of the British Isles. As a prime example, I now invite you to accompany me on a journey to the ancient English county of Staffordshire where I grew up, the origins of which date back to around 650AD.

"...the biggest bloody dog I have ever seen in my life..."

Late one evening in the early weeks of 1972, a man named Nigel Lea was driving blissfully across the Cannock Chase woods that dominate much of Staffordshire when his attention was suddenly drawn to a strange ball of glowing, blue light that seemingly came out of nowhere and slammed violently into the ground some short distance ahead of his vehicle and amid nothing less than a veritable torrent of bright, fiery sparks.

Needless to say, Lea quickly slowed his car down to what was a literal snail's pace. And, as he cautiously approached the approximate area where the light had seemingly fallen, was both shocked and horrified to the absolute core to see looming before him, "the biggest bloody dog I have ever seen in my life."

Very muscular and utterly black in color, with a pair of large, pointed ears and huge, thick paws, the creature seemed to positively ooze both extreme menace and overpowering negativity, and had a crazed, staring look in its yellow-tinged eyes.

For twenty or thirty seconds or so, both man and beast alike squared off against each other in classic stalemate fashion, after which time the animal both slowly and carefully headed for the darkness and the camouflage of the tall, surrounding trees, not even once taking its penetrating eyes off of the petrified driver as it did so.

Somewhat ominously it might be said, and only around two or three weeks later at the most, says Lea, a very close friend of his who he had known since his earliest schooldays was killed in an industrial accident, under very horrific circumstances, in the West Midlands town of West Bromwich.

Which today, Lea firmly believes – after having deeply studied, almost to the point of total obsession, the history of British Black Dog lore and the creature's associations with both deep tragedy and death – was directly connected with his strange and unsettling encounter on that tree-shrouded road back in 1972 – as do many others, as we shall later learn.

It is also interesting to note that this was not the only British-based phantom black dog encounter of 1972: on April 19 of that same year, at Gorleston, Norfolk, England, for example, a coastguard named Graham Grant was witness to a huge black dog that was seen charging along the nearby beaches – until it vanished into thin air, that is, never ever to return.

Then, at around 3.20-3.30 a.m. on a particular day in the latter part of September 1972, a nurse returning home from a late-shift at a Sheffield, England, hospital encountered a glowing-eyed, ghostly dog briefly padding around – in what was perceived by the witness as a "disturbed or confused" fashion – on her doorstep, before leaping off into the ethereal, autumn darkness.

Perhaps not merely a coincidence is the revelation that only hours earlier, the nurse had been directly involved in a tragically-unsuccessful attempt to save the life of a young car-accident victim who had been fatally injured in a head-on crash on a main road situated on the fringes of the city of Sheffield.

In a somewhat highly synchronistic fashion, today the now-retired nurse and her husband make their home in the Staffordshire town of Hednesford, right in the heart of the Cannock Chase, where Nigel Lea had his very own terrifying close encounter of the black dog kind more than forty years ago.

THE GHOST HOUND OF BRERETON

In the early-to-mid 1980s, truly surreal and sinister reports began to surface of a creature that became known at a local level as the Ghost Dog of Brereton – a reference to the specific area of Staffordshire from where most of the sightings originated. Brereton once had its very own identity; but today it is considered to be a part of the town of Rugeley – or Rudgeley, as it was originally known, according to the *Domesday Book*, and which translates as "the hill over the field."

With specific respect to the Brereton encounters, the phantom dog at issue was described as being both large and frightening, and on at least two occasions it reportedly vanished into thin air after having been seen by terrified members of the public on lonely stretches of ancient road late at night. In direct response to an article that appeared in the *Cannock Advertiser* newspaper during the winter of 1984/5 on the sightings of Brereton's infamous ghost dog, a member of the public from a local village, one Sylvia Everett, wrote to the newspaper thus:

"On reading the article my husband and I were astonished. We recalled an incident which happened in July some four or five years ago driving home from a celebration meal at the *Cedar Tree* restaurant at about 11.30 p.m. We had driven up Coal Pit Lane and were just on the bends before the approach to the *Holly Bush* when, from the high hedge of trees on the right hand side of the road, the headlights picked out a misty shape which moved across the road and into the trees opposite."

Mrs. Everett continued with her account:

"We both saw it. It had no definite shape, seeming to be a ribbon of mist about 18in. to 2ft. in depth and perhaps nine or 10ft. long with a definite beginning and end. It was a clear, warm night with no mist anywhere else. We were both rather stunned and my husband's first words were: 'My goodness! Did you see that?'

"I remember remarking I thought it was a ghost. Until now we had no idea of the history of the area or any possible explanation for a haunting. Of course, this occurrence may be nothing to do with the 'ghost dog' or may even have a natural explanation. However, we formed the immediate impression that what we saw was something paranormal."

Another person who may very well have seen the phantom hound of Brereton was Sally Armstrong. It was shortly after the breaking of dawn one day in late March 1987, and Armstrong, a now-retired employee of a Shropshire, England-based auctioneering company, was on her way to meet with a client, then living in Brereton, who was employed in the antiques trade. For a while at least, all was completely and utterly normal. But, things were only destined to change - and for the absolute worst, too, it can be convincingly argued.

Shortly before she arrived at the old cottage of the man in question, Armstrong was witness to a monstrous black-hued dog with wild, staring eyes that was sitting at the edge of the main road that runs through the locale of Brereton, and which was staring intently at her as she passed by it.

Somewhat unsettling: as Armstrong drove by the huge beast, she slowed down, quickly looked in her rear-view mirror, and could see that its head had now turned in her direction. It was, apparently, still focusing upon her each and every move.

Armstrong concedes that there was nothing to definitively suggest an air of the supernatural or the paranormal about the fiend-dog she saw more than a quarter of a century ago; however, that its huge presence seemed to both surprise and unsettle her for reasons that she cannot to this day readily explain or rationalise properly, leads Armstrong to conclude that: "...there was just something about it that makes me remember it this much later."

MAN AND ANIMAL

Possibly of deep relevance to the tale of the ghost dog of Brereton was the story of a man named Ivan Vinnel. In 1934, as a twelve-year-old, he had a very strange encounter indeed in his hometown of nearby Burntwood, Staffordshire.

The sun was beginning to set and the young Ivan and a friend were getting ready to head home after an afternoon of playing hide-and-seek.

The site of Nigel Lea's black dog encounter of 1972. Copyright Nick Redfern.

Suddenly, however, the pair was stopped dead in its tracks by the shocking sight of a ghostly "tall, dark man," who was "accompanied by a black dog" that had seemingly materialized out of a "dense hedge" situated approximately ten yards from the boys' position. Both man and animal passed by in complete and utter silence before disappearing – in typical and classic ghostly fashion, no less.

Ivan later happened to mention the details of the unsettling incident to his uncle, who then quietly and guardedly proceeded to tell him that he, too, had actually seen the ghostly dog on several occasions when he was a young child.

And, as is typically the case with ghostly hounds all across the British Isles, the beast was always reportedly seen in the same location: namely, faithfully pacing along the old road that stretches from the village of Woodhouses to an area of Burntwood situated near the town's hospital. And: weird reports from Staffordshire's out-of-place, dog-like beasts continue to surface to this very day.

A MYSTERIOUS DOG ON THE M6 MOTORWAY

It was in the latter part of June 2006 that all hell metaphorically broke loose, when reports flew wildly around the town of Cannock to the effect that nothing less than a fully-grown wolf was roaming and rampaging around the area.

Early on the morning of June 28, motorists on Junction 10A of the M6 Motorway near Cannock, Staffordshire jammed Highways Agency telephone-lines with reports of a "wolf-like creature" that was seen "racing between lanes at rush hour." Gob-smacked motorists stared with complete disbelief as the immense beast, described as being "grayish-black," raced between lanes, skilfully dodging cars, before leaping for cover in the nearby trees.

Highways Agency staff took the reports very seriously at the time, but publicly concluded that the animal was most "probably a husky dog." However, a spokesperson for *Saga Radio* – which was the first media outlet to arrive on the scene – said in reply to the statement of the Highways Agency that: "Everyone who saw it is convinced it was something more than a domestic dog. I know it sounds crazy but these people think they've seen a wolf."

The local newspaper, the *Chase Post*, which has always been *very* quick off-the-mark to report on incidents of mystery animals seen in the vicinity of Staffordshire's old woods, stated on July 6 in an article titled *Great Beast Debate on Net* that: "Internet message boards are being flooded with debates on our front-page revelation last week that a 'wolf-like' creature was spotted by dozens of motorists on the M6 hard-shoulder."

The *Chase Post* further noted, with justified pride and perhaps even a little welcome surprise, that: "Our own website has been thrown into overdrive by the story, which received around 2,600 hits from fans of the unexplained across the globe in the last week alone."

While the highly mystifying affair was certainly never ultimately resolved to the satisfaction of everyone involved – or, it might reasonably be said, to the satisfaction of *anyone* involved, for that matter - the final words went to the Highways Agency, a spokesperson for whom stated that:

"We have received a number of reports that the animal was captured. But we don't know where, who by, or what it was." Of course, this truly open-ended and somewhat vague statement did nothing to resolve the matter, at all.

Perhaps the event had indeed been due to the mistaken sighting of an escaped Husky; however, that does not in any way come close to explaining the eerie encounter of Jim Broadhurst and his wife that occurred while the pair was out for a morning stroll on the Cannock Chase, only a matter of days before the memorably-monstrous events of June 28, 2006 took place.

Broadhurst states that he and his wife had seen, at a distance of about one hundred and fifty feet, what looked very much like "a giant dog" striding purposefully through an opening in the woods. Broadhurst added that deep fear firmly gripped the pair when the creature suddenly stopped and looked intently and menacingly in their direction.

That fear was amplified even further, however, when the beast reportedly, and bizarrely, reared up onto two powerful hind legs and backed away into the thick trees, never to be seen again. The husband and wife, unsurprisingly, fled those dangerous and eerie woods – and have not returned since; ever-fearful of what they believe to be some form of "monster" lurking deep within the mysterious depths of the Cannock Chase.

Interestingly, and certainly unfortunately, in the weeks that followed the encounter, the Broadhurst family was cursed with a seemingly never-ending run of bad luck and disaster that did not abate until well into September of that same year.

THE CREATURE OF THE CATHEDRAL

Moving away from the Cannock Chase, there is the story of the Bradley family of Leeds, England who had the very deep misfortune to encounter one of the now-familiar hounds of hell in early 2009: at no less a site than the Staffordshire city of Lichfield's famous and historic cathedral; which has the distinction of being the only English cathedral to be adorned with three spires.

According to the Bradleys, while walking around the outside of the cathedral one pleasant Sunday morning they were startled by the sight of a large black dog racing along at high speed, and adjacent to the side of the cathedral. The jaw-dropping fact that the dog was practically the size of a pony ensured their attention was caught and held.

But that attention was rapidly replaced by overwhelming fear when the dog allegedly "charged the wall" of the cathedral and summarily vanished right into the brickwork as it did so! Perhaps understandably, the Bradleys chose not to report their mysterious encounter to cathedral officials, to the police, or to local media outlets.

Interestingly, a very similar beast – if not, perhaps, the very *same* one - is believed to have been seen only a short distance from the cathedral by a Scottish family with the surname of either Dobson or Robinson way back in the early-to-mid-

Lichfield Cathedral, Black Dog Territory

155

1950s. The details of this encounter are admittedly vague, scant and hazy in the extreme, however, and were passed on to me, merely as an aside and nothing else really, in the autumn of 1997 by a now-retired journalist who was working in the area at the time.

"...the size of a lioness..."

There is also the following, very significant story. In an article titled *Fresh Sighting of UFOs and Werewolves on Cannock Chase* that appeared in the *Birmingham Post* newspaper on January 15, 2010, it was reported that: "Resident, Jane McNally, recently had a run-in with a mysterious canine creature while out walking with her partner on Cannock Chase."

The *Birmingham Post* quoted McNally as saying: "I was walking with my partner and his dog. We put the dog back on the lead as we thought in the distance there was an enormous dog. As we approached the animal we realised this wasn't a dog and it just stared at us for a while – I said it looked like a fox, but the size of a lioness – it then turned into the wooded area, and we proceeded to walk on. As it turned its long, bushy black tipped tail, we realised it was definitely not a dog. I have just logged onto the net and went on to images of wolves, and can honestly say whatever we saw yesterday was the closest thing to a wolf."

SWYTHAMLEY'S NIGHTMARE

Two further stories of ghostly hounds seen in the county of Staffordshire come from paranormal investigator Tim Prevett, the first of which is focused around Swythamley Hall; a late-18th century country house that can be found near Leek, Staffordshire, and which, today, is classified as a Grade II listed building that has been converted into four separate residences.

The manor of Swythamley was held by the Crown following the dissolution of Dieuclacres Abbey and, thereafter, had several owners. It was acquired by the Trafford family in 1654, who replaced the original manor-house with a new construction around 1690. The family remained in residence until Edward Trafford Nicholls – who was the High Sheriff of Staffordshire in 1818 - sold the estate to Sir Philip Brocklehurst in 1832.

And, of the particular ghost-hounds of Swythamley, Prevett says: "One of the Traffords of Swythamley, while out hunting with dogs, is said to have leaped over a chasm. Having successfully cleared the precipice with his horse, the hunting hounds were not so lucky. The fell and perished in Lud's Church, where their spectral howls are still heard on occasion today. Their owner is also said to return."

Prevett adds: "A little way to the south west is Gun Hill, past which Bonnie Prince Charlie and his army passed in December 1745. The hill was also the site of a gallows. A black dog haunts this spot, and elsewhere en route to Derby via Leek and Ashbourne, where members of the Highlanders' rebellion perished. It is said the black dogs either mark or guard the Jacobites' final resting places."

THE CREEPY CANINE OF THE CEMETERY

Creepy canines haunt Staffordshire's German Cemetery. Copyright Nick Redfern

One of the strangest of all sagas began in April 2007, when a local, well respected group of paranormal investigators – the *West Midlands Ghost Club* – traveled out to the Cannock Chase woods of Staffordshire to investigate newly-surfaced reports of what some witnesses described as a large, hairy creature very much resembling a wolf and others a giant, fiendish hound.

But, there was something extremely weird about this particular dog or wolf: as well as walking like any normal animal would, this one had the amazing and uncanny ability to rear up onto its hind limbs, which it invariably did when anyone had the distinct misfortune to cross its malevolent path.

One of those whose encounter caught the attention of one of the club's investigators, Nick Duffy, was a mailman who was riding past the cemetery on a motorbike when he became spellbound by the sight of what, at first, he assumed was a large, wild wolf on the loose.

This would be extraordinary enough in itself, as the wild wolf is generally acknowledged as having become extinct in the British Isles centuries ago. That the creature was no mere normal wolf, however, became very obvious to the shocked man when it caught his eye, raised itself upwards on its back legs, and bounded away into the countless trees that envelop the cemetery.

The next witness to come forward to Nick Duffy and his colleagues was a local scout-leader who was walking around the cemetery when he experienced something profoundly similar. Quite understandably not wanting to speak out on the record, Duffy's source, too, initially assumed that the creature he saw lurking among the graves was a wolf - or possibly even a large dog, such as a Husky. It was neither.

On realizing that the animal was large and seemingly running wild, the man slowly and carefully retreated to the safety of his car and slammed the door, at which point, on hearing the noise, the beast rose up on its back legs - to an incredible height of around seven-feet, no less - and raced off into the heart of the woods. The shocking encounter was over. The controversy, however, was just getting started.

The local newspaper, the *Chase Post*, soon got in on the action and began publishing reports suggesting the werewolf secretly made its lair deep amid the many natural caverns and winding, old, man-made mines and shafts that exist deep below the surface of the Cannock Chase.

The beast, some speculated, possibly had a point of entrance and exit somewhere close to the cemetery – something which hardly generated much cheer in those that lived nearby. And that the sightings of the monstrous thing coincided with the mysterious disappearance of a sizeable number of pet dogs in the area, and that several deer had been found horribly mutilated and with significant organs torn out and flesh viciously removed too, only served to increase the escalating anxiety over the presence of the monster of the cemetery.

As the sightings of the creature continued, and the dog disappearances duly escalated, so did the controversy. Derek Crawley, the chairman of the *Staffordshire Mammal Society*, expressed his view that while a wolf could, in theory at least, make a home for itself on the Cannock Chase, in this case there were a couple of problems. First, there was that not insignificant fact that wolves should not have been running wild anywhere in Britain during the first decade of the 21st Century.

Plus, as Crawley also noted, wolves are very much pack-animals. But, the dog-like beast of the German cemetery seemed to be an overwhelmingly solitary beast. No one walking around the graves had ever seen more than one such creature on any given occasion.

Crawley did note, quite correctly, that there were a number of people, locally, who owned Huskies, and he opined that this may have been what people were seeing. Indeed, such a theory might have been considered not just a possibility, but a downright probability, had it not been for that troubling issue of the beast seen running on two legs as well as four.

Thus, with the witnesses steadfastly standing by their claims and assertions, the mystery remained. Or, it's correct to say it remained until the late summer of 2007, when the strange animal vanished either into the ether, some dark and mysterious realm of paranormal origins, or those shadowy tunnels beneath the old woods.

THE HOUND OF THE CASTLE

And then we have the account of Marjorie Sanders. Although Sanders' account can be considered a new one – at least, in the sense that it only reached my eyes and ears in August 2009, during which time I was on a week-long return trip to England – it actually occurred back in the closing stages of the Second World War, when the witness was a girl of ten or eleven.

At the time, Sanders was living in a small village not too far from the ancient and historic Tamworth Castle – which overlooks the River Tame, and which has stood there since it was built by the Normans in the 11th Century; although an earlier, Anglo-Saxon castle is known to have existed on the same site, and which was constructed by the forces of Ethelfreda, the Mercian queen and the eldest daughter of King Alfred the Great of Wessex.

According to Sanders, "probably in about early 1945," her grandfather had "seen a hellhound parading around the outside of the castle that scared him half to death when it vanished in front of him." For reasons that Sanders cannot now remember or comprehend, her grandfather always thereafter memorably referred to the animal in question as "the furnace dog."

Whether or not this is an indication that the spectral dog had the seemingly-ubiquitous fiery red eyes that so many witnesses have reported remains unfortunately unknown; but, it would not at all surprise me if that was one day shown to be the case.

Then, we have the brief but highly thought-provoking account of Gerald Clarke, a Glasgow baker, whose father claimed to have briefly seen a phantom hound with bright, electric-blue-coloured eyes on the grounds of a military base called Royal Air Force Stafford (which is situated only a short distance from the Cannock Chase) in the late 1950s, and while on patrol late one winter's evening.

As was the case with so many other witnesses to such disturbing entities, the elder Clarke quietly confided in his son that the creature "just vanished: first it was there and then it wasn't." And, now it's time to move even further afield.

EAST COAST BLACK DOGS

Perhaps the most famous of all of the phantom hounds of old Britain are those that are said to have frequented – and, in some cases, *still* frequent - the ancient roads and pathways of Norfolk, Essex, Suffolk, and Sussex. Their many and varied names include Black Shuck, the Shug Monkey, and the Shock. The Shuck and the Shock are classic black dogs; whereas, interestingly enough, the Shug Monkey is described as being a combination of spectral monkey and immense hound.

Even their very names have intriguing origins: While some researchers consider the possibility that all of the appellations had their origins in the word *Shucky* – an ancient east-coast term meaning *shaggy* – others suggest a far more sinister theory; namely that Shock, Shuck, and Shug are all based upon the Anglo-Saxon *scucca*, meaning *demon*; a most apt description, for sure.

THERE'S SOMETHING IN THE FOREST

Back in the winter of 1983, Paul and Jayne Jennings of Woodbridge, Suffolk, England, had an encounter of the black dog kind in – of all places - Rendlesham

Forest, which was home to Britain's most famous UFO encounter of all; a December 1980 event in which numerous military personnel from the nearby Royal Air Force Bentwaters military base encountered a UFO in the woods. But, UFOs aside, back to the matter of a certain black dog.

Both in their early twenties at the time of the incident, the Jennings were walking along a trail when they saw what Jayne Jennings described as "a big black dog that kept appearing and disappearing." When I asked her to elaborate, she explained to me that they had been walking along a pathway and on rounding a bend in the path came face to face with the dog.

It was a huge creature and, strangely, she said that while the head was unmistakably that of a large hound, the body was more feline in nature. For a moment the Jennings and the dog stared at each other. The dog was not aggressive, Jayne Jennings said. In fact, it had a mournful expression on its face.

Black Dog of Bungay.

But they were shocked when it vanished in the blink of an eye. They were even more shocked, however, when a moment later it reappeared and proceeded to "flicker on and off" four or five times before vanishing permanently. Paul Jennings told me that after the dog's final disappearance, the air was filled with a strange smell that resembled "burning metal."

It was hardly what you could call a positive experience for the terrified pair, and certainly not one they ever wanted repeating – which, most fortunately for them, it was not.

THE BUNGAY BEAST

It was August 4, 1577, when a terrifying event occurred at the village church in Bungay, Suffolk. An account written shortly afterwards, which can be found at the Parish Church of St. Mary in Bungay, tells the story of what took place. Although written in old English – which, to a degree, differs from today's English - its contents are decipherable.

Titled "*A Straunge and Terrible Wunder wrought very late in the parish Church of Bungay,*" it reads as follows:

"Immediately hereupon, there appeared in a most horrible similitude and likeness to the congregation then and there present a dog as they might discerne it, of a black colour; at the site whereof, together with the fearful flashes of fire which they were then seene, moved such admiration in the minds of the assemblie, that they thought doomsday was already come.

"This black dog, or the divil in such a likenesse (God hee knoweth all who worketh all) running all along down the body of the church with great swiftnesse and incredible haste, among the people, in a visible forum and shape, passed betweene two persons, as they were kneeling upon their knees, and occupied in prayer as it seemed, wrung the necks of them bothe at one instant clene backward, in so much that even at a moment where they kneeled, they strangely died.

Nick Redfern and Neil Arnold.
Copyright Nick Redfern.

"There was at ye same time another wonder wrought; for the same black dog, still continuing and remaining in one and the self same shape, passing by another man of the congregation in the church, gave him such a gripe on the back, that therewith all he was presently drawn together and shrunk up, as it were a peece of lether scorched in a hit fire; or as the mouth of a purse or bag, drawn together with string. The man albeit hee was in so strange a taking, dyed not, but as it is thought is yet alive; whiche thing is marvelous in the eyes of men, and offereth much matter of amasing the minde."

It was only shortly afterwards that the beast appeared at the church at nearby Blythburgh: "Placing himself upon a maine balke or beam, whereon some ye Rood did stand, sodainly he gave a swinge downe through ye church, and there also, as before, slew two men and a lad, and burned the hand of another person that was there among the rest of the company, of whom divers were blasted."

Today, the people of Bungay continue to celebrate and promote the legend of their very own equivalent of the Loch Ness Monster or Bigfoot. Indeed, even the local football team takes its name from the legendary animal that roamed around town all those centuries earlier.

"...both of them saw it..."

Then there is a manuscript housed at Nottingham County Library, England. Dating from 1952, it tells the brief but intriguing story of a Mrs. Smalley:

"Her grandfather, who was born in 1804 and died in 1888, used to have occasion to drive from Southwell to Bathley in a pony and trap. This involved going along Crow Lane, which leaves South Muskham opposite the school and goes to Bathley. Frequently, along that lane he saw a black dog trotting alongside his trap. Round about 1915 his great-grandson, Mrs. Smalley's son Sydney, used to ride out from Newark on a motorcycle to their home at Bathley. He went into Newark to dances and frequently returned at about 11 o'clock at night. He too often saw a black dog in Crow lane; he sometimes tried to run over it but was never able to. One night Sidney took his father on the back of the motorcycle especially to see the dog, and both of them saw it."

BLACK DOGS OF LONDON

Neil Arnold is one of Britain's most respected of all paranormal authors and sleuths, and whose research for his book *The Mystery Animals of the British Isles: London* has turned up some notable data on the city's black dog legends. Neil says:

"The old Newgate Prison, built in 1188 on the orders of Henry II, was situated just inside the City at the corner of Newgate Street and Old Bailey. The site was said to harbour one of London's most terrifying apparitions, that of an evil black hound. Legend dates back to the reign of Henry III, during a period of extreme famine, where holed up prisoners were alleged to have gorged upon one another to survive!

"One of these victims was said to have been a sorcerer of the darkest arts, who claimed near death that he would seek revenge on the inmates. Although the jail was demolished in 1902, the most fascinating account originates from the pen of a Luke Hutton, who was an inmate in the 1500s, and hanged in 1598.

"This oft-repeated version of the beast comes from 1638, entitled *The Discovery of a London Monster, called the Blacke Dogg of Newgate* in which the narrator tells of entering a pub where he gets into a conversation about the dog, which reads as follows (word for word): 'I maintained that I had read an old Chronicle that it was a walking spirit in the likeness of a blacke Dog, gliding up and down the streets a little before the time of Execution, and in the night whilst Sessions continued, and his beginning thus. In the raigne of King Henry the third there happened such a famine through England, but especially in London, that many starved for want of food, by which meanes the Prisioners in Newgate eat up one another altue, but commonly those that came newly in . . . there was a certain scholar brought tither, upon suspicion of Conjuring, and that he by Charmes and devilish Whitchcrafts, had done much hurt to the kings subjects, which Scholler, mauger his Devil Furies, Spirits and Goblins, was by the famished prisoners eaten up. . .'"

Neil continues:

"With vengeance promised by the prey: '. . . nightly to see the Scholler in the shape of a black Dog walking up and downe the Prison, ready with ravening Jawes to teare out their bowles; for his late human flesh they had so hungerly eaten, and withal they hourely heard (as they thought) strange groanes and cries, as if it had been some creature in great paine and torments, whereupin such a nightly feare grew amongst them, that it turned into a Frenzie, and from a Frenzie to Desperation, in which desperation they killed the keeper, and so many of them escaped forth, but yet whither soever they came or went they imagined a Blacke Dog to follow, and by this means, as I doe thinke, the name of him began.'"

THE REALM OF THE BLACK DOG

Moving on, Neil Arnold adds: "Richard Jones in *Haunted London* writes of 'The Realm Of The Black Dog' at Amen Court, Warwick Lane stating, 'Amen Court is a delightful, hidden enclave of seventeeth to nineteenth century houses, where the Dean and Chapter of St Paul's Cathedral live. At the rear of the court a large and ominous dark wall looms. Behind it once stood the fearsome bulk of Newgate Prison . . . . there remains a tiny passage, which was known as Deadman's Walk. The passage took its name from the fact that prisoners were led along it to their executions, and were buried beneath it afterwards.'"

Neil expands further: "With reference to the phantom hound Jones writes, 'This shapeless, black form slithers along the top of the wall, slides sloppily down into the courtyard and then melts away. Its manifestations are always accompanied by a nauseous smell, and the sound of dragging footsteps.'"

SOUTHERN BLACK DOGS

Turning our attentions away from London, Neil Arnold has more to discuss of a black dog nature from his home-county of Kent, in the south of England. He begins: "In my *Mystery Animals Of The British Isles: Kent* I wrote, 'A black hound was seen during the 1960s on the Wandsworth Road. Researchers claimed that the form was the ghost of an animal killed on the road. The hound would often be seen disappearing into 523 Wandsworth Road, and the haunting occurred for more than four months.'

"In the December of 1962 a proprietor of a fish restaurant situated at the sight of the haunting wrote a letter to the Society for Psychical Research commenting, 'I respectfully bring to your notice a phenomenon that has occurred at the above address, and trust that it may be of sufficient interest for your investigation, which I would welcome.

"In the last six or seven weeks of that period, a large black and beautiful dog was seen to pass from the rear rooms of the premises through the shop, and out into the street, from whence it would turn right, and lope away up the main road and out of sight.

"This visitation occurred six or seven times, always between 6:00 and 6:30 pm, and when we were sitting at a table, in the then empty shop, and with the rear door locked. On one occasion he brushed solidly against my wife's leg, and on each appearance was seen by three of us clearly.'

"Similar harmless ghost dogs have been seen in South East London where a phantom dog was said to prowl the Anchor Tavern, and another pub, the Spanish Galleon of Greenwich, was also said to be haunted by a large mastiff hound. However, the lore of the black dog often concerns hounds which are sinister, often appearing as omens of death or ill luck as discussed. Meanwhile a dog resembling a dachshund is said to haunt an area of Baker Street.

"A large, yellow-colored dog was once said to haunt the old Motley Club at Dean Street, in Soho. It was mentioned by Elliot O' Donnell that a man named Dickson, present at the premises before it shut down, observed on at least three occasions a yellow dog which confronted him on the staircase. On the first occasion the witness threw the dog a biscuit which it ignored and wandered by. On the second occasion the same thing happened but this time Dickson was startled to see the dog vanish into thin air. On the third occasion Dickson threw the dog a piece of meat, which it ignored, and so the man decided to prod the creature with his stick but the object passed through and the animal faded into nothing."

THE BLACK DOG IN THE SECOND WORLD WAR

Jon Downes, of the British-based Center for Fortean Zoology – one of the very few full-time groups in the world dedicated to the study of unknown animals such as the Chupacabras, lake monsters and sea serpents - says:

"Clues to the emotional *zeitgeist* of a community can be found in the most unlikely places. For example, during the long, hot summer that saw Europe plodding slowly and inexorably towards the most terrible war that mankind had ever known, a country and western song called 'Riders in the Sky' was extremely popular on both sides of the Atlantic. It told the story of an airborne `ghost rider` who drove a herd of cattle whose 'brands were still on fire and their hooves were made of steel,' and whose 'horns were black and shiny and their hot breath he could feel.'

"The hapless observer described how: 'A bolt of fear went through him as they thundered through the sky, For he saw the riders coming hard and heard their mournful cry. Yi-pee-yi-ay, Yi-pee-yi-oh, Ghost Riders in the sky.'"

Downes continues: "This haunting song was revived as an instrumental twenty-two years later by a group called *The Ramrods*, and it is this wordless version that is perhaps most well known today. What is far more important, however, is that the events recounted in the song are an almost exact account of a paranormal event called `The Wild Hunt` which has been reported from all over the Celtic lands of Europe."

THE WILD HUNT AND WILDER HOUNDS

Jon Downes elaborates further: "Belief in the Wild Hunt is found not only in Britain but also on the Continent, and the basic idea is the same in all variations: a phantasmal leader and his men accompanied by hounds who 'fly' through the

Cryptozoologist Jon Downes.
Copyright Nick Redfern.

night in pursuit of something. What they are pursuing is not clear; although Norse legend has various objects such as a visionary boar or wild-horse and even magical maidens known as Moss Maidens.

"Greek myth has Hecate roaming the Earth on moonless nights with a pack of ghostly, howling dogs and the phenomenon has also been reported from Germany, where, according to folklore, the procession includes the souls of unbaptised babies in the train of 'Frau Bertha,' who sometimes accompanied the Wild Huntsman, and which in the Franche Comte was believed to be King Herod pursuing the Holy Innocents.

"The Wild Huntsman everywhere was a demonic figure, who would throw unsuspecting peasants their share of 'game' with horrific consequences. This savage and tricky being is generally thought to be an aspect of Woden, a god who was characterized by his duplicity - as in parts of Germany and Scandinavia the Wild Hunt was known as 'Woden's Hunt.'"

Downes expands on the presence of the black dog at a time of death and disaster: "Certainly, the hounds are universally believed to be portents of war, death and disaster, and a belated traveler hearing them would fling himself face downward on the ground to avoid seeing them. The Devil's hunting pack, and the related phenomenon of the black Devil Dogs which are sometimes seen singly away from the Wild Hunt, are phenomena that have been reported on more occasions during the war years than on any other occasion - before or since.

"According to historian, Eric L. Fitch: 'A historical personage reputed to lead the Hunt is a character named Wild Edric, who held lands in the Welsh Marches in the eleventh century. In 1067 he led an uprising against the Normans and in 1069 sacked Shrewsbury. It appears that he was never defeated in battle and eluded capture altogether; in fact he made peace with William the Conqueror and actually joined his side. His death is not recorded and tradition has it that he did not die at all, but had to suffer eternal punishment for changing sides by leading a Wild Hunt. It is said that, along with his fairy wife Godda and his band of followers, he races across country in a furious ride.'"

Downes notes: "It would be interesting to find out whether German observers reported seeing their wild hunt, with 'Frau Bertha,' who seems to be the Germanic equivalent of Godda, during the months preceding the Second World War."

MORE WARTIME ENCOUNTERS

Jon Downes also offers us the following, thought-provoking statement: "Perhaps the most interesting thing about the sightings of the Devil Dogs - either *en masse* or singly during the war years - is the number of sightings by people who could not have been aware of the occult significance of the entity which they had been fortunate (or unfortunate) enough to encounter.

Downes cites the words of one such witness: "At the time, because of the war, my mother and I usually stayed with an elderly gentleman, who had kindly taken us in as 'refugees.' We only went back to the capital when the bombing ceased. The cottage where we lived is still in existence, in Bredon, Worcestershire. My encounter took place one late afternoon in summer, when I had been sent to bed, but was far from sleepy.

"I was sitting at the end of the big brass bedstead, playing with the ornamental knobs, and looking out of the window, when I was aware of a scratching noise, and an enormous black dog had walked from the direction of the fireplace to my left. It passed round the end of the bed, towards the door.

"As the dog passed between me and the window, it swung its head round to stare at me - it had very large, very red eyes, which glowed from inside as if lit up, and as it looked at me I was quite terrified, and very much aware of the creature's breath, which was warm and as strong as a gust of wind.

"The animal must have been very tall, as I was sitting on the old-fashioned bedstead, which was quite high, and our eyes were level. Funnily enough, by the time it reached the door, it had vanished. I assure you that I was wide awake at the time, and sat on for quite some long while wondering about what I had seen, and to be truthful, too scared to get into bed, under the clothes and go to sleep.

"I clearly remember my mother and our host, sitting in the garden in the late sun, talking, and hearing the ringing of the bell on the weekly fried-fish van from Binningham, as it went through the village! I am sure I was not dreaming, and have never forgotten the experience, remembering to the last detail how I felt, what the dog looked like, etc."

ADDITIONAL OBSERVATIONS OF THE BLACK DOG VARIETY

Commenting on the above, Jon Downes says:

"Events like this one are particularly interesting to the fortean investigator - primarily because they seem to provide supportive evidence for the theory that these `creatures` are, in fact, independent entities rather than hallucinations or delusions (caused, it has been suggested, by the witness having prior or preconceived knowledge of the folklore surrounding such `creatures.' In the case of a small child, however, this is almost certainly impossible.

"In East Anglia, there have been sightings of the local Devil Dog, known as *Black Shuck* for centuries. Unlike their counterparts elsewhere in Britain, these 'creatures' are often perceived as being particularly malevolent, and are often described as being physical manifestations of the Devil.

"The black dog which attacked Bungay Church in Suffolk in August 1577, for example, and which left several members of the congregation dead (and tell-tale demonic claw marks which can still be clearly seen on the wooden door of the church), is often considered to be one of these earthly visitations by the Lord of Darkness.

"None of the sightings of Black Shuck during the Second World War are as terrifying as the events chronicled in the previous paragraph, but they do tell us a great deal about the human psyche."

Downes cites the words of author and researcher, Graham McEwan:

"A curious case occurred at Hilly in Norfolk in 1945 when a man heard, but did not see, what he thought was Black Shuck. He became aware of a faint howling which slowly became louder, until it was 'ear-splitting.' It was accompanied by the sound of a chain being dragged along the road. The man, now quite frightened, broke into a run, slowing down as the howling died away. The witness later wrote: 'I later realized that this was the first time I had been afraid of a dog, my hair was standing on end, but why I could not understand . . . . I love dogs and have never been afraid of the fiercest in my life.'"

"...the airman saw a huge black beast..."

"Probably the most terrifying wartime encounter with Black Shuck," says Downes, "is this tantalizingly brief account from Nigel Blundell who wrote: 'Maybe it was Black Shuck who terrified a young American airman and his wife in the early years of the last war. They were staying in a flat-topped hut on the edge of Walberswick Marsh, Suffolk. One stormy evening they heard a pounding on the door. Looking out of the window, the airman saw a huge black beast battering itself against their temporary home. The couple pushed furniture against the door and cowered in terror as the assault went on, the beast hammering against each wall in turn, then leaping on to the roof. After some hours, the noise died away, but the couple could not sleep. At first light, they ventured cautiously outside to inspect the damage. But there was no sign of the attack, and no paw or claw marks in the mud. A similar black dog - the Mauthe or Moddey Dhoo - used to haunt Peel Castle on the Isle of Man. Soldiers on guard duty refused to patrol the ramparts alone. One boastful sentry who did so was found gibbering insanely and died three days later.'"

DOWNES' THOUGHTS ON THE BLACK DOG

Summing up, Jon Downes offers the following, thought-provoking words on the specific nature of the beast under our monstrous microscope:

"One peculiar thing about quasi-fortean phenomena is that they appear to happen in cycles. For example, during the eighteenth and nineteenth centuries there were a large number of reports of living frogs and toads found apparently entombed in solid rock. These phenomena seem to have died out during more recent times, and have been replaced within the pantheon of contemporary forteana by such phenomena as crop circles and sightings of the infamous, black, flying triangles.

"Black Dog sightings have followed a similar pattern. Whereas they have been reported intermittently throughout history, sightings began to tail off in the late nineteenth century. In the interests of brevity, we have only recounted a few of the accounts from the period that are on our files; but the fact that, as we have seen, there was a minor resurgence of them during the years when Europe was at war, is, we feel, somewhat interesting."

Downes closes as follows: "It is also interesting to note that whilst there have been postwar Black Dog sightings across Britain, these have been very few and far between, and it does seem as if our forefathers, who drew an arcane parallel between sightings of `The Wild Hunt` and imminent war and catastrophe, knew more about the nature of reality than we do."

Mark North, black dog authority.
Copyright Nick Redfern.

A CANADIAN CONNECTION

In 2007 the British Center for Fortean Zoology published an updated and revised edition of Mark North's acclaimed book, *Dark Dorset*, which detailed the many and varied mysteries of his home-county of Dorset, England. Around the time of the book's publication, I flew over to England and spoke with Mark about his thoughts on the black dog conundrum, and he told me:

"There are a lot of stories in there about the phantom black dogs. I've done a lot of investigations into the stories and myths around black dog tales. If you go back to the older tradition of black dogs, I think a lot of it could have been invented. On the Dorset coast, for example, there was a very big smuggling trade going on centuries ago. I think a lot of the stories of these animals were invented to frighten people and keep them away from the smuggling areas.

"What was also happening around this time is that Dorset had a lot of connections with Newfoundland and they used to do a lot of trading with the fishermen there. It was around this time that the Newfoundland dogs were brought over here, to this country.

"So, you have a new type of dog being brought over here, which was very large and that no one had ever seen before, and then you have these tales of large black dogs roaming around, and smugglers inventing these black dog tales. So, I think it could be that part of the story at least is that the Black Dog legends have their origins in these large, working black dogs brought over from Newfoundland."

Was it possible that Britain's entire mythology of ghostly black dogs was based solely upon the tall-tales of smugglers? Both Mark and I considered such an all-encompassing possibility to be highly unlikely, given the fact that sightings of such nightmarish beasts had been made all across the British Isles, and long before the smugglers of Dorset were up to their tricks.

In all likelihood, we concluded, those same smugglers had merely modified for their own ends already-existing black dog legends – something which worked even better for them with the introduction to the British Isles of the gigantic Newfoundland hound, which is indeed a formidable-looking animal. Ironically, however, the Newfoundland is actually a gentle animal noted particularly for its love of people.

And as Mark also told me: "Back in the 1600s and 1700s, when many of these stories started, people were very superstitious. Back then, it was a completely different world. And that's what I like about it: it was very innocent in some ways. You've got this superstition of these black dogs there that turn everything around and it made it a completely different world. You could go into some of the old woods, and on the moors, and it would have been like being in a different world, where anything might have happened."

Thus, in Mark's view, there is a very real black dog mystery, but it was one that had been ingeniously exploited by smugglers to scare people away from their plundered hoards – no wonder, then, that the mystery is steeped in both confusion and controversy!

NEWFOUNDLAND OR NIGHTMARE

On June 9, 2007, Martin Whitley, a professional falconer, born and bred in the county of Devon, contacted the research organization *Big Cats in Britain* with the following story: "I was flying a hawk on Dartmoor with some American clients, when one of them pointed out this creature. It was walking along a path about 200 yards away from us. It was black and gray and comparable in size to a miniature pony.

"It had very thick shoulders, a long, thick tail with a blunt end, and small round ears. Its movement appeared feline; then 'bear-like' sprang to mind. There was a party climbing on the Tor opposite, making a racket, but this it ignored completely."

Big-cat researcher Merrily Harpur noted: "Martin's American clients took a series of photos. They show the Dartmoor landscape, the school party on the Tor, and in the middle distance an animal which seems to change shape in each frame, from cat, to bear, to pony, to boar, to various breeds of dog."

Martin was adamant that the animal was no dog: "I have worked with dogs all my life and it was definitely not canine. I have also seen a collie-sized black cat in the area, about ten years ago, and it was not that – this was a lot bigger."

Not everyone was in agreement, however. Shortly after the photographs were provided to *Big Cats in Britain*, copies were also sent to Jon Downes – the Director of the Devonshire-based Center for Fortean Zoology - who confided in me by telephone late one night that, despite the admittedly odd fact that the creature in the pictures did appear to change in shape from shot to shot, he was convinced that it was nothing stranger than a large dog of physical, rather than paranormal, origins; and suggested that the "morphing" effects were merely a byproduct of the camera's technical limitations.

Jon was not alone in his opinion. Perhaps inevitably, Britain's media soon latched onto the story. And they soon claimed the answer to the puzzle, too. The *Daily Mail*, in an article titled *That's not the Beast of Dartmoor...it's my pet dog*, revealed that they had spoken with a woman named Lucinda Reid, who lived close to the area, and who was convinced that the photos provided by Martin Whitley actually showed her two-year-old, 168-pound Newfoundland dog, Troy! Certainly, Newfoundlands are huge beasts and can look both imposing and terrifying to the untrained eye. Lucinda told the newspaper:

"I was in stitches when I read that someone thought Troy was the Beast of Dartmoor. I spotted that it was him right away – you can tell by the shape and the way he is walking. We go up to that spot on Dartmoor all the time. It is only ten minutes away from our home and Troy loves to run about there. A lot of people don't have a clue what he is, because he's so big."

Lucinda continued: "Troy frightens the life out of everyone because of his size and he doesn't look like a dog from a distance. He sometimes disappears off round the rocks on his own, and that's when he must have been photographed. But Troy is certainly nothing to be afraid of, he's a big softie. So, if anyone else sees him on the moor – there's no need to panic."

But, given that the locale was none other than definitive black dog territory – namely, Dartmoor - was the hunting ground of the devilish black hounds of centuries-past, the theory persisted that Troy was not the culprit, after all. The legend, almost inevitably, lived on.

Now, with the cases addressed, let's take a look at the theories that have been advanced to explain the presence of these unearthly creatures in our midst.

"...the guardians of the road to hell..."

In his definitive book on the subject *Explore Phantom Black Dogs*, author and researcher Bob Trubshaw wrote thus:

"The folklore of phantom black dogs is known throughout the British Isles. From the Black Shuck of East Anglia to the Mauthe Dhoog of the Isle of Man, there are tales of huge spectral hounds 'darker than the night sky' with eyes 'glowing red as burning coals.' The phantom black dog of British and Irish folklore, which often forewarns of death, is part of a worldwide belief that dogs are sensitive to spirits and the approach of death, and keep watch over the dead and dying. North European and Scandinavian myths dating back to the Iron Age depict dogs as corpse eaters and the guardians of the roads to hell. Medieval folklore includes a variety of 'Devil dogs' and spectral hounds."

FROM MAN TO BEAST

Dr. Dave Clarke, a long-time Fortean, who has a PhD in folklore, says: "One enduring folk belief is that human beings, as well as devils, witches and fairies, could shape-shift and appear in animal form. This type of story appears in trial records, pamphlets and folklore throughout the middle ages where animal familiars are identified with the devil. Earlier accounts lack the preoccupation with demonic creatures. An early list of shape-shifting apparitions was prepared by a Cistercian monk in North Yorkshire around 1400. It contains accounts of ghosts changing forms from human to crow, dog, goat, horse and even a haystack. These are described as human souls trapped in purgatory, appealing for help from the living to escape their predicament."

"...their spirits take permanently the form of animals..."

Elliott O'Donnell was the author of numerous classic titles on all manner of mysteries, but it is his 1912 book, *Werewolves*, that has a bearing upon the very matters under the microscope – namely, the black dogs of Britain.

O'Donnell presented a fascinating body of data in his near-legendary book, which is essential reading for anyone wishing to acquaint themselves with hard-to-find data on all manner of strange beast, including black dogs, and not solely the werewolves of the book's title. Nevertheless, O'Donnell's words are deeply applicable to this particular debate concerning the real nature of the British black dog.

He wrote: "It is an old belief that the souls of cataleptic and epileptic people, during the body's unconsciousness, adjourned temporarily to animals, and it is therefore only in keeping with such a view to suggest that on the deaths of such people their spirits take permanently the form of animals. This would account for the fact that places where cataleptics and idiots have died are often haunted by semi and by wholly animal types of phantasms."

O'Donnell's words relative to "idiots" and "such people" might not be perceived by the tedious politically-correct brigade of today as being particularly heart-warming, but they do, without doubt, offer a theory that is fascinating to muse upon. And, there are other parallels, too, that can be found in folklore. They also deal with the matter of man becoming terrible animal when physical life ends, and at which point a new life - and a highly strange life, I might add - duly begins.

THE DOGMEN OF NEWGATE

Bob Trubshaw notes: "Newgate Gaol was the scene of a haunting by 'a walking spirit in the likeness of a black dog.'" So the story went, says Bob, "Luke Hutton, a criminal executed at York in the late 1590s, left behind an account of the phantom hound. Published as a pamphlet in 1612, *The Discovery of a London Monster, called the black dog of Newgate* suggested the dog was the ghost of a scholar imprisoned in Newgate who had been killed and eaten by starving inmates."

A BROTHERLY BLACK DOG

Then there is the very weird tale of William and David Sutor. The dark saga all began late one night in December 1728, when William, a Scottish farmer, was hard at work in his fields and heard an unearthly shriek that was accompanied by the briefest of glimpses of a large, horrific-looking, dark-coloured dog. And on several more occasions in both 1729 and 1730, the dog returned, always seemingly intent on plaguing the Sutor family.

It was in late November of 1730, however, that the affair ultimately reached its apex. Once again the mysterious hound manifested before the farmer, but this time, incredibly, it was supposedly heard to speak in English, and uttered the following, concise words: "Come to the spot of ground within half an hour."

The shocked William did so; and there waiting for him was the spectral animal.

"In the name of God and Jesus Christ, what are you that troubles me?" pleaded the terrified William. The hound answered that he was none other than David Sutor – William's brother - and that he had killed a man at that very spot some thirty-five years earlier.

William cried: "David Sutor was a man and you appear as a dog."

To which the hound replied: "I killed him with a dog; therefore I am made to appear as a dog, and I tell you to go bury these bones."

Finally on December 3, and after much frantic searching and digging, the bones of the murdered man *were* finally found at the spot in question, and were duly given a respectful, Christian burial within the confines of the old Blair Churchyard. The dog – David Sutor in animalistic, spectral form, legend maintains – vanished, and was reportedly never seen again.

"...man has in him two spirits – an animal spirit and a human spirit..."

The last missive on this admittedly highly controversial aspect of the British Bigfoot controversy goes to Elliott O'Donnell:

"According to Paracelsus, Man has in him two spirits – an animal spirit and a human spirit – and that in after life he appears in the shape of whichever of these two spirits he has allowed to dominate him. If, for example, he has obeyed the spirit that prompts him to be sober and temperate, then his phantasm resembles a man; but on the other hand, if he has given way to his carnal and bestial cravings, then his phantasm is earthbound, in the guise of some terrifying and repellent animal."

While O'Donnell's words were meant as a collective warning to his many and faithful readers, frankly, the latter sounds far more appealing and adventurous than does coming back as some chain-rattling spectre of human proportions. Give me terrifying and repellent, rather than sober and temperate, any day of the week!

OVERSEAS PARALLELS

And now we turn our attentions to the work of Simon Burchell, the author of *Phantom Black Dogs in Latin America*. Running at 38 pages, it is obviously very much a booklet rather than a full-length book. But that doesn't detract from the most important thing of all: its pages are packed with case after case, each offering the reader little-known and seldom-seen information on the definitive Latin American cousin to Britain's more famous counterpart.

And the reason I reference Burchell's title is because his observations on the beast may very possibly offer us more than a few answers to our questions concerning its British cousin.

What impresses and intrigues me most of all about Burchell's publication is the truly startling wealth of similarities between those creatures seen centuries ago in England, and those reported throughout Latin America in the last 100 years: namely:

• the diabolical, glowing eyes;

• the association that the phantom hound has with life after death;

• how seeing the beast may be a precursor to doom and tragedy;

• its occasional helpful and guiding qualities;

• the fact that the animal is usually witnessed in the vicinity of bridges, crossroads, and cemeteries – which are classic locales where paranormal activity occurs time and time again; its ability to shape-shift and change in size;

• and not forgetting the most important thing, of course: namely, its perceived paranormal origins.

Burchell also reveals how the legends of the phantom black dog of some Latin American nations – such as Guatemala – have been exploited by those with draconian and outdated morals. For example, there are widespread tales of people that enjoy having a drink or several incurring the dire wrath of the phantom black dog – which, as Burchell says: "...was certainly popularized by the Catholic Church which used this legend and others as moralizing tales."

Winged hounds – whose appearances and activities smack strongly of the modern day Chupacabras of Puerto Rico and UFO lore – are discussed; as are copious amounts of data that make a link with tales of a truly dark and satanic nature.

Burchell also reveals intriguing data suggesting that at least some tales of the black dog might be based upon cultural memories and stories of very real, large and ferocious hounds brought to the New World by the Conquistadors centuries ago – "savage and ferocious dogs to kill and tear apart the Indians."

That said, however, it is clear that the overwhelming majority of reports of the phantom black dog in Latin America parallel those of Britain to a truly striking, eerie and extraordinary degree – in the sense that they appear to be something other than flesh-and-blood entities.

A Brit, Burchell lived in the highlands of western Guatemala for three years, and knows his stuff. And his is a great little publication written by someone with a passion not just for his subject matter, but for the cultures and countries that appear within its pages.

As Burchell states:

"Although the Black Dog may appear at first glance to be a British or north European phenomenon, it exists in essentially the same form across the entire length and breadth of the Americas. Much has been written upon the presumed Germanic, Celtic or Indio-European origin of the legend but such an origin would not explain how a highland Maya girl can meet a shape-shifting Black Dog at a Guatemalan crossroads. It appears that the Black Dog, much like the poltergeist, is a global phenomenon."

CONCLUSIONS

And there we have it: a tale of a monstrous entity – the fiery eyed black dog – that is equal parts macabre, mystifying, bizarre, terrifying, supernatural, paranormal, eerie and even devilish. As for its origins: well, it seems that the beast – in some fashion, at least – is linked to death, looming death, tragedy, disaster and negativity.

In other words, it's a not a creature with which you particularly want to cross paths. And those origins are clearly most ancient in nature, dating back to the Middle-Ages and possibly even much earlier than that. And that sightings of the hounds of horror extend to the present day and are even celebrated - such as by the people of Bungay, Suffolk – demonstrates the sheer, overwhelming power and allure that the black dog still holds over the people of Britain.

And, as a result of a very curious set of circumstances, theories, sightings, tales and more, the very existence and legend of Britain's black dog directly set in motion the wheels that led Sir Arthur Conan Doyle to write one of the most famous and loved novels of all time: *The Hound of the Baskervilles.*

Regardless of the precise nature and intent of the legendary beast, I say: long-live the spectral black-dog of the British Isles. And long-live *The Hound of the Baskervilles*, which, without its real-life counterpart, would never, ever, have seen the light of day.

Thus, in a very strange and decidedly roundabout fashion, each and every one of us who love Sir Arthur Conan Doyle's adventures of Sherlock Holmes and Dr. Watson have a monstrous beast to thank for one of the world's most famous literary classics! It doesn't get much stranger than that!

REFERENCES:

- *Explore Phantom Black Dogs*, Bob Trubshaw (Editor), Heart of Albion Press, 2005.
- *Dartmoor Mystery Beast*, Merrily Harpur, www.forteantimes.com, August 6, 2007.
- *That's not the Beast of Dartmoor…it's my Pet Dog*, *Daily Mail*, August 3, 2007.
- *The Hunter with the Stony Visage*, www.bbc.co.uk, October 27, 2005.
- *The Dark Huntsman* and *Wistman's Wood*, www.legendarydartmoor.co.uk.
- *The Hound of the Baskervilles: Hunting the Dartmoor Legend*, Philip Weller, Halsgrove, 2001.
- *Dark Dorset*, Mark J. North & Robert J. Newland, CFZ Press 2007.
- *There's something in the Woods*, Nick Redfern, Anomalist Books, 2008.
- *Monster Hunter*, Jonathan Downes, CFZ Press, 2004.
- *Wildman*, Nick Redfern, CFZ Press, 2012.
- *The Mystery Animals of the British Isles: Staffordshire*, Nick Redfern, CFZ Press, 2012.
- *The Mystery Animals of the British Isles: London*, Neil Arnold, CFZ Press, 2011.
- *The Mystery Animals of the British Isles: Kent*, Neil Arnold, CFZ Press, 2009.
- *Phantom Black Dogs in Latin America*, Simon Burchell, Heart of Albion Press, ??
- *Animal Ghosts: Or Animal Hauntings and the Hereafter*, Elliott

O'Donnell, Kessinger Publishing, 2003.

- *Mystery Animals of Britain and Ireland*, Graham McEwan, Robert Hale Ltd., London 1987.

- *Werewolves*, Elliott O'Donnell, Kessinger Publishing, 2003.

- *Strange Staffs*, Tim Prevett, *Paranormal Magazine*, February 2009.

- *In Search of Herne the Hunter*, Eric L. Fitch, Capall Bann Publishing, 1994.

- *The World's Greatest Ghosts*, Roger Boar and Nigel Blundell, Reed International Books, Ltd., 1994.

BIG BLACK DOGS AND PHANTOM HOUNDS IN AMERICA
By Andrew Gable

PART ONE: MARYLAND AND DELAWARE

Legends of black dogs and phantom hounds are widespread throughout the Chesapeake Bay region, which was one of the earliest areas settled by the English. The tales of British black dogs were combined with werewolf traditions and typical ghost stories, as well as possibly with cryptozoological sightings of weird creatures, to create traditions that are like the British ones, and yet unlike them at the same time.

BLACK DOGS OF WARFIELDSBURG

The tiny village of Warfieldsburg in Carroll County is haunted by a black dog.

The tales of Snarly Yow were enough to scare the daylights out of any believer.

Recounted by Maryland folklorists Annie W. Whitney and Caroline C. Bullock is the story of two men who were riding along near the Ore Mine Bridge at dusk around 1887. They saw a large black dog which passed through a fence, crossed the road, and passed through another fence. Whitney and Bullock also recount the tale of a man who stood under a tree near a bridge, possibly the Ore Mine Bridge, because he was told a phantom black dog would come by. The dog appeared, and according to him the dog followed him for a brief time before vanishing. Yet another instance was of a man who saw a black dog dragging a length of chain. This black dog can apparently never appear more than once to the same person, and it is said that the crack of a whip near it will cause it to vanish. In some variants of the story, the dog is the phantom of Leigh Masters, a notorious Carroll County landowner who was supposedly quite cruel. Masters is also associated with the haunting of Avondale, his manor house.

There was a case in 1975 in which a group of motorists supposedly struck a large black dog standing on a road near Warfieldsburg. They felt the impact of the strike and felt the animal under the wheels, but when the car passed by the black dog was standing in the road, baring its teeth at them before vanishing.

BLUE DOG OF ROSE HILL

Perhaps the oldest ghost story of Maryland is that of the Blue Dog of Rose Hill. Near the town of Port Tobacco (Charles County) is a rock covered in reddish discolorations. Called the "Peddler's Rock," it supposedly marks the spot where a trader was killed at some point in the latter part of the 1700s. In true ghost story fashion, there are many variants of the tale. Some have it that the body was found lying on the rock, some that the body was buried. Some have it that the victim was not a trader, but a returning Civil War soldier. In any case, the man's money was left behind, and his dog - a great blue-tinged mastiff, almost black - was killed during the murder. After the crime, the men returned to seize the treasure and were warded off by howling and then charged by a large, luminous dog.

During the Civil War, men under the command of General Joseph Hooker supposedly tried to retrieve the peddler's treasure but were, like the murderers, frightened away by howling and the approach of a large hound. I don't know of any confirmation of this story, but in the early 1860s General Hooker was, indeed, engaged in maneuvers around Washington, D.C. (The number of camp followers attached to Hooker's army, by the way, were the source of hooker, a common slang term for prostitute). As recently as February of 1971, locals claimed to hear the howling of the dog coming from the vicinity of the Rock.

Many of the dog-beasts were said to be able to stand erect and rip the throats out of human victims.

It could be just another variant of an urban legend or a wholly separate story, but the city Frederick (Frederick County) has its own Blue Dog of Rose Hill. The grounds of Rose Hill Manor off Route 355 in the northern part of the city are also haunted by a phantom blue dog. This blue dog was the pet of a previous owner of the manor. The owner had buried treasure "six feet from the old oak tree" on the property. The ghostly dog appears at midnight, wanders the grounds, and vanishes as mysteriously as it appeared. Now-deceased Maryland researcher Mark Chorvinsky of "Strange Magazine" investigated the tales of the Frederick Blue Dog.

SNARLY YOW

"Snarly Yow" is the name given to a phantom hound which haunted a section of the National Pike near Turner's Gap (Frederick County). The hound was first mentioned by Madeleine V. Dahlgren in 1882. Her book, "South Mountain Magic," details no less than a dozen sightings of the beast. One account is from a Daniel Mesick, whose father kicked at a huge dog near Dame's Quarter. His foot passed directly through it. Sticks, rocks and even bullets were recorded as having passed through the beast in Dahlgren's accounts. Other accounts have stated that the dog left physical traces and frightened horses to the extent that they threw their riders. The dog was seen numerous times by a minister at a small church in Glendale. A staple of Frederick County legendry for years, the Yow was seen in 1962 near Zittlestown. In this instance, it was headless, white, and dragged a chain along behind it.

The South Mountain area is also the traditional home of a number of werewolves.

FENCE RAIL DOG

The Fence Rail Dog is an enormous hound, nearly ten feet in length, which haunts a stretch of Route 12 near Frederica in Delaware. Mentioned by Charles J. Adams III, a Pennsylvania-based author on paranormal topics, the dog appears in the wake of automobile accidents on the road. Not much information is at hand, but as folklore from around the globe speaks of dogs as a sort of psychopomp – or spirits which guide the dead to the afterlife – its appearance in the wake of death may be an example of this.

RED DOG FOX

The Brandywine Creek State Park in northern Delaware near Wilmington is home to appearances of a large dog or fox which is often seen to rise up into the apparition of Gil Thoreau, an outdoorsman. Once again, not much information is known on this creature.

BULLBEGGER CREEK

It isn't technically in Maryland or Delaware, but in the northern portion of the small finger of Virginia on the Delmarva Peninsula is a feature called Bullbegger Creek. There is also a nearby village called Bullbegger. British readers will be familiar with the term, which refers to a phantom or goblin that haunted several regions across the isle. Traditions do exist in Virginia of free-roaming humanoid phantoms which change into black dogs, but I can't place those traditions geographically and can't say definitively whether this accounts for Bullbegger Creek's name. It is certainly an odd name, however! I wouldn't doubt there are some sorts of traditions are around there.

As can be seen from the above cases, the phantom hounds found in this region of the eastern United States are both similar to, and different from, the British cases. Chain-dragging seems to be a fairly common feature of the accounts, as it is in the cases of the Gytrash and other English hounds. Only the dog haunting Warfieldsburg is reputed to follow individuals as is common in the British lore. Another common feature of the stories (also common to Pennsylvania lore, as will be discussed later) is a clearly phantasmal nature, and in several of the instances the dog is clearly defined as the phantom of a specific individual.

An interesting facet of the case is that the dog traditions seemed to, for the most part, die off in the 1970s, the late 1960s and 1970s being the timeframe that Bigfoot sightings began in earnest in Maryland. Also interesting is that some sightings, particularly of Frederick County's "Dwayyo" in 1973, do have a rather canine cast to their features. One wonders whether some of what are reported as Bigfoot sightings are actually sightings of black dogs

PART TWO: PENNSYLVANIA
ADAMSTOWN BLACK DOG

In the northern corner of Lancaster County lies the small burg of Adamstown. The town is haunted by no less than four separate phantoms – two female ghosts called the White Lady and the Black Lady, a headless swine, and, most relevant to this volume, a small black dog which appears seemingly at random. The dog follows pedestrians and then vanishes as mysteriously as it appeared.

HANS GRAF CEMETERY

A prominent urban legend in Lancaster County circles around a cemetery on the outskirts of Marietta, near the tiny village of Rowenna. Properly called the Shock Cemetery (a name infamous in black dog circles in its own right), and also known at times as the Wildcat Cemetery, the burying ground is called the Hans Graf Cemetery in most parlance. While the graveyard doesn't hold the grave of Hans Graf, one of the earliest settlers of Lancaster County (a popular misconception), the name is inspired by a plaque on the surrounding wall which states that "Within this God's acre rest the descendants of Hans Graf." The cemetery is actually far from an "acre" - it's barely as big as my living room. Bizarrely, the cemetery has no gate or other entry - it is bounded by an unbroken stone wall roughly three feet high.

This tale has been a particular passion of mine for some years. Stories I've heard associated with the cemetery include mysterious lights within its bounds, winds with little to no apparent origin, that walking the walls seven times by the light of a full moon will cause death, and that walking the walls backwards thirteen times summons some manner of ghoul. The most common tales, however, are those of a phantasmal white dog which haunts its grounds. Many are the tales of people who've heard a barking dog as they approach or enter the cemetery. The spot is a favorite one for local paranormal investigators, and several have received EVP voices from the cemetery. One investigator has seen a white dog or wolf appear and vanish within the grounds.

On the trip I made to the cemetery, I noted that though the cemetery as a whole was disgustingly overgrown, there was a roughly man-sized spot in the corner bare of vegetation. The spot was also present on several subsequent trips I made. I vaguely seem to recall something about a spot where nothing would grow in the version of the tale I heard - but as that was years ago, I can't swear to it. As I first approached the walls, I did indeed hear a dog barking. Although my dog was in the car, I'm certain that's not

It is not uncommon to hear tales of shapeshifting from demon dog to full-fledged werewolf.

what this was. I found some graffiti on the back wall which may have been simply that, but which appeared to be some runic lettering in the Futhark language as well. I personally saw or experienced nothing, but back in the car my dog was apparently reacting to something, frantically jumping back and forth and finally cowering in the back seat.

MR. ETLINGER AND MR. ELLINGER

In 1909, Pennsylvania folklorist Henry W. Shoemaker penned "The Black Wolf of Oak Valley." In this story, an outlaw by the name of Silas Werninger was cornered in his home, but committed suicide rather than be captured by his pursuers. He was buried in the forest near his home, and after his death a large black wolf emerged from the grove and menaced townspeople. A witch advised the people to dig up Werninger's remains and bury them in consecrated ground in order to dispel the phantasmal wolf.

This tale was a thinly-veiled reference to real events which took place in Centre County, Pennsylvania, in 1896. The true name of the outlaw was William Etlinger, and he was indeed cornered in his cabin near the town of Woodward after taking his wife and children hostage. Etlinger committed suicide amidst the wreckage of his home, which was burnt by authorities in an effort to flush him out. He was, indeed, buried in the mountain forests near his burnt cabin as nobody would claim the body for burial; and his body has, indeed, been removed from its wooded grave to the town cemetery.

Although there are ghostly legends associated with the Etlinger debacle, they seem to involve the appearance of a phantasmal cabin on the burnt foundations where his once stood. So how did the black dog become associated with the legend? For one thing, northern Pennsylvania and more specifically the exact region where these events happened has historically had a population of troublesome black wolves. It isn't inconceivable that a black wolf loitered around Etlinger's grave in order to get itself a free meal and that this was the reason the body was moved.

A more intriguing possibility is provided by no less than the governor of Pennsylvania in the early years of the 20th Century, Samuel Pennypacker. Pennypacker was a tireless researcher into the folklore of the area where he resided - near Schwenksville in Montgomery County. Writing in 1907, the governor uncovered tales of the local ne'er-do-wells, the Ellingers. The Ellingers, he discovered, were originally blacksmiths (William Etlinger was also a blacksmith, according to some contemporary news accounts), but went on to operate a tavern along the Skippack Pike where they robbed and murdered a number of travelers. The creek-side forests near the Ellinger tavern were the haunt of many a phantom for years afterward, ranging from headless horses and calves to ghostly fireballs and skeletal shepherds.

There were also tales of white demonic dogs associated with the Ellinger ruins. Around 1890, a man named Frank Ziegler was riding on the road near the ruins of the tavern when his horse froze in fear. From out of the ruins came a massive white dog which gradually dissolved into shadow. In 1896 Henry Wireman encountered a monstrous phantom "with eyes as large as plates" near the ruins - although it isn't specified whether this was caniform, the dinner-plate eyes are certainly a feature of many black dog reports.

Another man - Henry Landis, a principal at a Philadelphia school - recounted how his horse froze near the tavern immediately before the appearance of another white dog, which on this occasion reared onto its hind legs and snapped at the horse. As Landis frantically rode off, he glanced back to see the still-bipedal dog gradually fade away as it did on the previous occasion.

As both a folklorist and a contemporary, it seems highly likely that Pennypacker and Shoemaker would have communicated. I find myself wondering whether Pennypacker mentioned these legends to Shoemaker - and whether he, in turn, vaguely remembered the stories of blacksmiths named Ellinger as he wrote the tale and remembered it as stories about a blacksmith named Etlinger.

DEATH RODE A PALE...WOLF?

In his "*American Myths & Legends*," folklorist Charles Skinner recounted a tale from Warren County (not Venango, as the title of the tale implies). A huge white wolf lived on the Cornplanter Reservation (now inundated beneath the waters of Lake Kinzua), and was associated in particular with the Jacobs clan of Native American huntsmen. Sightings of the wolf were thought to be a sure sign of misfortune to follow. A group of hunters caught wind of the stories and took to the chase – during this hunt, Jim Jacobs, patriarch of the clan, encountered the white wolf and was killed in an accident a short time later (this detail likely dates the story to the late 1870s, as Jim Jacobs – who definitely was a real figure – was killed by a train in 1880). At the conclusion of this hunt, however, the white wolf plunged over a gorge to elude capture and vanished in mid-air. A record-sized wolf was, indeed, killed on the Cornplanter Reservation in the late 1870s; also, a popular tale associated with Jim Jacobs claims that he killed a huge wolf in a snowstorm when only a child – the white wolf could have been the phantom of that one.

THE DOGS OF LOCK HAVEN

An urban legend circulating among the students of Lock Haven University and the townsfolk concerns a large hilltop cemetery near the grounds of the college. Said to be used for Satanic rites (but then, according to legend, what cemetery isn't?) and also in the vicinity of several Indian burial grounds, according to a 2009 *"Lock Haven Express"* article, the cemetery is reputedly haunted by a number of black canine forms, which are usually concentrated near a certain mausoleum in a back corner. Sloan Hall, the section of the university nearest the haunted cemetery, is in turn haunted by several phantoms. One of these is an eerie and mobile black mist, which may have some sort of connection to the dogs.

THE HELL HOUND TOLD YOU NOT TO!

In his pioneering book *Lo!* (1931), Charles Fort mentioned the tale of a talking dog. The actual tale, mentioned in a Pittsburgh newspaper, was far more sinister than Fort's humorous recounting made it seem: a small dog walked in front of two men and greeted them with a rather cheerful "Good morning!" But then the dog made a second utterance, "I speak for myself," and walked on. One of the men lunged to grab the dog, which moved out of his way and said, "Don't touch me." The man didn't listen, and severely scorched his hand when it made contact with the conversant canine.

THE WEREWOLF AND MS. PAUL

May Paul, who lived on her family's farm along the Schwaben Creek in Northumberland County, gradually befriended an old hermit. The old man often came and sat on a log, watching her herd her family's sheep. The other wolves in the area were frightened off by the mere sight of the old man. One night (in the 1850s or thereabouts) a local farmer shot a huge gray wolf, which he then tracked to a hut where he discovered said hermit dying of a gunshot wound. The Pauls later claimed that in subsequent years, their sheep were never the targets of wolf attacks, even though neighbors lost their livestock to the carnivores. Was the spirit of the werewolf protecting the flock even after his death? The area of the Paul's farm is now called *Wolfmannsgrob* – "the wolfman's grave."

THE WHITE WOLF OF SUGAR VALLEY

Henry W. Shoemaker recounts the story of a huge white wolf seen in this region of Clinton County near Loganton. First encountered by Philip Shreckengast, the white wolf killed livestock and generally made itself a nuisance. The people of Sugar Valley sought the aid of Granny McGill, a witch, who suggested that a black lamb, born under a new moon in the autumn, be tied near a trap. The plan worked and the wolf was captured. John Schrack of Carroll had the pelt, which had shaggy hair like a sheep or goat rather than the short hair of a wolf (I am endeavoring to determine whether this pelt is still in existence). The head of the wolf was reputed to keep wolves away from Jacob Rishel's sheep paddock, to flash green light from its eyes at night and to move its jaws.

WAYNE SPOOK WOLF

In his 1920s book on the lore of the wolf in Pennsylvania, Henry W. Shoemaker recounts the tale of George Wilson of Wayne Township, Clinton County, who long believed a neighbor of his was a werewolf. He shot a large brownish wolf in the foreleg with a silver bullet one night, and soon afterwards the suspected witch was found to have a broken arm. Then, a few years later, Wilson again shot a werewolf when a three-legged wolf was found on his property. I'm personally uncertain whether Shoemaker meant that it was completely missing a leg (three-legged animals in general were held to be portents of evil among the forests of Pennsylvania), or whether a lame animal was meant, thereby implying it was the same wolf previously shot.

The weird world of the strange has a contented home at the Albany Rural Cemetary.

CHARLES FORT LIES BURIED NEARBY – THE RED-EYED HOUNDS OF ALBANY'S RURAL CEMETERY

By Claudia Cunningham – The "MIB Lady"

One cannot help but get the feeling that the spirit of Charles Fort is keeping close tabs on the paranormal events taking place in the Albany Rural Cemetary.
(Photo by Penny Lane)

Tim Beckley must have figured that my favorite Sherlock Holmes tale is "The Hound of the Baskervilles," which I have on an old VHS video tape and have played many times. It's a great story and it parallels so much of the information we have on the sightings of phantom hounds and devil dogs. I am not surprised to learn that in some ways it is based on historical cases of these specters that Sir Arthur Conan Doyle obviously knew about.

I have been friends with Tim now for several years. He calls me "the MIB Lady" because I have collected quite a number of stories about the notorious men-in-black, especially those encounters that have taken place near where I live in upstate New York. We have done several radio talk shows together discussing the matter, including Coast to Coast AM and The Para Cast.

Initially, I told the editor of "The Conspiracy Journal" that I knew of a haunted cemetery where Charles Fort, the great researcher and writer, is buried, along with one of our lesser known presidents, Chester Arthur. It's the Albany Rural Cemetery just outside of the state capitol of New York and as far as I am concerned it's rather spooky.

* * * * *

And perhaps the site where Fort and his entire family are entombed is a fitting locale for dastardly black hounds and phantom dogs from hell to be seen. Fort collected such beastly stories throughout his writing career and placed them in the volumes that make up "The Complete Works Of Charles Fort" (available in a 1000-plus page, 4 volume, large print set available directly from the publisher of this current work).

Often the hounds were found to be hideous killers of farm animals and even household pets that had wandered out upon the moors. As a case in point, let us take these typical examples that have been culled from Fort's intensive studies. Are these references to a phantom hound, or just some annoying "large dog," or something too thorny to contemplate?

In the month of May, 1810, something appeared at Ennerdale, near the border of England and Scotland, and killed sheep, without devouring them, sometimes slaughtering seven or eight of them in a night by biting into the jugular vein and sucking the blood. That's the story. The only mammal that I know of that does something like this is the vampire bat. It has to be accepted that stories of the vampire bat are not myths. Something was ravaging near Ennerdale, and the losses by sheep farmers were so serious that the whole region was aroused. It became a religious duty to hunt this marauder. Once, when hunters rode past a church, out rushed the whole congregation to join them, the vicar throwing off his surplice on his way to a horse. Milking, the cutting of hay, and the feeding of livestock was neglected. For more details, see "*Chambers' Journal*," 81-470. On the 12th of September, someone saw a dog in a cornfield and shot it. It is said that this dog was the marauder, and that with its death the killing of sheep stopped.

For about four months, in the year 1874, beginning on January 8th, a killer was abroad in Ireland. In "*Land and Water*," March 7, 1874, a correspondent writes that he had heard of depredations by a wolf in Ireland, where the last native wolf had been killed in the year 1712. According to him, a killer was running wild in Cavan, slaying as many as 30 sheep in one night. There is another account, in "*Land and Water*," March 28. Here, a correspondent writes that in Cavan sheep had been killed in a way that led to the belief that the marauder was not a dog. This correspondent knew of 42 instances, in three townships, in which sheep had been similarly killed – throats cut and blood sucked, but no flesh eaten. The footprints were like a dog's, but were long and narrow and showed traces of strong claws. Then, in the issue of April 11th of "*Land and Water*," came the news that readers had been expecting. The killer had been shot. It had been shot by Archdeacon Magenniss, at Lismoreville, and was only a large dog.

This announcement ends the coverage in "*Land and Water*." Almost anybody, at least in the distant past, before suspicions regarding conventional journalism had developed to what they are today, who read these accounts down to the final one, would say, "Why, of course! It's the way these stories always end up. Nothing to them."

But it is just the way these stories always end up that has kept me busy. Because of my experiences with the "pseudo-endings" of mysteries, or the mysterious shearing and bobbing and clipping of mysteries, I delved more into this story that was said to be no longer mysterious. The large dog that was shot by the Archdeacon was sacrificed not in vain, if its story shut up the minds of readers of "*Land and Water*," and if it be desirable somewhere to shut up minds upon this earth.

See the "*Clare Journal*," issues up to April 27th: the shooting of the large dog, with no effect upon the depredations; another dog shot; and the relief of the farmers, who believed that this one was the killer; still another dog shot, that again was supposed to be the killer; then the killing of sheep continuing. The depredations were so great as to be described as "terrible losses for poor people." It is not definitively said that something was killing sheep vampirishly, but that "only a piece was bitten off, and no flesh sufficient for a dog ever eaten."

The scene of the killings shifted.

"*Cavan Weekly News*," April 17, reported that near Limerick, more than 100 miles from Cavan, "a wolf or something like it" was killing sheep. The writer says that several persons, alleged to have been bitten by this animal, had been taken to the Ennis Insane Asylum, "laboring under strange symptoms of insanity."

It seems that some of the killings were simultaneous near Cavan and near Limerick. At both places, it was not reported that any animal known to be the killer was shot or identified. Given that these things may or may not be dogs, their disappearances are as mysterious as their appearances.

There was a marauding animal in England toward the end of the year 1905. London's "*Daily Mail*," Nov. 1, 1905, reported "the sheep-slaying mystery of Badminton." It is said that, in the neighborhood of Badminton, on the border between Gloucestershire and Wiltshire, sheep had been killed. Sergeant Carter, of the Gloucestershire Police, is quoted as saying, "I have seen two of the carcasses myself, and can say definitely that it is impossible for it to be the work of a dog. Dogs are not vampires, and do not suck the blood of a sheep, and leave the flesh almost untouched."

And, going over the newspapers, just as we're wondering what's delaying it, here it is:

London's "*Daily Mail*," December 19: "Marauder shot near Hinton." It was a large, black dog.

So then, if in London any interest had been aroused, this announcement stopped it.

We go to newspapers published nearer the scene of the sheep-slaughtering. "*Bristol Mercury*," November 25, reported that the killer was a jackal which had escaped from a menagerie in Gloucester. And that stopped mystification and inquiry, in the minds of readers of the "*Bristol Mercury*."

While no black phantom dogs with glowing red eyes or MIB were seen, researchers Tim Beckley and Claudia Cunningham scope out the area around the gravemarker of Charles Fort searching for anything unusual.

Suspecting that there had been no such escape of a jackal, we go to Gloucester newspapers. In the "*Gloucester Journal*," November 4, in a long account of the depredations, there is no mention of the escape of any animal in Gloucester, nor anywhere else. In following issues, nothing is said of the escape of a jackal, nor of any other animal. So many reports were sent to the editor of this newspaper that he doubted that only one slaughtering thing was abroad. "Some even go so far as to call up the traditions of the werewolf, and superstitious people are inclined to this theory."

We learn that the large, black dog had been shot on December 16th, but that in its region there had been no reported killing of sheep, from about November 25th. The appearance of the data leads to another scene-shifting. Near Gravesend, an unknown animal had, up to December 16th, killed about 30 sheep (London's "*Daily Mail*," December 19). "Small armies" of men went hunting, but the killing stopped, and the unknown animal remained unknown.

I go on with my yarns. I no more believe them than I believe that twice two are four.

* * * * *

I have a friend, Linda, who initially told me all about the Albany Rural Cemetery and the creepy, eerie stories associated with this massive city of the dead. And believe me, there are quite a few of them!

One day Linda was driving along its many twisting and turning roads, passing by large mausoleums and musty crypts. There are a number of historical figures, like mayors and governors, not to mention the man who spent his entire life investigating the strange and unknown.

It was a rather nice day, as Linda spins her account. It was warm and sunny, but there were several shadowy patches she could drive through that emitted a cool breeze of a sort in contrast to the brilliant glare that encompassed her car, blinding her at times.

She went up a hill and around a curve and pulled over to stop. She felt someone was following her. Suddenly, she was astounded to see a massive black SUV, almost military-like, so close behind her it could have parked in her rear seat. The vehicle looked like it had just pulled out of the showroom, it was so neat and polished – just like in the tales "Mothman Prophecies" author John Keel wrote about the vehicles the men-in-black were known to arrive in as they went about their task of silencing UFO witnesses.

Most astonishing of all is the fact that while the roads were paved with gravel she never heard a sound as the strange vehicle pulled up close and eventually passed her. As the SUV crept along, she noticed the windows were completely black and – most fear-provoking of all – it turned down one of the side roads that would take you back to the main entrance to the cemetery . . . only when Linda tried to follow in close pursuit the road ended onto a chain fence which it would have been impossible to drive through.

Later, as she drove by the main office to leave the cemetery, she saw the car parked in the middle of the road as if it were waiting for her. One moment there was a "person" standing next to the vehicle only to vanish – blink out – in her rearview mirror.

Eventually, I did some checking around and found that others had encountered vanishing black cars, more men-in-black and a couple who fly over the headstones at dusk in their pajamas.

This is in addition to the legends of the big black dog that wanders about at night with its blazing red eyes. One couple claims to have heard the clumpity, clump, clump of some heavy animal paws right along the road where my friend Linda says the SUV vanished through a chained off area. They were apparently walking their own dog, possibly a poodle, when they were overcome with fear and concerned for the safety of themselves and their pet and decided to pick up the pace. When they got under what they thought was the safety of some street lights, they turned around and looked into the face of a huge black dog with red eyes – at least they thought it was a dog – and the funny thing is that their own dog merely walked on without reacting to this "monster"-looking beast.

The phantom creature walked really fast, keeping up with the couple as they ran near the gates. As they watched, the dog simply blinked out as if it had never existed. This is a very common urban legend around these parts, but where there is smoke there is usually fire.

PROFESSOR JAVA'S AND MY OTHER DUSTY DOG STORIES

Not too far away is Professor Java's, located in Albany on Wolf Road (is it a coincidence that it is so justifiably located?) where it is said that an Indian woman has been seen floating in through the back door, but quickly disappearing. Bottles have been known to fly off the shelves behind the bar and people have heard a ghost baby crying as well as the sound of a howling dog who seems troubled by something. To confirm these rumors, I went to the restaurant and had dinner there with a girlfriend once and we DID hear a dog barking faintly. I talked with a barmaid to confirm this, and she said the week before the situation was really bad. On one particular night bottles would shatter and fall off the shelves as if being pulled down by an invisible hand.

I have two mysterious ghostly dog stories of my own to contribute to the strange canine legacy. They may not seem so scary, but I can vouch that they are true.

Our dog Napoleon – a mix of Doberman and Lab – died while my grandmother was living with us. My grandmother was very attached to the dog, as we all were. He lived to be 15 years old, but we were still very unhappy about losing him. About a week or so after he passed on, my grandmother had just gotten into bed and had turned the light off. In the dark, she heard Nappy's little chain that he wore around his neck rattling and actually felt the thump-thump-thump-thump of his tail hitting the side of the bed, like he used to do when he was happy to see someone. My grandmother had a history of such paranormal experiences. She said she saw my uncle who died in World War II standing directly in front of her, and even had a sighting of my deceased father shortly after his passing. Naturally, because of her familiarity with the afterlife, I wasn't too surprised to hear that Nappy had paid Gram one last visit.

Also, my mother had a little Yorkie, Jack. I had given her Jack after her little dog Tiffany died. Jack was quite a character, a sprightly and lively Yorkshire Terrier. Everyone was in love with him. My grandmother had died, as did little Tiffany, so I thought Jack would be just the kind of dog to cheer mom up. He was all personality and charm . . . if you can describe a dog that way. My mother was devoted to him. Sadly, he developed diabetes and his last years were spent in agony. He had to be put to sleep. I thought I would lose her because she cried night and day. So I moved mom into my place in Delmar for two years before we moved together back to her home in Glenmont.

My mother was in my guest room asleep one night and she told me the next morning she awoke to see a big black butterfly gently fly across the room. The wings were very lacey looking, and it floated into her bathroom and disappeared. She was amazed and wondered if she dreamed it.

Then a month later I knew I had to replace Jack because my mother wasn't any better, so my friend who runs the Greene County Humane Society recommended I come and fetch a charming Pekingese named Stella to replace Jack. Once I saw her I fell in love with her and, being a quiet lap dog, she would be perfect for my mother, who is in her 90s. I drove down to Hudson to have a look at her, and promised I'd be back in a couple of weeks to bring her home. My mother was still grieving and I wanted to give her time to pull herself together before bringing Stella home, as I thought she wasn't ready for another dog.

One Saturday, before getting Stella, we went to a thrift store and my mother said, "You know, I think the black butterfly was Jack telling me he was in Heaven." A sentimental and charming thought. Then she asked me to look around for a figurine with a butterfly on it. I said, "Look at what you're leaning on!" and there was this big gold butterfly with lacey wings! There are no coincidences in life. It is still on her dresser next to Jack's picture.

The night before I brought Stella home, mom saw the butterfly again, and we think this was Jack saying, "It's OK to replace me . . ."

It's funny, but I bought a book on animals in the afterlife and the first paragraph said that animals have a way of telling us they are OK after they pass, and they will send you butterflies, which stand for eternal life. And he did. Funny, but that first year after losing him all we saw was butterflies in the yard . . . even into November!

Tim Beckley notes that Harry Houdini may have also appeared as a butterfly as proof of life after death because apparently he wasn't able to come through a medium utilizing direct voice communications or physical materialization. Beckley says that another immensely popular celebrity he met is said to have "come back" to Earth in a similar manner, but for "delicate" privacy reasons he cannot name this well known personality, though he once had a TV show that was enormously popular and made him a household name to this day.

I am sure Charles Fort would have had a comment or two on these personal tales as well as the ones he was able to document on his own. Black dogs and phantom canines are the thrust of this work and obviously had a deep impact on Sir Arthur Conan Doyle and the writing of one of my favorite works, "The Hound of the Baskervilles."

The Man Who Fell From A Clear Blue Sky

by

William Kern

All Rights Reserved 2012

William Clifford Kern
6460-65 Convoy Court
San Diego, California 92117
May 21st, 2012

I have often wondered if "changelings," especially human/wolf changelings (hulfs) have not gotten a bad rap in the pages of contemporary literature. Certainly, there is ample anecdotal evidence to indicate that "werewolves" have existed and that they may have been responsible for gruesome crimes. But what if the hulfs were innocent of the crimes and have only been the scapegoats to cover up the crimes of other humans? This brief story examines such a possibility.

How Dark The Blaze of Noon
O dark, dark, dark, amid the blaze of noon,
Irrevocably dark, total eclipse...
Total eclipse! no sun, no moon!
All dark amidst the blaze of noon!

THE MAN WHO FELL FROM A CLEAR BLUE SKY
by
William Kern

At The End Of The Universe Lies The Beginning Of Life

Because it occurs in Time, there is no beginning to this adventure and, therefore, it will have no ending; at least no ending that the reader might recognize as an ending. It is a tale about people and the world they inhabit, about the world and the various people in it, about how people view and struggle with the world that often seems to thwart their every move, and how the world (and the cosmos for that matter) uses and consumes the creatures that dwell in it.

There is no great, earth-shattering moral to the story, unless the reader finds something his or her mind is listening to as they read, and connects those unspoken unthoughts to this tale. If there is an underlying thought, it will be to question whether or not humans and other creatures have any control over their existence while they are dwellers on this strange and often hostile world.

Since the story has no chronological beginning, it might as well begin today; this morning as I was strolling down the street on my way to the market to purchase food for my evening meal. I had twice seen an old man (or a man who appeared old, but who may have been middle-aged). He had the look and demeanor of a wretched homeless person and, yet, he walked with a stride and purpose that told me he was going somewhere important to him and that to get there was important. A most purposeful stride that was taking him to a meaningful destination, a dreadful mission. I was determined, out of curiosity, if nothing else, to follow him and find out what he was up to. I probably should have minded my own business.

*****

The old man looked like an oily rag someone had thrown into a pond; he just kind of floated through the world all sloshy and raggedy and older than the scaly serpent itself. No one paid much attention to him; first he was there then he wasn't and few noticed either way. He was gutter rain and trash blowing across the street. Everyone knew he was there but no one cared. He was in the corner of your eye, the corner of your mind; he was sneeze or clear your throat or scratch an itch. He happened to the world automatically like he was invisible most of the time and probably that was the way he wanted it. The only reason the old man came to my attention at all was because I spotted him twice in the same day almost the same hour all wrinkly and brown dirty mail pouch tobacco barn siding skin, tattered clothes, dull brown eyes, dull brown greasy hair, streaks of gray, dull brown lips that looked like they hadn't cracked a smile in a thousand years walking in front of me the same way I was going with his gnarled dull brown hands permanently semi-clenched like dead chicken feet, sculling himself along the sidewalk with a stick he had found somewhere and I wondered where he lived and how he managed to survive in a world that cared little or nothing for homeless things.

I recalled someone mentioned that they had heard the old man had fallen from the sky and no one bothered him because the brassface police and the street thugs were scared to death of him saying he was immortal and invincible powerful filled with magic.

Everyone thought he was a magician from another world and who was to say otherwise?

It took some doing just to catch up with him and I thought maybe he even slowed down some so I could get up beside him without running and I said hi but he just kept rowing himself down the sidewalk like he either didn't see or hear me or did but didn't give a damn so I said hi again and he said go away or I'll hit you with this stick you nosy damned kid stop bothering me or I'll bust your head like a rotten punkin so I sidestepped a little but kept on walking with him and pretty soon he just stopped dead without warning and I took two steps before I could stop and he swung the stick like swoosh an inch from my face and I put up my arm and caught a mighty whack on the palm of my hand goddamn I hollered and he grinned like that was about the funniest thing he had seen in a long time.

Okay he says come along and I'll tell you the story of how I happened to fall from the sky to land on this here miserable piece of real estate. How did you know I asked and he said that's what everyone who follows me wants to know so why would you be any different and I rubbed my hand with my other hand and walked with him into a dark gloomy alley between two old derelict buildings the city hadn't got around to tearing down and through a kind of doorway that seemed to appear from the darkness and into a black room with a couple of small boxes next to a bigger box like your old basic table and chairs and he lit a candle on the big box using a match from a folder that I couldn't even see until the light came up and I could see that the old man and me and the three boxes and the candle and the folder of matches were the only things in the room about sixty feet square, a room so large the candle light barely reached the graffiti walls, the peeling scarred gray dull concrete windowless walls ciphered with lifetimes of chalk and spraypaint, sad memories and forlorn wisdom.

The raggedy man seemed to waver in the flickering candle glow, staring at his hands, flexing and unflexing his fingers and marveling at the motion as if he had never really seen such wonders before that very moment.

We sat and he rested his chin in the palms of his upturned hands, staring into the flickering candlelight. He seemed to have died as soon as he sat for he did not move did not blink and I thought he did not even breathe for almost a minute.

The mirror people, he said of a sudden, cast me here when I least expected it to happen. I'd known for some weeks, couple of months really, that the people in the mirror were real, were alive, were watching me, every move I made, even when I wasn't in front of a mirror. They knew what I was doing, knew what I was thinking because they were doing and thinking the same thing. I began to fear sleeping, thinking the dopplegangers would come to get me in the darkness while I was dreaming of pretty girls and sweet cherry blossoms falling like pink snow.

Not certain what made me think of it the first time. I wasn't even in front of a mirror. I began to wonder if the image—the mirror image—extended beyond what could be seen in the glass. Look here, if you step slightly to one side of the mirror you can see the door to the bedroom. If you step the other way you can see the shower or the wardrobe. And a little more you can see down the hallway leading into the living room. You can't see the living room because it is around corners and behind walls but isn't the living room there all the same? Everything in your house or apartment is there, in the mirror. Even the world beyond your front door, the very cosmos itself, is in the mirror; you just have to be able to figure out how to see around the corners and through the walls.

You get so interested in the image in the mirror that it becomes you, and you forget who you were, who you are, who you could become. You become the person in the mirror.

I had everything I wanted. I envied no one, wanted no one else's life. Having survived the experience of living on Earth for a full forty years, I felt I was unique, unlike anyone else. I began to imagine that I had discovered some great universal secret, this new world in the mirror. It was the place where ghosts live, where spooks and haunts and creatures of the night reside until we think them into existence. I was reborn into a completely new reality and, having realized that, I had just begun to live.

The images in the mirror were from a parallel universe just waiting to be explored, just waiting there in the silvered glass, drawing me closer with every glance.

I began to obsess on this idea, wondering before I slept or soon after waking, if there was another being, a doppleganger, reclining on a bed identical to mine, only mirror-image, who was thinking about me lying in bed thinking about him. I began to fear that one day, when I least expected it, one of those beings in the mirror world would come and snatch me away.

I worried that I was mad and hoped that I was prepared for it but I knew I wasn't.

They didn't come for me at all. I went to them as easily as if I walked through a doorway into another room, just slipped right into the mirror one early Fall morning as if I'd been sucked up by a vacuum and landed in a backwards world. Everything seemed perfectly normal but in the back of my head I knew my world, what I thought of as the real world, was on the other side of the mirror. I wanted to go back but didn't know how. Going back was not as easy as crossing over.

I jumped from my world of 1851 to the first reflected world of 1951, a full one hundred years into their future. But the mirror world of 1951 was, I believe now, unlike the world that would have existed in 1951 where I originated. Perhaps it was or wasn't. I don't know anymore. I thought I had died and that I was in the world of death. I was certain God had forsaken me as punishment for my sins, which at that time were legion. I was afraid, scared stupid for a long time, but soon I accepted my life as the real life and began to suspect that the life I'd had on the other side of the mirror was an illusion.

As soon as I grabbed a hold of the mirror world, strange new things began to happen. I would wake up and be in a different world every morning, go to sleep in a different world every night. I almost couldn't keep up with it at first. But it was not long before I couldn't remember my life before I fell into the mirror.

Things happened slowly at the beginning like I was being prepared for my new world carefully, but soon came one adventure after another, a carousel whirling past me so quickly everything was a blur. I can't remember the first hundred years clearly but I do remember a couple of things that happened before I fell back through the mirror to land here. Now all I can think about is going back to find the people I knew there, in the last world into which I had fallen, the people I loved, the people I long for.

"You said 'the first hundred years,' " said I. "Were you there that long?"

"Twice as long, perhaps thrice as long. It is not in me to remember so many years, so many adventures. Sometimes I think I am dreaming it all, even now here with you. But I was going to tell you about the people I cared for, wasn't I?"

"Yes, tell me," I said, and he pursed his dull gray lips and nodded sagely. Presently he spoke and when he did his voice was thin and dark and ancient.

* * * * *.

Gold and frankincense and myrrh. The earth exploded beneath a new star. I walked under the vast electric midnight sky. Wise men arrived at last but they did not stop to ask for directions; they knew where they were going. The oak tree, naked in the shadow, was not interested in cherry blossoms or dancing cranes in far away Japan. An imprisoned monk sipped warm tea before a dusty window while he peered at the four strangers, barely visible on the road below. It was quiet except for the faint white voices of geese winging southward in the high and lonely sky.

The sea darkened; the tall cliffs, newly washed by crashing high tide, stood as mute guardians against the invincible intruding waves.

How cold it was.

The gray pink fog, never far behind, accompanied the winter wind, pushed, stirred up the loose, torn off bits of seagrass, ready or not, and dragged them into the relentless surf, carried them to where, scattered all about, remained the rumpled souvenirs of heaven's flame, all one pile.

Unarmed but for faith I walked across the dying embers of the universe, holy golden funeral pyre, low and crackling, where the bleating wind swirled the ashes as they rose to the nameless hill in the mist.

Rain, falling like hard, rusted nails, a sudden late autumn shower. I was newly baptized. I reached out and touched the rook's impulsive call, a massive melody agonizing downward from the greening shade. The planets hesitated. Martyrs with ashen faces looked up briefly from the temple, sputtering madness, incredulous, then withdrew into their lairs, heads bowed beneath uncombed hair.

All was still once more.

A green frog, its form freshly painted by the clinging mist, sprang into an old pool, plopping into the sound of water. My footsteps alarmed the rooks and they flew madly just above the withered reeds, protesting my approach. Soon will come the first soft snow, enough to bend the leaves of the fragile jonquil and in the frog's cry was a portent of the winter death to come.

Still shivering, I longed for cherry blossoms and butterflies, for brightly colored Maples and sun-filled skies. Last days of autumn, first days of winter. No one traveled the road now but I, steeped in thoughts and loneliness as dawn ascended. Far down the stream I could see the rough wooden bridge that joined the path leading to the stone house on the cliff. The ammonia-colored moon was hidden now and then by angry dark clouds; the stars were gone. Around the harvest pool more frogs leaped away as I longed for the warmth of home. I thought I would not like to die here in this place behind the mirror, in this dream, in this gloom where there was no joy, no sky, no moon, no stars, no flowers.

How cold it was, how cold. No familiar sky, no familiar earth, but still the snow will fall.

In the pale light I stared into the stream and saw my father's face. The clouds parted for a moment and I could see the Milky Way Galaxy at the bottom of the dark water. When I looked up it was already gone. I was naked in the darkness. I stirred the water with my hand, remembering the vision of the stars but only a slight muddiness appeared.

CRYPTID CREATURES FROM DARK DOMAINS

The imprisoned monk, having finished his warm tea, was playing his flute all out of tune. The horizon was glowing lighter in the east. Soon the sun would rise, still lost to my sight above the black clouds. In the half light I longed for love and the cold wind turned to rain again, smudging the clouds that snaked through the stream. The bridge was not far but I leaped across the narrow stream and struggled up the far bank in the mud, too eager for the shelter and warmth of the hearth.

A lightning flash in the faraway sky. Between the forest trees I saw the shape of a creature watching as I approached. When the lightning flashed again, it was gone. It saw all it needed to see.

In that morning's mad world, visions of the hulf.

I was cold and now I was smeared with mud to my knees. I mounted the trail to the stone house above on the windswept cliff. The footpath was slick and the going was slow.

Dreams in my head like wet heavy rain, like soot on a broken window, like a soft and terrible machine, like a skulking young hulf and when she growled I could hear under the purling little girl voice the dark, lean, terrible animal living in the heat of her throat.

This hulf had been stalking me for at least an hour, from the moment I left the safety of the village where she wished not to show herself, and I could tell from the sound of her panting it was a female. I never saw her clearly, but I knew she was there in the underbrush trying to keep pace with me and I wondered if she was hungry, if she would pounce upon me and kill me.

But it had been an hour and still she had only followed and I pondered to what purpose.

I stopped and peered into the dense brush then upward at the house above me on the headland, longing all the more for its safety and comfort.

"Hulf," said I with a gentle voice, "Why do you not come out to the path where the ground is firmer, where we may walk together to the house yonder?"

Silence in the bush, then a low purling, then a stirring and parting of the green, and she crept into view first on all fours—I started at the sight of her— then she stood with amazing agility, smiling a little smile, her eyes keen upon me, her hands curled as if to attack but her back straight and strong. When she spoke her voice was remarkably masculine and deep, a counterpoint to the siren female whisper above it as if she spoke with two voices at once.

"I am not good at tracking," she intoned through her white wolf teeth and dark red hunger, wondering aloud if we humans had to sleep with the fear of waking someday to find we, too, were changing into the hulf, part human and part wolf, sometimes more of one than the other and I just smiled back at her with deliberate silence, eyes narrowed and piercing, until she turned away to gaze with feral curiosity at the stone house above us on the rocky promontory.

"And are you going there?" she asked presently.

"I am."

"May I go with you?"

"If you wish it." And I wondered if she had children and if they, too, were hulfs living in the dystopian world of terror and blackness beneath the city streets, beneath the darkness, beneath the thin line between self and the unspeakable world of monsters and murder.

"My forerunners were human like you," she said. "It was only after the disease accident that we became the hulf living on the swiftness of our limbs. I was only thirteen years alive when I began to change. Now I am twenty years alive and I have had no children." She thrust out her ample bare human breasts and laughed gaily, almost a puppylike yelp. "Not yet."

"Did you think perhaps to kill me and have me for breakfast back there?" I asked.

"Briefly," said she, "but I suppose I am too much human and too little wolf to do it." And nothing else.

And so we walked to the house together without further conversation.

I felt, for a moment, that she wanted to reach out and take my hand, to walk swinging it gaily back and forth like a child at a circus with her father. But, perhaps, it was I who wanted to hold the hulf's hand so that both she and I would feel more at ease.

I did and she did not draw away.

When we reached the house I began to search for the key in my kit while she gazed about at the mist-covered trees and brush, the spider webs bejeweled with glistening droplets of crystal rain, and she soon spied an enormous rook perched upon a barren limb, preening and combing its feathers fastidiously.

Here the hulf mustered up some urge to commune with nature. Perhaps she wished to see some design among the fallen leaves and receive some backtalk from the mute sky or the frantic rook, open to any gesture on the part of nature to grant a brief respite from fear of what she had become. The hope of such a moment of transcendent beauty and communion seemed worth the wait for that which she interpreted as that rare, random granting of a miracle.

The rook, arranging and rearranging its feathers, seemed like a fastidious spinster in comparison with the strange form of the sad hulf. It was an object set out on the landscape for no particular purpose, because her real desire was some backtalk from the recalcitrant human. Neither rook nor sky nor human spoke, but the hulf herself was very wordy, full of parenthetical phrases, uttered half whispers, concerned not with the actual landscape but with her own thoughts. She finally reattached these thoughts to the landscape by declaring that the rook might be a tasty morsel, a repast enjoyed in the company of bejewelled columbines.

She was aglow, was the hulf, in the notion that she might have been the first of her pack to travel this high mountain trail, delighted by a rook on a bare branch autumn morning, and last summer's berry canes and vines binding the sagging fence, and the stone house of a human who had actually taken her hand and urged her upward to the lonely headland.

I left most of my wet and muddy garments on the screened porch, then fetched towels. The she hulf had no idea what to do with a towel, so I showed her by first drying her and then myself. She allowed me to touch her without the least bit of shame.

Her hair was long and unkempt although it seemed not to be dirty. Her upper torso was as human as any human girl I had ever seen but her lower torso was covered with a soft, light colored downy fur. Except that her face appeared to protrude a bit more than normal at the jaw, she was quite a striking looking girl. The most unusual features were her legs and feet. The heel was high, exactly like a canine's and she walked on toes which terminated in canine claws. She had slightly pronounced canine teeth.

A month earlier creatures such as that she hulf filled me with disgust and revulsion; now I watched her with admiration and, perhaps, something more; adoration, or if not adoration, then empathy.

I struck a fire on the hearth which at first filled her with temerity. I sat before the flames to show that the fire would only harm her if she fell into it or got too near. She crept toward it, cautious and inquisitive, soon sat with her legs beneath her haunches and gazed at the hypnotic curling.

In the light I could see that she was beautiful, almost diaphanous, both in form and in features. Her dark wolf eyes turned toward me and caught me stealing her beauty. She smiled softly and I blushed.

"Have you a name?" I asked.

"Name?"

"Yes, a name. What do the others call you?"

"They call me to them by saying 'hulf'."

"And the others," I asked, "are they also addressed as 'hulf'?"

She nodded to affirm it.

I could not refer to her as 'hulf'; it was not in me to do it. "May I call you by a human name?"

"Yes," said she absently, still mesmerized by the dancing fire.

"I'll call you Cybele, then. Is that alright?"

"See-bee-lee," she repeated and nodded her head slightly.

"My human name is Guillaume," I said. "Close friends call me Gill."

"Gill." She nodded again as she repeated the name and her old stones and mossy voice made it sound like thunder echoing from faraway mountains.

Hulf and human, Cybele and Gill, we took breakfast of hot chocolate and honeyed biscuits under one roof together, moon in a field of clover and among all the moon gazers at the ancient temple grounds below, there was not one nearly so beautiful as the hulf. I was enchanted and she was the enchantress.

Later I dozed in my chair before the hearth, wrapped in a soft comforter, and she lay upon a cushion at my feet, refusing my invitation to sit in the facing chair, saying the position of sitting as a human was too difficult for her, too uncomfortable, too foreign. By mid morning, we slept soundly and the fire burned down to cold ash.

When I awoke, she was gone, the door closed securely behind her and I felt strangely and sadly alone, longing for her to return, cold and empty inside.

She had taken the towel and I wondered why.

The wise men, ever erudite and pedantic, had told us that we might all change eventually into the hulf and laws were passed after that forbidding anyone to kill them. Generally speaking, the hulfs presented no danger to those of us who had not changed. Even so, most people shunned them and tried to drive them away. As long as there was adequate food, the hulfs stayed to themselves, formed their own communities as packs and were civil to each other and to humans.

But when food was not plentiful, or when the populations of hulfs outgrew the food supply (they were prolific breeders), there would in some towns occur an occasional kill and human bones would be found in the ditches and fields. Then the humans would put their guns by their doors and sit by the fires all night, alert for sounds of skulking creatures outside in the darkness, some of the men looking for any excuse to reduce the populations of the changelings, never thinking that the victims might have been killed by other humans.

* * * * *

I dreamed of a man of power standing at a podium with his hand raised to heaven, invoking the wisdom of God. The man of power said God told him the hulfs were evil and should all be killed. Next morning he was found torn to shreds on his living room floor.

All in my dream.

A week later one of the pundits who advocated the deaths of the hulfs was found torn to shreds on his living room floor. I think it was a coincidence that it happened the way I dreamed it.

* * * * *

Winter drew closer with each passing hour and I grew keen to close the house and go to my apartment in the village below. I put it off day after day hoping the she-hulf would return. I did not want her to find the house locked and empty.

Strange that I should have been so concerned for her. The thought of her living in the dystopian world of terror and blackness beneath the city streets, beneath the darkness, beneath the thin line between self and the unspeakable world of monsters and murder filled every hour of every day of my life.

A linnet sang, and through a thicket of barren larches the late moon shone. That cool morning was swept away into the sea. All along the road to the village not a single soul, only the autumn dawn came, seen but not heard; the branches of the forlorn trees poured rainwater into puddles when they leaned, then, with the solitaire for a soul, they slept peacefully, awaiting the first snows already lurking above the peaks to the north.

Dark autumn old age settled down on me like heavy clouds or dying birds and dead morning glory vines secured the gate in the old fence; the hand of death strangling the life from the world. Crossing half the sky, as I stared at the raging gray ocean below, massive clouds promised snow and, later, a sudden winter shower sent the noisy rooks diving into the shelter of the eaves.

Day and night. Night and day. Even those long and dreary days and nights were not long enough to empty my mind of the she hulf Cybele. No words can express how sad I was, propped unceremoniously against the great window frame staring dumbly at the darkening seasons outside.

I wished she were there to listen to my words. The world is wearisome when there is no one to share it. I stalked from room to room through that house of dreadful night.

Raindrops spiraled down from unknown universes, carrying their precious cargoes of microscopic life. The seas darkened and the wild geese had all gone to their breeding grounds far to the south. I wished I had gone with them. From every direction winter approached. The house had become a trap; I yearned to close it and go to the village.

But I determined to wait one more day for Cybele.

When I awoke the next morning (late, for I slept fitfully), there was a light covering of fresh snow upon the ground. Thin, it would melt by noon. A foot from the bottom step of the porch was a yellow patch where something had pissed in the snow. I began to look from window to window, front and back, side to side, for signs of Cybele, hoping she had returned, hoping she was waiting, worrying that she would be cold and wet. At first nothing, then, near the shed behind the house I saw her crouching to examine something in the tall, brown grass. When she stood, she was holding a tiny rabbit. She pulled the towel from her shoulders and wrapped the bunny in it and held it close to her breasts.

I opened the back door and she turned toward me and came in, just like that, without a word, and went in to sit before the fire newly built upon the hearth.

"Something for this tiny?" she asked, and I brought some greens from the refrigerator, watched amazed as she caressed it and fed it until it slept in the warm towel.

I wondered aloud, unfortunately, if she was saving it for a meal and she glared at me with accusing eyes. "That is offensive. This is an orphan who has survived the first snow of winter here on this high place. To think that I would kill it is a knife in my heart. Never ask such things of me again."

I apologized sincerely and she turned away with a nod to begin caressing once more the orphaned survivor of the first snow of winter. I felt terrible to have misjudged her so.

"When you were here before," I began to ask.

"Yes?"

"Why did you take the towel?"

"I needed it for this tiny," she answered and the occult wisdom of the response slammed into my brain like a hammer. Had she really foreseen the discovery of the cold little orphan? I suspected she had.

* * * * *

"Can you imagine it?" he asked me, still staring into the candle flame.

"I can. But did you close the house and go to the village as you had planned?"

"No. After Cybele returned I never even thought of it again. We spent the first months of winter there, a mild winter as it turned out, and I was often able to go into the village for provisions. I bought girl clothes for her, warm things because it seemed to me she was often uncomfortable with the cold. She was rarely without a towel for a shawl, although it may have been a security blanket rather than a hedge against the cold. It pleased her to receive the gifts and I must admit it pleased me to give them."

"Did you fall in love with her?" I asked.

"Oh, yes, of course, from the very beginning, despite knowing it was an impossible thing for both of us."

"Did you...ah...sleep with her?" I asked as delicately as possible.

He smiled wryly and looked away into the darkness at the edge of the light. "Always that imprudent question. The answer is no, I did not; something I often thought of and more often regretted having not done. She was an innocent child and I was two hundred years old. I thought to protect her and she thought of me as her guardian. To kiss her, to caress her would have been the same as to destroy her innocence for no purpose. You see that it was... not possible. But you are wondering why I am here and she is not. A long story and a sad one."

"Why do you say you were two hundred years old?" I asked.

"Quite simply because I was at least that old. I am even older now that I am here. When I fell into the mirror, or to be more precise, when my image and I exchanged places in the mirror, the year was 1851. I landed in an alternate world of the hulfs where it was, by my time reckoning, 1951, and now I am here where, if I reckon aright, it is the year 2054. I have been here for two years and each day of that I have been trying to figure out how I can return to the world of the hulfs. I am beginning to fear that it is not possible."

"You do not look like a two hundred years old man," said I, appraising him with a sideways glance and thinking he might be more than a little bit mad.

"I have not aged a day since I fell into this strange world. I am still forty years old although I have lived nearly two hundred and fifty years."

"Is that, do you think, a paradox of the parallel universe?

"I imagine, although I have not really given it much thought. But, probably, it is."

"But you are safe here and secure. No one has any thought to harm you. Why do you feel you must return?" I asked.

He was quite for a time, rocking gently back and forth on the creaky wooden box chair.

"Because I had promised to lead them to safety, to a sanctuary, where they could live without fear of the humans but I was unable to complete the journey. We began our dangerous journey without much planning in the last days of winter, escaping from men who would murder us.

"It was terrible. We were constantly hungry and thirsty. I was always cold and wet and I feared that if the humans did not find and kill me, I would perish from disease or exposure to the elements.

"Sometimes we walked; sometimes we ran, always hiding during the day and making our way through unfamiliar lands at night. We had fled for hundreds of miles in those months of late winter and early spring and I began to think that we might reach our destination safely within just a few more days.

"And, then, one morning, I awoke to find myself here in this abandoned building, with not a clue as to what might have happened to the others. I believe, or I want to believe, that my mirror self continued with them and completed that mad journey to freedom.

"But I must know the truth. If I do not return, I fear they may all perish. Time may not be the same for them as it is for me. A hundred years or a thousand may have passed for them. They may have already reached their haven safely, or they may have perished, but I must find out.

"It is I who is now living in the dystopian world of terror and blackness upon the land, beneath the darkness, beneath the thin line between self and the unspeakable world of monsters and murder.

"My dear God, I am at an age now and at a time where life stops giving and begins to take. What a mockery our bodies make of us when they are finished with us. It would be better if we simply evaporated when we grow too old and weary to go on living; a puff of smoke drifting skyward and that would be the end of us."

* * * * *

It was cold enough to make the devil swear on the evening the others came, the other hulfs, two dozen to be sure, slipping into the yard under cover of darkness and asking entrance to the house. I struggled to understand the meaning of their visit until Cybele explained that a vaccine had been formulated that would protect humans against the disease that had affected the hulfs. The hulfs, living in their dystopian world of terror and blackness beneath the thin line between self and the unspeakable world of monsters and murder, could not be protected; they would continue to change until they perished from the disease or were killed by humans.

And I came to understand that evening the true reason Cybele had taken the towel. It bore my scent and that scent had led the pack around the village, through the forest and up the steep incline to my doorstep, the beginning of their hazardous and fearful escape from certain death.

The world I had thought secure now changed into something new and foreboding. The hulfs, all of the pack to which Cybele belonged, were asking that I lead them away to a place of safety in the South; a place they were told about by others who had journeyed there and returned to spread the word that a haven existed for any hulf brave enough to chance it. They could no longer travel safely in the world of humans now that a preventive had been found. Hulfs were hunted and killed without mercy. They had become expendable, a sacrifice to science. Six from their pack had already been slain.

I was filled with dread for the hulfs, but most especially for Cybele and the pups, and, at the end, I agreed to lead them to the unknown sanctuary in the South. I had no idea where to begin. In wiser days, when I was younger and stronger, I might have made a plan for salvation before the night was over but that evening I was stymied and loathe to dice with death. And, oh, I could see in their eyes, their shining eyes, their hopeful eyes, the growing fear that I might abandon them to the mad guns cursing in the village below, and some began to decry their hope in knowing tones.

Picture it; we fools, I and they, now all with the dying and the dead, standing mute around the fading hearth and wondering, all of us, we miserable fools, they and I, how we might tend toward this task. Darkness never seemed so dark; dread never seemed quite so dreadful as on that smothering night.

Now here I am, sleeping on a bed of nails with one foot in the fire. Some days when you wake up, you think you are the same person who went to sleep in your bed the night before.

Believe me, you aren't.

In wiser days, in days before I first fell into the mirror (oh, how I wish I knew how it happened,) I had no thoughts of heroic adventures. I worked and enjoyed my life as most nineteenth century forty-year-old men did, giving little or no thoughts to the lives and wants of others, even of those I thought I loved. Live and let live, you see.

Now, here in this place where I am imprisoned, I can think of little else save Cybele and the others and trying to find a way to get back to them. Yes, I know the mirror me must have taken them to their sanctuary, but I dearly want to know if they made it or not.

"Perhaps," said I, "you don't want to know. What if you learn they didn't safely reach their destination? What if you find they and you—the mirror you— perished before you reached the sanctuary?"

"Perished? How perished?"

"Accident or at the hands of others," I said.

"The humans, you mean?" the raggedy man asked.

"Or perhaps other hulfs who saw you as a threat...or see you as a threat, as the case may be or may have been."

"I think they would not ever have done that, and yet..." he let the thought slip away as his mind drifted back to that time moments ago or hundreds of ages past when he had promised to lead the hulfs to safety in the south of whatever world he had found himself in.

"No," he said at last, "If my double had been killed or even injured there, I could not have come here, or I would have come here injured, and I did not".

"Are you certain that's how it works?"

"Yes."

"Always?"

His piercing grey eyes bored into me. "For me, at least, up to this point."

He stood slowly and languidly, stretching his lean frame wearily. "You should go now," he said at length. "I want to continue my experiments with the transference, to see if I can discover what beam or current existed on the occasions that I fell into these alternate worlds."

"But have you a mirror?" I asked.

"Pieces that I have salvaged from the trash bins. They are not adequate, I think, since I have been unable to effect a transfer. Perhaps you might fetch one for me and bring it tomorrow."

"Several, perhaps. Large or small?"

"Small," he said. "About this size." He made a circle with his arms, finger-tips touching.

"Then I shall bring two when I take my lunch hour."

"Oh, of course," he said quietly. "I forget people here must work for...things."

He promised to continue with his story the following day and, after getting a list of things he could use—not the least of which was a boxful of food and toiletries, bottles of drinking water and clean clothes—I bid him farewell.

I turned and looked back at him as I left the building and saw that he was again sitting on the hard wooden box with his mouth working chants and silent, unspoken dreams that seemed to fall away from him like smoke and summer rain. He made little gestures with his thin, gnarled fingers, pointing and waving, brushing his thoughts away and inventing others from the still, dark air.

*****

I did not go to work the following day. I called in for a vacation day and went directly to a hardware store to purchase the two mirrors, then, with the boxes of supplies and the mirrors, I drove to the abandoned building where I expected to find the traveler waiting for me. He was not there. I lighted the candle to dispel the darkness and sat to wait for him. It was nearly ten o'clock before he rowed himself through the open doorway holding in his right hand a small book.

"Library," he said, by way of explaining where he had been. "I have no library card, so I had to steal it." He held the book toward me so I could read the title. Currents From The Void, was imprinted on the spine. His eyes gleamed with some sort of ethereal light, almost glowing with electric fire, and for a moment I was frightened that I was in the presence of a demon. I started backward but he pointed to some debris beyond the ring of light; wooden stands that I had not seen. He placed the book upon the box he used as a table.

"You'll return it for me, won't you?" he asked.

"What?"

"The book. You'll return it?"

"Oh, of course."

He began arranging the wooden stands near the table. "If you want to see ghosts," he said, "just look into the mirror. Or, better still, have the two mirrors look at each other." As he spoke, he went busily about placing the two mirrors in a way that they directly faced one another, each reflection creating an infinite passageway into and out of the other.

"According to the book, by placing these two mirrors facing one another, the light energy reflected back and forth between them might create a vortex, an energy beam or current, that might create a transfer of my mirror double from his

210

world to this one."

"And you to his," I said.

"Precisely, exactly, yes."

Light might be coaxed out of empty space, he explained, when in the presence of reflective surfaces. It was, he said, a process known as the "Casimir Effect" where two metallic plates or mirrors placed in close proximity to one another can result in an attraction between the two, despite there being no charge running into the plates to create an electromagnetic force. The reflecting coatings of mirrors is silver, an excellent conductor of electricity.

"The attraction seems to come from the fact that virtual photons—that is, particles of light energy that only exist for a limited time and space—exist in greater numbers outside the two plates, rather than between them. The resulting force, though miniscule, is still strong enough to be measured." He wagged a finger at the book. "I read it there."

He motioned me to the table and sat, then began sorting through the food and clothes I had brought. He constructed a large sandwich and ate parts of it while he examined the clothing and toiletries, humming and nodding, nodding and humming, until he had selected a shirt and trousers, shoes and stockings that suited him.

"These will do nicely. Thank you."

I nodded and managed a smile. "Sturdy togs for traveling," said I. "In case you are thinking of traveling, I mean."

"Yes. Now or tomorrow or next week, if I can transfer."

"And if you cannot?

"I will keep trying."

He ate slowly, deliberately, as he explained his arrangement of the mirrors. In all the years of thinking of mirrors, it had never occurred to him, he said, to place two of them facing each other, precisely aligned so that one reflected the other and nothing else, either to the sides or to the top or bottom. Mirrors so placed should be able to collect and store virtual photons, if even for a fraction of a second, and be reflected as light, vibrating back and forth, reflected back and forth endlessly, infinitely, billions of times per second, creating a magnetic field, a beam, a current exactly like a river, a physical bond between the mirrors upon which one might travel to the far fields of space and time.

"And, according to this fellow in the book, the virtual photons do not merely create light where none exists; ethereal light, it also retains the images of everything that passed before it and all that passed in one's life. Images, sound, sensations and actual memories. That is why I experienced so many adventures when I exchanged worlds the first time. I was living and reliving the lives of every mirror double with whom I was reacting. When I at last slipped into that one life of the gent who lived in the stone house upon the headland, all the others faded away."

"So you think that you can step into this virtual energy and be whisked away back to the world of the hulfs?" I asked. "What makes you think you can go back to the world you left? This is like a time machine of some sort. Aren't you afraid you will appear on another world in the middle of a war, or in the middle of a plague, or some other mass extinction?"

He shook his head with dark, brooding eyes. Clearly he was not afraid of any of those possibilities. Or he simply refused to acknowledge them. He was focused upon returning to Cybele; intent upon saving her from the guns of the madmen who wanted only to kill the hulfs.

"The mirrors create light and memories from empty space where none actually exists," he cried, hands above his head, sweeping the air as if to clear it of debris and call down blazing shards of fire and brimstone. "If I step into the current, the dopplegangers will also step into the current of their mirrors at the same time because we are always doing exactly the same things with the mirrors, and we should transfer; I there and he, here. Or I to some other world and he to another, rather than I to his and he to mine. That is the chance one takes when posing before the mirror. The world to which I transfer will be like this one in nearly all respects. See, I had never thought of using two mirrors before. I always tried to use a single mirror. But in my home in the year 1851 there were two mirrors in the room, facing each other. And in the home upon the headland, there was but a single mirror in the great room. In none of the rooms were there two mirrors facing each other. It did not occur to me that the mirrors would actually produce the current of virtual energy that could project me into another existence, a parallel universe, a mirror cosmos."

"How, then, did you transfer here?" I asked.

He finished eating the sandwich and wiped his mouth upon the sleeve of his ragged coat. His eyes grew empty and he drew down a somber face. "Ah," he said at last, "that is the story, isn't it? That is the error. That is the flaw I could not see."

The raggedy man fell into a deep silence, still and hardly breathing. "What if I fail?" he said at last. "What if I cannot transfer? Perhaps my plan for the mirrors is a fantasy and all that happened before was simply some kind of mad coincidence. What if I cannot return to lead them to safety?" He sagged, with his neck drawn down into his shoulders, and he shook his head forlornly.

"Then one day, when this world had ended, she will join you. Cybele, I mean. You will be together somewhere, somewhen," I said and touched his arm reassuringly.

He drew away and stared at me incredulously. "Do you really imagine the cosmos is so tender, so gracious, so kind? How came I here before I completed my task if that is so?"

I told him I didn't know the answer to that but that I felt certain if his love for the she-hulf was strong enough, they might meet again in another life.

"Strangely enough," he said with narrowed eyes, "I have some memories of such things, although I cannot be certain they are not memories of dreams or nightmares or hallucinations. I remember living briefly and dying on the planet Mars." He looked up quickly, fixing me with his fierce, mad gaze, assured himself I did not think him possessed, and looked away into the shadows at the edges of the room. "Perhaps it is a sort of madness brought about by the mirror world in which I dwelled for some many years. And it is all of them who share my concern equally."

"What?"

"I want to return to save all the hulfs; not just Cybele, although she does concern me most, I confess."

I cleared my throat of the tight dryness I felt there. "Perhaps, when their world has ended, they will appear here to be with you," I said.

"Their world has already ended. It is no longer their world. They were driven out, brutalized, and to appear here would be the worst of all situations! Can you imagine what would happen to them in this world if they suddenly appeared as hulfs, as I left them? They would be murdered just as quickly here as there and perhaps even more brutally. Are they dead now? Were they ever alive? Am I alive or dead? I don't even know anymore. But I shall surely die if I cannot return to learn if they were saved. I can feel myself growing older and closer to the fate that awaits all humans since I fell to this place."

"You can try," I said softly. "Only try."

"Yes." He nodded gravely. "Only try."

"Perhaps, if you are successful with the mirrors, you will find them again," I said as I watched him arrange and rearrange the mirrors. "Perhaps you will find Cybele again."

"One must be lost in order to be found. They are not lost; it is I who has gone missing." He stared at the grafitti-covered walls with empty eyes. "Why do you test me?" he growled. "Have I not been tested enough these last two-hundred years?"

He was clearly challenging whatever god he thought might be listening at that moment, shamelessly, as if he had no shame at all.

"Oh, dear Cybele! Jack! Pups! Apollo! Naomi! Why, Shiatan, do you test me so?" He breathed a long, quivering sigh and turned back to me. "I must complete my arrangements here to learn if I can create the vortex or energy field that will carry me on to the next world, or back to that world which I so long to see again."

* * * * *

We do not know what we do not know. And we fools; all of us, could not know what awaited us when we planned so carefully our perilous escape. Had I known the dangers, the sadness, the treachery we would encounter, I might have told the hulfs that we could not go. But, we planned through the winter, often huddling around the blazing fire late into the evenings, that we should begin soon after the first promising warm days of spring.

We heard no fearful reports from the village of more killings and we sank into a kind of trusting denial, thinking that everything would be alright, believing that the villagers had decided to try to live with the hulfs; even if in an uneasy peaceful coexistence. These were naive, foolish dreams. The reason we heard no gunshots or further reports of death was because nearly all the hulfs had been killed by mid-winter, and only a few had managed to flee to the south, to safety, or the promise of it.

But we did not know these things for we remained secluded in the stone house on the headland, rarely venturing out for fear of being seen, and only I, at that, and only to go into the village for provisions that we needed to survive. The plan had been to always keep a small store of supplies to take with us, food and water we could not buy or find as we moved southward, and to live off the land as much as possible.

It was easy to plan but, as we were to discover, nearly impossible to accomplish. In late winter and early Spring, there is little growing from the cold earth to sustain man or beast. Seeds and berries and herbs still lay dormant beneath patches of lingering snow. It is a wonder any of us managed to survive at all.

Cybele came to me early one late winter morning, wrapped in the blanket she had become accustomed to carrying with her, still sleepy-eyed from her warm pallet in the cellar.

"We have been talking and thinking," she said.

"Yes?"

"Some are thinking of leaving in a few days even if you choose not to lead us."

I was astonished. "But, why?" I asked.

"They... some of them... are afraid. They say they can smell death in the village. They say they cannot hear the voices of the other hulfs. They are afraid."

"And you?"

"Yes," she responded softly. "I, too, am afraid. Not of staying until warmer days, but of their fear and what it might drive them to do. They do not trust the humans; some are beginning wonder if even you might betray them. I worry that some harm may come to you."

Do you care for me that much? I wondered, and saw in her eyes that she did.

"Did they send you to speak with me?" I asked.

"I told them I would do it because I trust you. I know you will not deceive us."

I turned away from her and held my hands toward the fire, rubbing warmth into my fingers and arms. At length I faced her. "We shall leave in two days. Tell them that. No, I shall tell them myself after all are awakened and have eaten."

And, so, for two days we packed our provisions—scant few that we had—wrapped our bedding and selected clothing so that all would appear at a distance to be humans, placed as much as we could into two small carts and enjoyed, on that last afternoon in the stone house, a substantial meal.

After sunset at middle March, the hulfs all dressed as humans dress and we ventured into the night. I did not even bother to lock the house, knowing even then that I should never return. It was still quite cold.

There was no moon that night.

* * * * *

One of the problems with being the last of your kind is that, if things do not work out, if your plans for the future fail and your dreams go awry, then you and your blood line shall soon cease to exist. Nothing will remain of you to remind future generations that you were even here, except, perhaps, some myths and legends whispered around an evening hearth. It was likely that the two dozen hulfs who had stayed with me through the winter and a few dozen more from the village were the only ones who had managed to escape the guns and axes of the humans. How many others had already fled to the sanctuary in the south and found safety we could only guess.

I had done all I could to encourage the hulfs, to convince them we could reach the unknown sanctuary had we but the courage, stamina and perseverance to accomplish it. Secretly, I hoped my promises would not be revealed to be the hollow mutterings of a fool.

The arrow of time moves forward only. Things done can never be undone but, perhaps, they can be repeated or duplicated or reenacted differently, or dreamed again on a new night with less terrifying conclusions. Perhaps. Perhaps.

*****

Sometimes we walked; sometimes we ran, always hiding during the day and making our way through unfamiliar lands at night. It was dreadful. We were constantly hungry and thirsty. I was always cold and wet and I feared that if the humans did not find and kill me, I would perish from disease or exposure to the elements. In moments of fevered madness I even imagined that the hulfs would kill me as I slept and eat me.

We had fled for hundreds of miles in those months of late winter and early spring and I began to think that we might reach our destination safely within just a few more days. We began to see signs, trails and pathways, hulf prints, bits of hair clinging to the brush, that indicated we were on or near the road leading to the sanctuary. We fell into a kind of complacency, thinking that beyond the next turn or over the next hill we would find our salvation.

It did not occur to me that if we could see and follow the signs, the human hunters could follow them as well. And, so, we were caught in their trap.

I plodded beside one of the carts keeping my eyes fixed on the top of a tree which showed against the sky above the pines. The trees might mean that a stream or lake was near. I was a good foot taller than the largest of the male hulfs and had been walking with my shoulders hunched forward under my heavy tattered and dirty shirt so I would not present a noticable target in case we were observed by humans who might be lurking in the forests.

My height made walking difficult, for I had to cut down my normal stride to accommodate my speed to the progress of those pulling the carts. After months of stumbling along behind them my back and shoulders ached unmercifully.

We had been twenty-six in number when we left the headland in March and we had moved slowly but unfaltering, sometimes covering as much as twenty miles in a night. Now there were only twenty-two of us. Four had sickened and died within the first month, and those of us who remained had weakened from hunger and exposure.

As our provisions dwindled, we transferred as much as we could to the largest of the carts and abandoned the smaller in a copse beside a stream where we had stayed for two days and nights.

The single cart and its load had become a living thing, a determined, nearly unmovable object, everlastingly pitting its weight against our strength.

I shifted the two pistols hidden under my coat and shivered a little. I had hoped to find warmth and sunshine as we trekked southward, gentle breezes that might restore strength to all of us. The hope had become a jest. Bitter cold had followed implacably from the moment we had left the great stone house on the headland above the village.

It would settle down with deathly frostiness as soon as the sun was gone, numbing us into mindless zombies and shivering the uncomplaining pups, lying so still in the bottom of the cart.

I lost all track of time. Not until we crossed a broad, winding ice-free river whose banks were lined with crocus and Queen Anne's Lace did I realize we had journeyed into Spring. It was the twenty-fourth of June! Three long, miserable

216

months since we had begun our escape from certain death. In that time, not one of us had been injured or killed by the humans, although we often saw them in the distance watching us as we passed and once we were pursured by hunters on horses. They gave up the chase when their mounts were unable to follow us through the dense forests.

But it was there, in the forest, that we found the abandoned homes and farms, the abandoned hopes and dreams, of the humans who had succumbed to the disease of the hulfs. Empty houses stared back at us with sightless eyes, the dreams of their owners dead and forgotten, leaving populous, prosperous villages to be overrun by encroaching forests.

In the wagon, I heard one of the she-hulfs moan. I halted the company and walked to the back, lowering the heavy tailboard. A she-hulf lay in one corner, the piled-up provisions towering above her, a lovely girl barely in her mid-teens, scarcely heavy enough to depress the thick pallet beneath her. At the sight of me she smiled, but her lips were colorless and pinched, and her golden eyes were bright with fever.

"What is it?" I asked.

"She is pregnant, Gill," Cybele said behind me. "The pup will come soon. Are we near any place where we can stop?"

"There must be something soon." I placed a hand on her forehead, felt the heat and smoothed back her golden hair. It was damp beneath my fingers. Cybele took out a cupful of water, then raised her with an arm beneath her shoulders and let the girl drink.

She took but a swallow. Cybele found a cloth, moistened it from the cup, and gently bathed her forehead and temples.

She moaned again. For an instant we stood staring down at her swollen belly, rounding the folds of the long cloak which covered her. Her lean face was tight with despair.

"How did this happen?" I asked.

Cybele's eyebrows went up a half inch. "How? Do you not understand the mating?"

"Yes, of course," I stammered. "But I mean when did this happen, how without my seeing or knowing?"

"The males are stealthy and filled with cunning, Gill. Wherever we're going, we'd better hurry, or we'll have a pup before we get there."

I straightened and pulled the covers over the she-hulf, then swept back my long unshorn hair. The company plodded on through the early morning toward a sagging house across a meadow of knee-high grass.

The sun glowed bronze through a haze, and was already riding above the towering tops of the trees. The temperature was slowly rising and the mist swept from the meadow on a light breeze.

We did not see the humans, coiled like a panther, waiting at the edge of the trees, waiting to shoot and hack with their terrible guns and axes, waiting to kill us all, hulfs and human alike, as if we were all so much garbage to be disposed of at the command of madmen.

Within minutes after reaching the house, I had a fire going and a kettle filled with vegetables hanging on a tripod.

The heat repelled the coldness. Squatting down beside the flames, for a time we could almost believe that we had reached the end of the journey. The woods around us seemed friendly, like the windrow of some quiet farm. The cart was as secure as a small fortress. The girl on the bed inside it was young and healthy and happy, and seemed safe from any harm. I lifted her gently and carried her into the old house while Cybele carried in the padded pallet. When she was comfortable, I went outside to sit by the fire.

The stew began to simmer. I rose and went to talk to the other hulfs, who had all gathered to sleep at the edge of the woods, to get a feel for their hopes, and to give them encouragement for the journey ahead of us.

I stopped in the half-darkness of the trees. Behind me the clearing showed bright, giving me the sensation of standing outside a window and looking into a lighted room. I lowered my hands to close about the coolness of the pistols and stood frozen, looking at the sandy ground marked with human boot-prints.

I moved a few steps forward, bent over as if in a dream, and touched a piece of rope circling one of the trees. From there I moved on quietly to touch three others. All were covered with blood. I could see that from the flickering rays of the rising sun which danced through the trees, bringing light from the clearing.

I knelt and pulled one of the pistols from my belt, scanning the brightening forest for signs of humans or hulfs. At a distance, I could see the form of a man behind one of the trees, his fat belly and face silhouetted against the light from the clearing.

I leveled the pistol and cocked the hammer. Suddenly, someone grabbed me about the neck and pulled me backward, snatching the pistol from my hand at the same time.

"They have taken four of us," a voice rasped in my ear. It was Jack, the Alpha male.

"Taken? Where are they taking them?" I croaked.

"To death with their knives."

"Oh, God, oh, God."

"Your god cannot help them now," Jack said as he released me from his powerful grip.

"How many are they?" I asked.

"I counted nine with knives and guns. They knew we were coming, Gill. I think they have been following us for days."

"Why could you not smell them?"

"They have covered their clothing and skin with a lotion that masks their scent. But I have smelled that scent since the day we were at the river."

We sat in silence for some time, waiting for the assault that we knew must surely come. Jack leaned back against the base of a tree and raised his snout to the sky, his nostrils flaring.

"They are still here," he said.

"Where are the other hulfs?"

"They have gone by ones and twos back to house. There is some safety there."

"I'm sorry, Jack," I said weakly, close to tears.

"For what?"

"For the hulfs. For the deaths of the hulfs."

"It was not your fault. Come."

We went back and stood leaning against the cart. Steam came up from the kettle of water and hovered above the simmering stew.

My back grew cold, and I draped a blanket about my shoulders, reaching again for the pistols in my belt, to assure myself they were still there, ready and deadly. Many times I heard a rustle, but it was only wind in the treetops.

The fire had died and twice been replenished when we heard the young she-hulf scream. Hours later, she gave birth to a son. Some of the females bathed the tiny, squalling pup, wrapped it in clean old linen, and laid it beside its mother.

Her lips moved feebly. "I'm very tired."

"You have a son," someone said in the shadows.

She closed her eyes. After a while, Cybele put her hand on the girl's ashen face and found it cold.

Across the clearing a shot flashed out from the trees, then, closer, another one. I ran out to crouch behind the shelter of the cart, pistols out and ready.

"Come inside, fool," Jack growled. "The air will not stop their bullets but perhaps the timbers of the house will."

He grabbed my arm and dragged me inside where most of the survivors were clustered together for protection.

Hideous and demonic figures broke from the trees, yelling and screaming. I held my fire, then coolly picked out the nearest hunter and shot him. He fell, his arms sprawled wide. Another was killed seconds later.

"Seven more," I thought. "And I have but ten more rounds."

It didn't seem to matter, for the thought of the dead she-hulf, herself no more than a child, lying in the next room had crept deep into my soul.

There was a noise outside. Hurried steps bounded up on the porch, and someone knocked at the door. I flung it open.

A hulf I did not recognize stood outside in a long leather coat. "There's firing!"

"Where?"

"Just south of here. Not very far."

"Where were you?"

"In the forest, following the nine humans who took the four hulfs. I turned from the trail and heard firing as I was coming in."

At a soft command, water was dumped on the flaming logs, raising a cloud of ruby-colored steam. More water came, and the fire died.

I stood by the half-opened door waiting for the humans to attack in force. Jack and some of the other hulfs watched at the windows.

Cybele stood, and was trembling. "Be careful, Gill."

"I'm always careful, girl. I've been careful all my life. Too careful, perhaps. Now is the time for madness and action or we shall all perish." I pulled her close and kissed her. "Nothing living shall kill me tonight."

"Nothing but another human's gun," she whispered, pressing her fingers to her lips as if to seal the kiss there forever. "Be careful."

I motioned for Jack and two of the other hulfs to go with me into the forest to get behind the hunters. Together we went down from the porch and crept around to the back of the house.

Cybele watched without speaking. My eyes swept the camp, darkened now except for the sputtering fire.

When we had reached the edge of the forest, I turned to Jack and indicated that he and one hulf should go to the left while I would take the other hulf to the right. The idea was to get behind the humans and kill them one at a time.

"We'll circle to meet and home in on the noise of any firing. Watch for an ambush."

I had no worries about Jack. He could travel the woods in daylight or darkness with the speed and silence of a spectre.

When I was certain we were behind the humans, I stopped and listened. There was no sound of firing, but somewhat northward I heard a soft whistle. An instant later, to the left, it was answered by another. The hulf touched my shoulder.

"Not humans," he said quietly.

I nodded and we moved forward toward the sound.

"Let's push on. There'll be no more firing. Whatever it is, their work is done. The two dead humans have spooked them. They're probably wondering how hulfs could have killed their comrades."

We approached a clearing and pulled up short. There was smoke in the air, and the smell of burned powder. To our right were the last few embers of a dying fire in the camp where the humans had waited.

Jack, with the other hulf in tow loomed from the shadows, ghost-like, to stand beside us.

"We've circled the clearing," Jack said grimly. "We found the bodies of the four taken earlier. They were skinned and their paws cut off. They took the heads of the two females."

"Come away from the fire," I said, "in case they are watching. We'll make easy targets in the glow of this smoke."

"The seven hunters are over there," Jack said, pointing toward the south. "They are all together, hiding, afraid. No one is watching for us."

"In that case," I said, "they will be easy pickings for my pistols."

"Are you certain you want to do that?" Jack asked. "You are human; they are humans. Is it not murder in the eyes of your laws?"

"Self-defense is not murder."

"It is if one is a hulf."

I had no answer for that. I checked the pistols to make certain I had ten rounds. I silently wished I had more. "The Lord provideth, and equally taketh away."

"Nonsense," Jack growled. "But do what you must. I will take these hulfs back to the house to protect the others. Be careful; someone or something besides the hunters is in this forest tonight."

They moved silently, drifting away like the smoke from the dying campfire.

Tomorrow you'll christen the baby and bury his mother with a few words from the Scriptures, I thought, as I made my way into the forest toward the hunters. I tried to think of words of Scripture I could say and found I could not remember any. They were lost two hundred years behind me.

It was strangely silent as I crept forward into the greening forest. There were no animal sounds, no bird calls, no human voices from the camp now only yards away. Smoke from their fire curled upward and was borne away on the breeze. The sun was now already above the trees and I could see the hunters slumped around the meager fire as if asleep.

I stopped at the edge of the small clearing. No one was on watch. I looked for the bags holding the hulf skins and heads, but could not see them anywhere. From my left came a single soft whistle and from the right, moments later, came an answer.

"Not human," the hulf had told me.

I eased forward until I was less than ten feet from the nearest sleeping hunter. There was a pungent smell of death in the camp. I searched again for the bags of hulf skins and realized with a start that the hunters were not sleeping at all—they were dead; killed where they sat by some unseen and unheard creature.

Horrified, I stood and backed away from the goulish scene, then turned and began to run as fast as I could through the tangled brush. I had not gone ten yards when two large male hulfs stepped into view before me. I tried to stop, tried to turn away, but one grabbed me around the neck and flung me to the ground, mouth open wide to crush my throat.

"Hold!" came a harsh command from the shadows.

I looked beyond the hulf to see a large, muscular male appear from behind a tree. He waved his arm and the hulf holding me down sprang away, leaving me breathless and choking.

The great hulf stepped to my side and bent near me, sniffing and snorting. I feared then that he would kill me himself.

He straightened and relaxed a bit. "You have the scent of a she-hulf on you," he said. "The young one with the newborn pup in the house yonder. And another, perhaps, as well."

I could not answer, only nod affirmatively.

"Do you lead them to the sanctuary?"

Nodding again.

"We have been watching you for some time, wondering where you are going, what you are doing. This morning we thought you had led them here into the trap to be killed by the humans."

I shook my head no.

"I see that. If you seek the sanctuary, you are leading them in the wrong direction. You took the wrong trail at the river two days ago and you are moving away from the sanctuary. It is a trap the humans have devised by leaving bits of fur and paw prints to make it appear as though hulfs have gone down the one path while they swept away the tracks from the other."

I swallowed away the dryness in my throat and managed to sit upright. I looked back toward the hunter's camp. "Did you... ?"

"Of course we did. We cannot leave this baggage alive to kill our brothers and sisters. Some of the hulfs are already cleaning the campsite of the refuse so other hunters will never know what happened there. More are back at the river to make sure the trap signs are removed. It is something we try to do every day. It is why we are here."

"How many are you?" I asked.

He raised his head suspiciously and eyed me askance. "We are many," he said simply. "But you are now only nineteen, counting the newborn pup."

"The mother died," I said quietly.

He grimaced and looked away into the forest, growling deep in the heat of his throat. Presently, he turned back to me. "Eighteen, then. Do you have lactating females to care for the pup? If you do not, we will take him and our camp will raise him."

"I don't know. I'll ask when I return."

"Come." He extended his hand—still human but lengthened and distorted and clawed and covered with dark fur—and snatched me from the ground as easily as he might lift an infant. "We have much to do this day."

I wanted to ask his name but knew he would only say, 'hulf,' if he answered at all.

*****

"I would spend days in those intercrossing mirror worlds which ran into one another, trembled, vanished, only to reappeared again," the raggedy man said softly.

"I gave my mind, my body, my soul to those fathomless distances, those echoing vistas, those separate universes cutting across my own and existing, despite my consciousness of them, in the same place at the same time. That extended reality, separated from me by the smooth surface of silvered glass, drew me towards itself by a kind of unknowable, intangible touch, dragging me into the gleaming surface, as if into a mysterious abyss.

"I was drawn towards the apparition which posed before me when I came near the mirror and which strangely doubled my being. I tried to imagine how this other was different from me, how it was possible that my right hand should be his left, and that all the fingers of my hands should change places.

"My thoughts were confused when I attempted to probe that enigma, to solve it. In this world, where everything could be touched, where voices were heard I lived, actually, and in that reflected world, which it was only possible to imagine, was he, the phantom, the ghost. He was almost myself and yet not really myself; he repeated all my movements, but not a single one of those movements exactly matched my own.

"He, that other, that phantom, knew something I could not divine, he held a secret hidden from my understanding; a secret that would soon come crashing down upon me to fill me with terror and wonder.

"But I noticed that each mirror had its own separate and special world. Put two mirrors in the very same place, one after the other, and there will arise two different universes. And in different mirrors before which I posed, there would rise before me different apparitions, all of them similar to me but never exactly like me and never exactly like the others.

"According to the strange conditions of their worlds they take the form of the person who poses before the glass but under this borrowed image they each preserved their own personal characteristics.

"There were some worlds of mirrors which I loved; others which I hated. I did not love all my doubles. I felt most were hostile toward me, if only because they were forced to drape themselves in my likeness.

"There were some whom I despised. There were others, on the other hand, whom I feared, who were too strong for me and who dared in their turn to mock me to do as they demanded.

"I smashed the mirrors where these hostile doubles lived. I would not look into them. I hid them, gave them away, even broke them into pieces.

"But every time I destroyed a mirror I wept for hours, knowing that I had broken to pieces a distinct, distant universe. And hateful, terrible faces stared up at me from the broken fragments of the worlds I had scattered upon the floor."

*****

I returned to the abandoned house, accompanied by twelve guardian hulfs, eight of them adult males, four of them adult females, but they were certainly not all who were in the forest that night.

Our frightened company were huddled in one corner of the room sharing the vegetable stew. They were elated when they saw the guardians and and began enthusiatic conversations. Some of them knew a few of the guardian hulfs as being from the village from which they, themselves, had recently fled.

The alpha male guardian hulf asked about the newborn pup and learned we had no lactating females. He told one of his females to take the pup and, because she was lactating, she began nursing it. He let us know that they would take the pup to their camp and raise it as their own.

I named the alpha male Apollo and the nursing female Naomi, although I never addressed them by those names because I feared it might offend them to be called by human names.

Cybele brought me a cup of still warm stew. "Are you okay?" she asked. "You look strange and you are so quiet."

"I'm okay now that I am back here with you. It was a cruel morning and a sad one."

"It is not your fault that the hulfs were taken. Don't punish yourself for something you cannot or could not prevent." She looked at the cup of stew I held in my trembling hands. "Drink now," she said tenderly.

I lifted the cup and drank a bit of the broth. "The hulfs have told me we are going in the wrong direction," I said. "We will have to go back to the river where the trails diverged, or cut across from here if there is a trail which will take us to the sanctuary."

"Yes, there is a secret way, but it leads to a large lake where we may take a ferry across. It is but two days through the forest. If the ferry is not there, or if the captain will not or cannot take us, we will have to go around. It will be a month or more if we go around; only four days if we can cross."

"Then let us hope we can cross," I said as I finished the cup of stew. "Did anyone say how far the sanctuary is from the lake?"

"Two more days." Cybele said. "They said we would be safe from harm once we cross the lake."

"Or journey around it."

"Yes." She looked away briefly and shifted awkwardly. "You kissed me, Gill," she said so softly that I had to lean forward to hear.

"Yes, I did. Should I not have done it? I didn't mean anything wanton by it. It is a human gesture toward someone they care about. It is meant to reassure the other that everything will be okay."

"For someone you love?"

"Well, yes, I suppose that's the way to say it."

"And do you love me?"

"Dear Cybele, I have loved you from the first day when we met on the path to the stone house."

"You never told me."

"Because it is not possible for us to be together. We live in different worlds. You have the world of the hulfs and I ... ."

She touched my lips with a finger. "I, too, have loved you and no other since that first day. But I know we cannot be together. Our different worlds will not allow it. Still, we can be companions for many years."

I did not have the heart or the courage to tell her how different our worlds really were, that I might one day simply vanish, fall into a mirror and simply vanish. I could not screw up the courage to explain it, to tell her that I was two hundred years old and that if I did not vanish into a mirror, I might just drop dead. I wanted so badly to say it, but I could not. And so the traitor in me said, "Yes."

*****

The raggedy man began to weep. Not aloud, not pitifully, but silently. Tears

225

crept down his brown, wrinkled cheeks to fall into his lap.

"I'm sorry," he said after a time. His lips tembled. He shook his head from side to side. "I'm sorry. I loved her so."

"And she loved you."

"And I deserted her at her hour of need...at their hour of greatest need... by doing that which I feared so much. I fell into this world where I have lived as a pauper, longing only to return to my most beloved Cybele."

*****

In the days when the hulf disease began, there was little trouble between the hulfs and men. They lived apart— the men in the villages and farms and the hulfs in the swamps and thickets and on the wide grassy meadows between the villages.

Sometimes a horse or cow would stray into the marshes or meadows to become a meal, and sometimes the hulfs would find one already dead, and drive off the vultures and feral cats, and feast well to their heart's content for days.

The hulfs of the old time were clumsy of foot and dull-coloured, with rough fur and large heads, many of them misshapen and ugly. They came every spring north into the villages, after the willows turned green and before the fruit trees flowered, when the grass on the wide meadows grew long. They came only in small groups then, each pack an alpha male and two or three females with a pup or two, having their own hunting territory, and they went again to hunt in the foothills when the Harlequin Maples were red and the antelope came down from the mountains.

But, as the disease evolved, the hulfs became sleek and swift, brave and cunning; the males strong and handsome, the females lithe and lovely. The pups were simply beautiful to behold by the time I had fallen into their world.

It was their custom to hunt in the open, going into cover only in the heat of the day. They avoided the long stretches of tangled forest, preferring the openness of meadows and farms near the edges of the villages where they often found portions of food thrown out by humans.

It was difficult, if not impossible, to come upon them unawares. They were not fighters; their teeth were only for prey, but if they were provoked or threatened, once they began, no living thing came near them; no other living creature could withstand their power and ferocity.

And in those early days when men seemed to be trying to account for the disease and to find a cure, humans, by and large, seemed harmless; indeed, many wanted to do all they could to help the sad and hopeless hulfs.

But no utterance of prophecy warned the hulfs of the terrible savagery that was to come, of the clubs and guns and axes to be wielded to drive the packs from the villages into the dystopian world of terror and blackness beneath the city streets, beneath the darkness, beneath the thin line between self and the unspeakable world of monsters and murder that was to replace the wide meadows and the freedom of the earth.

*****

Season changes had compensations. The bitter cold, which lasted for intense, shivering periods that winter and sent us sometimes from our beds to shiver about the edge of a roaring fire, equally rid the encampment of the pesky insects and brought great flocks of wild ducks and geese into the nearby rivers and lakes.

Relief from the cold came with spring, but the insects returned, and a new caution was necessary against the deadly snakes and panthers and bears which had come out from hibernation to bask in the sun.

But it was worth trudging through the thin, lingering snow and ankle-deep icy marshes just to smell again the sweetness of blossoming trees and flowers, and to know that the fish of the lakes and streams would soon begin to rise again to be snatched by a quick, clawed hand.

*****

Most humans, and especially their children, had never seen hulfs closely, but soon they saw them every day as they began to raid out from their lairs on the edges of the villages, joining and raiding together in search of food. The hulfs in the countryside came together in larger and stronger packs, forming communities around many of the abandoned farms that dotted the countryside.

The bears and panthers had become afraid of them, and when they caught wind of a hulf they turned aside. When the humans saw this, they, too, became afraid of the hulf living on the swiftness of their limbs and the deep, dark, red heat of their throats.

And many humans began to keep guns and axes beside their doors to drive away or kill any hulf who might stray too close. They surrounded themselves with fear and loathing, never suspecting they might, one day, also become a creature of the darkness to be loathed and feared by those who loved them but a day before.

*****

Apollo and Naomi came to me in the evening to say that they would lead us to the secret trail to the lake, would take us as far as they could before turning back to guard and protect any others who might seek the sanctuary by the same path we had traveled.

Naomi was nursing the pup and I watched unabashed the tender scene, knowing that the pup would be safe and loved, growing someday to a strong adult, running free and hunting the marshes and meadows of the sanctuary.

"Sanctuary is but eight days away if you are fortunate enough to cross the lake. But the ferry is not always at the lake," said Apollo. "If it is taking others across, and if it left only a day before, or the morning before you arrive, it will be eight days before it returns. It is not safe on this side of the lake. Human bounty hunters have discovered the pier and they lurk nearby, waiting for some luckless straggler to arrive... ."

"Then they kill!" Naomi growled, slashing the air with her fingers. "And they take their skins and the feet of the males and the heads of the females back to the villages to prove they have killed those who make the pups so they can claim their bounties."

"They are paid small fees for males," Apollo said. "Larger fees for the females because when they kill a female, they are killing the future of the packs. Fewer pups means we soon will be gone forever."

*****

"I am weary," said the raggedy man. "I should find a place to bathe and change into these clothes you have brought me. Then I must arrange my mirrors and try to return to Cybele."

I looked at my watch and realized that it was evening. Outside, the sun was already on the horizon and it would soon be dark.

"Is there anything I can do to help?" I asked.

"Not really. If the mirrors are arranged properly, I will vanish and some other man or creature will appear in my place. If not, then we will continue our conversation tomorrow."

"If you go—fall into the mirror, I mean—will the man who replaces you know what happened in the world where you left the hulfs?"

"If he is from that world, yes, I suppose he will. But it has been two years. How many adventures will he have survived in so long a time?"

"Yes," I said softly. "How many adventures?"

"And he might not be from the world of the hulfs. He might be from the past, or from a future so distant that he would not recognize this world at all. It might not even be a human."

"I see," I said, standing to go. I reached out and took the raggedy man's wrinkled brown hand in my own. "If I do not see you again, then I wish you a safe journey and hope you find those you left behind and loved so much."

The raggedy man said nothing, stood with lips pursed and eyes bright with tears. He took the book from the large box and gave it to me.

I walked away, then, without looking back.

And, so, the raggedy man's story ends. When I returned the next morning, everything was gone. The boxes, the mirrors, the food and clothing, the easels, even the folder of matches and the candle had vanished as if they had never existed at all.

No man or creature was lurking in the dark building to explain what had transpired the previous night. I want to believe that the transfer occured and that the newcomer, eager to escape the filthy delelict building, had thrown everything into the trash bin to hide any evidence of his arrival and had then gone into the outside world to live another fantastic adventure.

I want to believe that the raggedy man returned to the world of the hulfs, returned to Cybele, and lived with her in the sanctuary until the end of his days.

But I would never know.

Only the paw prints of a large canine were lightly visible upon the dusty concrete floor. But the pattern was of two paws only, as if the creature walked upon its hind legs in the manner of a human.

I had one more task to do. I took the book to the library on my way to work, dropping it unnoticed into the night return slot.

I never saw the raggedy man again and realized he had never told me his name and had never explained why or how he had fallen into this world.

END

CRYPTID CREATURES FROM DARK DOMAINS

231

Made in the USA
Las Vegas, NV
02 May 2023

71459728R00131